INTRODUCTION

This Snapshot guide, excerpted from my guidebook *Rick Steves' Italy 2011*, introduces you to the hill towns of central Italy. Here in Italy's heartland, you'll enjoy an idyllic landscape, time-passed medieval hill towns, and tree-lined meandering backcountry roads. Dine on Italy's heartiest food in an atmospheric farmhouse, and taste a glass of wine poured by a proud vintner whose family's name has been on the bottle for generations.

I've included a mix of towns and cities, some undiscovered, some deservedly popular. Choose among the back-door towns of Volterra and Civita, the wine-lovers' towns of Montepulciano and Montalcino, touristy towered San Gimignano, manicured Pienza, trendy Cortona, fit-for-a-duke Urbino, classic Orvieto, tradition-steeped Siena, and spiritual, artsy Assisi—or even better, visit them all.

To help you have the best trip possible, I've included the following topics in this book:

• **Planning Your Time,** with advice on how to make the most of your limited time

• **Orientation,** including tourist information (abbreviated as TI), tips on public transportation, local tour options, and helpful hints

• **Sights** with ratings:

　　▲▲▲—Don't miss

　　▲▲—Try hard to see

　　▲—Worthwhile if you can make it

　　No rating—Worth knowing about

• **Sleeping** and **Eating,** with good-value recommendations in every price range

• **Connections,** with tips on trains, buses, and driving

Practicalities, near the end of this book, has information on money, phoning, hotel reservations, transportation, and other helpful hints, plus Italian survival phrases.

To travel smartly, read this little book in its entirety before you go. It's my hope that this guide will make your trip more meaningful and rewarding. Traveling like a temporary local, you'll get the absolute most out of every mile, minute, and euro.

Buon viaggio!

HILL TOWNS OF CENTRAL ITALY

San Gimignano • Volterra • Montalcino • Pienza •
Montepulciano • Cortona • Orvieto • Civita di Bagnoregio

The sun-soaked hill towns of central Italy offer what to many is the quintessential Italian experience: sun-dried tomatoes, homemade pasta, wispy cypress-lined driveways following desolate ridges to fortified 16th-century farmhouses, atmospheric *enoteche* serving Tuscany's famously tasty wines, and dusty old-timers warming the same bench day after day while soccer balls buzz around them like innocuous flies.

The hill towns of central Italy—in Tuscany, Le Marche, and Umbria—retain their medieval charm, and are best enjoyed by adapting to the pace of the countryside. So, slow...down...and savor the delights that these villages offer. Spend the night if you can, as many hill towns are mobbed by day-trippers.

Planning Your Time

How in Dante's name does a traveler choose from Italy's hundreds of hill towns? I've listed some of my favorites in this chapter. The one(s) you visit will depend on your interests, time, and mode of transportation.

Multi-towered San Gimignano is a classic, but because it's such an easy hill town to visit (1.25-hour bus ride from Florence), peak-season crowds can overwhelm the town's charms. For rustic vitality not completely trampled by tourist crowds, out-of-the-way Volterra is the clear winner. Wine aficionados head for Montalcino and Montepulciano—each a happy gauntlet of wine shops and art galleries (Montepulciano being my favorite). Fans of architecture and urban design appreciate Pienza's well-planned streets and squares. Art-lovers and those enamored by Frances Mayes' memoir *(Under the Tuscan Sun)* make the pil-

ARIGhARIA

HILL TOWNS

Hill Towns of Central Italy

grimage to Cortona. Urbino, well off the tourist track and quite remote, is known for its huge Ducal Palace. The grand, classic town of Orvieto is famous for its wine, ceramics, and colorful cathedral. But my longtime favorite is the tiny, obscure hill town of Civita di Bagnoregio (pictured on previous page). Assisi and Siena, while hill towns, are in a category by themselves. Bigger and with more major artistic and historic sights, they each get their own chapter.

For a relaxing break from big-city Italy, settle down in an *agriturismo*—a farmhouse that rents out rooms to travelers (usually for a minimum of a week in high season). These rural B&Bs—almost by definition in the middle of nowhere—provide a good home base

MonTerchi, Arezzo

Hill Towns: Public Transportation

TO GENOA
TO MILAN
TO VENICE
CINQUE TERRE
FERRARA
LA SPEZIA
BOLOGNA
LUCCA
FLORENCE
CARRARA
EMPOLI
FIESOLE
RAVENNA
PISA
A B POGG.
CORTONA
RIMINI
SALINE
CAM.
TERENTOLA
GUBBIO
PESARO
LIVORNO
SIENA
PERUGIA
URBINO
FALCONARA
CECINA
C D E
ASSISI
CHIUSI
SPELLO
CIVITA
TODI
FOLIGNO
SPOLETO
VITERBO
ORVIETO
ANCONA
TARQUINIA
CIVITAVECCHIA
ORTE
CERVETERI
TO BARI & BRINDISI
ROME
TO NAPLES
DCH

A - VOLTERRA
B - SAN GIMIGNANO
C - MONTALCINO   NOT TO SCALE
D - PIENZA
E - MONTEPULCIANO

---BUS
— RAIL
✈ AIRPORT

from which to find the magic of Italy's hill towns. I've listed several good options throughout this chapter.

Getting Around the Hill Towns

Bigger destinations (such as Cortona and Orvieto) are doable by public transportation, but most hill towns are easier and more efficient to visit by car.

By Bus or Train

Traveling by public transportation is cheap and connects you with the locals. While trains link some of the towns, hill towns—being on hills—don't quite fit the railroad plan. Stations are likely to be in the valley a couple of miles from the town center, usually connected efficiently by a local bus.

Buses are often the only public-transportation choice to get between small hill towns. If you're pinched for time, it makes sense to narrow your focus to one or two hill towns, or rent a car to see more.

By Car

Exploring small-town Tuscany, Le Marche, and Umbria by car can be a great experience. But since a car is an expensive, worthless headache in Florence and Siena, wait to pick up your car until the last big city you visit (or pick it up at the nearest airport to avoid big-city traffic). Then use the car for lacing together the hill towns and exploring the countryside.

A big, detailed regional road map (buy one at a newsstand or gas station) and a semiskilled navigator are essential. Freeways (such as the toll autostrada and the non-toll *superstrada*) provide the fastest way to connect two points, but the smaller roads, including the super-scenic S-222 through the heart of the Chianti region (connecting Florence and Siena), are more rewarding. For more joyrides—from Siena to Montalcino, and from Montalcino to Montepulciano.

Parking throughout this region can be challenging. Some towns don't allow visitors to park in the city center, so you'll need to leave your car outside the walls and walk into town. Don't drive or park in any area with signs reading *Zona Traffico Limitato (ZTL)*—often above a red circle. Parking lots, indicated by big blue *P* signs, are usually free and plentiful outside city walls. In some towns, you can park on the street; nearby kiosks sell "pay and display" tickets. I'd advise, when possible, parking in guarded lots, which are worth the expense to reduce the threat of theft (no guarantees, though).

San Gimignano

The epitome of a Tuscan hill town, with 14 medieval towers still standing (out of an original 72), San Gimignano (sahn jee-meen-YAH-noh) is a perfectly preserved tourist trap. There are no

important interiors to sightsee, and the town is packed with crass commercialism. The locals seem corrupted by the easy money of tourism, and most of the rustic is faux. The fact that this small town supports two torture museums is a comment on the caliber of the masses who choose to visit. But San Gimignano is so easy to reach and visually so beautiful that it remains a good stop. I find the place enchanting at night.

In the 13th century—back in the days of Romeo and Juliet—feuding noble families ran the towns. They'd periodically battle things out from the protection of their respective family towers. Pointy skylines, like San Gimignano's, were the norm in medieval Tuscany.

San Gimignano's cuisine is mostly what you might find in Siena—typical Tuscan home cooking. *Cinghiale* (cheeng-GAH-lay, wild boar) is served in almost every way: stews, soups, cutlets, and, my favorite, salami. Most shops will give you a sample before you commit to buying. The city is well known for having some of the best saffron in Italy; look for it on menus at finer restaurants (it's fairly expensive). Although Tuscany is normally a red-wine region, the most famous Tuscan white wine comes from here: the inexpensive, light, and fruity Vernaccia di San Gimignano. Look for the green "DOCG" label around the neck for the best quality.

HILL TOWNS

San Gimignano

① Hotel l'Antico Pozzo
② Hotel la Cisterna
③ Palazzo al Torrione
④ To Ponte a Nappo Rooms &
Co-op Supermarket
⑤ Le Vecchie Mura Camere &
Ristorante
⑥ Locanda il Pino
⑦ Trattoria Chiribiri
⑧ Dulcis in Fundo Ristorante
⑨ Locanda di Sant'Agostino
⑩ Gelateria Pluripremiata
"di Piazza"

Orientation to San Gimignano

While the basic ▲▲▲ sight here is the town of San Gimignano itself, there are a few worthwhile stops. From the town gate, head straight up the traffic-free town's cobbled main drag to Piazza della Cisterna (with its 13th-century well). The town sights cluster around the adjoining Piazza del Duomo.

Tourist Information: The helpful TI is in the old center on Piazza del Duomo (daily March–Oct 9:00–13:00 & 15:00–19:00, Nov–Feb 9:00–13:00 & 14:00–18:00, free maps, sells bus tickets, books rooms, tel. 0577-940-008, www.sangimignano.com).

The town offers a two-hour **guided walk** in English and Italian several days a week (April–Oct Sat–Sun at 11:00, €20; includes admission to Civic Museum and Tower; pay and meet at TI). Two-hour guided walks into the surrounding countryside are also available on request.

Arrival in San Gimignano: The bus stops at the main town gate, Porta San Giovanni. There's no baggage storage anywhere in town, so you're better off leaving your bags in Siena or Florence. You can't drive within the walled town. There are three pay lots a short walk outside the walls; the handiest is Parcheggio Montemaggio, just outside Porta San Giovanni. The one below the roundabout and Co-op supermarket is least expensive (€1/hour, €6/day, Giubileo 1).

Helpful Hints: Thursday is **market** day on Piazza del Duomo (8:00–13:00), but for local merchants, every day is a sales frenzy. A public **WC** is just off Piazza della Cisterna (€0.50), and another is around the corner from Porta San Giovanni. A little electric **shuttle bus** does its laps all day from Porta San Giovanni to Piazza della Cisterna to Porta San Matteo (€0.50, 2/hour, buy ticket from TI, *tabacchi* shop, or from coin-operated machine on bus).

Self-Guided Walk

Welcome to San Gimignano

This quick walking tour will take you across town from the bus stop at Porta San Giovanni through the town's main squares to the Duomo, and on to the Sant'Agostino Church.

• *Start, as most tourists do, at the Porta San Giovanni gate at the bottom end of town.*

Porta San Giovanni: San Gimignano lies about 25 miles from both Siena and Florence, a good stop for pilgrims en route to those cities, and on a naturally fortified hilltop that encouraged settlement. The town's walls were built in the 13th century, with gates like this that helped regulate who came and went. Today, modern posts keep out all but service and emergency vehicles. The small square just outside the gate features a memorial to the town's WWII dead. Follow the pilgrims' route (and flood of modern tourists) through the gate and up the main drag.

About 100 yards up, on the right, is a pilgrims' shelter (12th-century, Pisan Romanesque). The Maltese cross indicates that this was built by the Knights of Malta. It was one of 11 such shelters in town. Today, only the wall of this shelter remains.

• *Carry on, up to the town's central Piazza della Cisterna. Sit on the steps of the well.*

Piazza della Cisterna: The piazza is named for the cistern that is served by the old well standing in the center of this square.

A clever system of pipes drained rainwater from the nearby rooftops into the underground cistern. This square has been the center of the town since the ninth century. Turn in a slow circle and observe the commotion of rustic-yet-proud facades crowding in a tight huddle around the well. Imagine this square in pilgrimage times, lined by inns and taverns for the town's guests. Now finger the grooves in the lip of the well and imagine generations of maids and children fetching water. Each Thursday, the square fills with a market—as it has for more than a thousand years.

• *Notice San Gimignano's famous towers.*

The Towers: Of the original 72 towers, only 14 survive. Before effective city walls were developed, rich people fortified their own

homes with these towers: They provided a handy refuge when ruffians and rival city-states were sacking the town. These towers became a standard part of medieval skylines. Even after town walls were built, the towers continued to rise—now to fortify noble families feuding within a town (Montague and Capulet–style).

In the 14th century, San Gimignano's good times turned very bad. In the year 1300, about 13,000 people lived within the walls. Then in 1348, a six-month plague decimated the population, leaving the once-mighty town with barely 4,000 survivors. Once fiercely independent, now crushed and demoralized, San Gimignano came under Florence's control and was forced to tear down its towers. (The Banca Toscana building occupies the remains of one such toppled tower.) And, to add injury to injury, Florence redirected the vital trade route away from San Gimignano. The town never recovered, and poverty left it in a 14th-century architectural time warp. That well-preserved cityscape, ironically, is responsible for the town's prosperity today.

• *From the well, walk 30 yards uphill to the adjoining square with the cathedral.*

Piazza del Duomo: The square faces the former cathedral. The twin towers to the right are 10th-century, among the first in

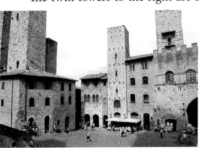

town. The stubby tower opposite the church is typical of a merchant's tower: main door on ground floor, warehouse upstairs, holes to hold beams that once supported wooden balconies and exterior staircases, heavy stone on the first floor, cheaper and lighter brick for upper stories.

• *On the piazza are the Civic Museum and Tower, worth checking out (see "Sights in San Gimignano," later). You'll also see the...*

Duomo (or Collegiata): Walk inside San Gimignano's Romanesque cathedral. Sienese Gothic art (14th century) lines the nave with parallel themes, Old Testament on the left and New Testament on the right. (For example: the suffering of Job opposite the suffering of Jesus, Creation facing the Annunciation, and the birth of Adam facing the Nativity.) This is a classic use of art to teach. Study the fine Creation series (top left). Many scenes are portrayed with a local 14th-century "slice of life" setting, to help lay townspeople relate to Jesus—in the same way that many white Christians are more comfortable thinking of Jesus as Caucasian (€3.50, €5.50 combo-ticket includes mediocre Religious Art Museum, daily April–Oct 10:00–18:40, Nov–March 10:00–16:40).

From the church, hike uphill (passing the church on your left) following signs to *Rocca e Parco di Montestaffoli*. Keep walking until you enter a peaceful hilltop park and olive grove within the shell of a 14th-century fortress. On the far side, a few steps take you to the top of a little tower (free) for the best views of San Gimignano's skyline; the far end of town and the Sant'Agostino Church (where this walk ends); and a commanding 360-degree view of the Tuscan countryside. San Gimignano is surrounded by olives, grapes, cypress trees, and—in the Middle Ages—lots of wild dangers. Back then, farmers lived inside the walls and were thankful for the protection.

• *Return to the bottom of Piazza del Duomo, turn left, and continue your walk across town, cutting under the double arch (from the town's first wall). In around 1200, this defined the end of town. The Church of San Bartolo stood just outside the wall. The Maltese cross indicates that it likely served as a hostel for pilgrims. Continuing on down Via San Matteo, you pass a fascinating array of stone facades from the 13th and 14th centuries—now a happy cancan of wine shops and galleries. Eventually you reach...*

Sant'Agostino Church: This tranquil church, at the opposite end of town (built by the Augustinians who arrived in 1260), has fewer crowds and more soul. Behind the altar, a lovely fresco cycle by Benozzo Gozzoli (who painted the exquisite Chapel of the Magi in the Medici-Riccardi Palace in Florence) tells of the life of St. Augustine, a North African monk who preached simplicity. The kind English-speaking friars (from Britain and the US) are happy to tell you about their church and way of life, and also have Mass in English on Sundays at 11:00. Pace the tranquil cloister before heading back into the tourist mobs (free, €0.50 lights the frescoes; April–Oct daily 7:00–12:00 & 15:00–19:00; Nov–March Tue–Sun 7:00–12:00 & 15:00–18:00, Mon 16:00–18:00). Their fine little shop, with books on the church and its art, is worth a look.

Sights in San Gimignano

Civic Museum and Tower (Museo Civico and Torre Grossa)—This small, fun museum, consisting of just three unfurnished rooms and a tower, is inside City Hall (Palazzo Comunale). The main room, called Sala di Consiglio (a.k.a. Danti Hall), is covered in festive frescoes, including the *Maestà* by Lippo Memmi. This virtual copy of Simone Martini's *Maestà* in Siena proves that Memmi doesn't have quite the same talent as his famous brother-in-law. Upstairs, the Pinacoteca displays a classy little painting collection, with a 1422 altarpiece by Taddeo di Bartolo honoring St. Gimignano. You can see the saint, with the town—bristling with towers—in his hands, surrounded by events from his life.

As you exit, be sure to stop by the Mayor's Room (Camera del Podesta). Frescoed in 1310 by Memmo di Filippuccio, it offers an intimate and candid peek into the 14th century. The theme: profane love. As you enter, look to the left corner where a young man is ready to experience the world. He hits his parents up for a bag of money and is free. Almost immediately he's entrapped by two prostitutes, who lead him into a tent where he loses his money (above the window), is turned out, and is beaten. Above the door from left to right see a parade of better choices: marriage, the cradle of love, the bride led to the groom's house, and newlyweds bathing together and retiring happily to their bed.

The highlight for most visitors is a chance to climb the **Tower** (Torre Grossa). The city's tallest tower, 200 feet and 218 steps up, rewards those who climb it with a commanding view. You leave via a delightful stony loggia and courtyard out back.

Cost and Hours: €5, includes museum and tower, audioguide may be available for €2, daily March–Oct 9:30–19:00, Nov–Feb 10:00–17:30, Piazza del Duomo.

San Gimignano 1300—This new attraction is a trip back in time. Located inside the Palazzo Ficarelli in the town center, it features a scale model of San Gimignano at the turn of the 14th century. You can see the 72 original "tower houses," peek into cross-sections of buildings, and view scenes of medieval life within the city walls

Cost and Hours: €5, daily 8:00–20:00, June–Sept until 23:00, Via Berignano 23, tel. 0577-941-078, www.sangimignano1300.com.

Sleeping in San Gimignano

Although the town is a zoo during the daytime, locals outnumber tourists when evening comes, and San Gimignano becomes peaceful and enjoyable. Drivers can unload near their hotels, then park outside the walls in recommended lots. Hotel websites provide instructions.

$$$ Hotel l'Antico Pozzo is an elegantly restored 15th-century townhouse with 18 tranquil, comfortable rooms, a peaceful interior courtyard terrace, and an elite air (Db-€140 and higher depending on the room, air-con, elevator, Wi-Fi, near Porta San Matteo at Via San Matteo 87, tel. 0577-942-014, fax 0577-942-117, www.anticopozzo.com, info@anticopozzo.com, Emanuele).

$$$ Hotel la Cisterna, right on Piazza della Cisterna, offers 49 predictable rooms, some with panoramic view terraces (Sb-€78, Db-€100, Db with view-€120, Db with view terrace-€145, 10 percent discount with this book, buffet breakfast, air-con, elevator, Wi-Fi, good restaurant with great view, closed Jan–Feb, Piazza della Cisterna 23, tel. 0577-940-328, fax 0577-942-080, www.hotelcisterna.it, info@hotelcisterna.it, Alessio).

$$$ Ponte a Nappo, run by enterprising Carla Rossi (who doesn't speak English) and her son Francesco (who does), has seven comfortable rooms and two apartments in a kid-friendly farmhouse. Located a long half-mile below town, this place has killer views (Db-€110, 2-to-6-person apartment-€130–220, air-con extra, free Wi-Fi, parking, pool, free loaner bikes, 15-minute walk

Sleep Code

(€1 = about $1.25, country code: 39)
S = Single, **D** = Double/Twin, **T** = Triple, **Q** = Quad, **b** = bathroom,
s = shower only. Unless otherwise noted, credit cards are
accepted and breakfast is included (but usually optional).
English is generally spoken, but I've noted exceptions.

To help you sort easily through these listings, I've divided
the rooms into three categories based on the price for a
standard double room with bath:

$$$ Higher Priced—Most rooms €100 or more.
  $$ Moderately Priced—Most rooms between €70-100.
    $ Lower Priced—Most rooms €70 or less.

Prices can change without notice; verify the hotel's
current rates online or by email. For other updates, see www
.ricksteves.com/update.

or 5-minute drive from Porta San Giovanni, tel. 0577-955-041,
mobile 349-882-1565, fax 0577-941-268, www.accommodation
-sangimignano.it, info@rossicarla.it). A picnic dinner—lounging
on their comfy garden furniture as the sun sets—is good Tuscan
living. About 100 yards below the monument square at Porta San
Giovanni, find Via Vecchia (not left or right, but down a tiny road)
and follow it down a dirt road for five minutes by car. They also
rent a dozen or so rooms and apartments in town (each described
on their website).

$$ Palazzo al Torrione, just inside Porta San Giovanni, is
quiet and handy, and generally better than most hotels, though
they don't have a full-time reception. Their 10 modern rooms
are spacious and tastefully appointed (Db-€80, terrace Db-€100,
Tb-€98, terrace Tb-€113, Qb-€120–130, 10 percent discount with
this book, breakfast-€5, communal kitchen, parking-€6/day, inside
and left of gate at Via Berignano 76; operated from *tabacchi* shop 2
blocks away, on the main drag at Via San Giovanni 59; tel. 0577-
940-480, mobile 338-938-1656, fax 0577-955-605, www.palazzo
altorrione.com, palazzoaltorrione@palazzoaltorrione.com, Vanna
and Francesco).

$ Le Vecchie Mura Camere offers three good rooms above
their restaurant in the old town (Db-€60, no breakfast, air-con,
Via Piandornella 15, tel. 0577-940-270, www.vecchiemura.it, info
@vecchiemura.it, Bagnai family).

$ Locanda il Pino is tiny (five rooms), but has a big liv-
ing room. It's dank but super-clean, quiet, and run by English-
speaking Elena and her family above their elegant restaurant just

inside Porta San Matteo (Db-€55, no breakfast, easy parking just outside the gate, Via Cellolese 4, tel. 0577-940-415, locanda @ristoranteilpino.it). While far from the bus stop, this is a good value for those with a car.

Eating in San Gimignano

Trattoria Chiribiri, just inside Porta San Giovanni, serves home-made pastas and desserts at remarkably fair prices. It's petite with tight seating and, though hot in the summer, is a fine value (€6 pastas, €8.50 *secondi*, daily 11:00–23:00, Piazza della Madonna 1, tel. 0577-941-948, Beatrice and Maurizio).

Dulcis in Fundo Ristorante, small and family-run, proudly serves local cuisine with a modern twist, gourmet presentation, and slow-food values in a jazz ambience (€12 pastas, €15 *secondi*, meals served Thu–Tue 12:30–14:30 and 19:30–22:00, closed Wed, Vicolo degli Innocenti 21, tel. 0577-941-919).

Le Vecchie Mura Ristorante is my choice for good service, great prices, tasty home cooking, and the ultimate view. It's romantic indoors or out. They have a dressy, modern interior where you can dine with a view of the busy stainless-steel kitchen under rustic vaults, but I'd come for the incredible cliffside garden terrace. Cliffside tables are worth reserving in advance by calling or dropping by: Ask for "front view" (€8 pastas, €12 *secondi*, Wed–Mon dinner only from 18:00, last order at 22:00, closed Tue, Via Piandornella 15, tel. 0577-940-270, Bagnai family).

Locanda di Sant'Agostino spills out onto the peaceful square, facing Sant'Agostino Church. It's cheap and cheery, serving lunch and dinner daily—a great place for salads, pizza, or a rustic dish of pasta. Dripping with wheat stalks and atmosphere on the inside, there's shady on-the-square seating outside (€8 pastas, €12 *secondi*, daily 11:00–22:00, closed Tue off-season, also closed Jan–Feb, Piazza Sant'Agostino 15, tel. 0577-943-141, Genziana and sons).

Picnics: The big, modern **Co-op supermarket** sells all you need for a nice spread (Mon–Sat 8:30–20:00, closed Sun, at parking lot below Porta San Giovanni). Or browse the little shops guarded by wild boar heads within the town walls; they sell boar meat *(cinghiale).* Pick up 100 grams (about a quarter pound) of boar, cheese, bread, and wine and enjoy a picnic in the garden at the Rocca or the park outside Porta San Giovanni.

Gelato: To cap the evening and sweeten your late-night city stroll, stop by **Gelateria Pluripremiata "di Piazza"** on Piazza della Cisterna (at #4). Gelato-maker Sergio was a member of the Italian team that won the official Gelato World Cup (daily 8:00–24:00, tel. 0577-942-244, Dondoli family).

San Gimignano Connections

Bus tickets are sold at the bar just inside the town gate or at the TI.

From San Gimignano by Bus to: Florence (hourly, less on Sat–Sun, 1.25–2 hours, change in Poggibonsi, €6.25), **Siena** (8 direct/day, 1.25 hours, €5.50), **Volterra** (4/day Mon–Sat; on Sun only 1/day—usually crowded—with no return to San Gimignano; 2 hours, change in Colle Val d'Elsa).

By Car: San Gimignano is an easy 45-minute drive from Florence (take the A1 exit marked *Firenze Certosa*, then a right past tollbooth following *Siena per 4 corsie* sign; exit the freeway at Poggibonsi). From San Gimignano, it's a scenic and windy half-hour drive to Volterra.

Volterra

Encircled by impressive walls and topped with a grand fortress, Volterra sits high above the rich farmland. More than 2,000 years ago, Volterra was one of the most important Etruscan cities, a city much larger than the one we see today. Greek-trained Etruscan artists worked here, leaving a significant stash of art, particularly funerary urns. Eventually Volterra was absorbed into the Roman Empire, and for centuries it was an independent city-state. Volterra fought bitterly against the Florentines, but like many Tuscan towns, it lost in the end and was given a fortress atop the city to "protect" its citizens.

Unlike other famous towns in Tuscany, Volterra feels not cutesy or touristy...but real, vibrant, and almost oblivious to the allure of the tourist dollar. A refreshing break from its more commercial neighbors, it's my favorite small town in Tuscany.

Orientation to Volterra

Compact and walkable, the city stretches out from the pleasant Piazza dei Priori to the old city gates.

Tourist Information: The helpful TI is on the main square, at Piazza dei Priori 19 (daily 10:00–13:00 & 14:00–18:00, tel.

0588-87257, www.volterratur.it). The TI's excellent €5 audioguide narrates 20 stops (2-for-1 discount on audioguides with this book).

Arrival in Volterra: Buses stop at Piazza Martiri della Libertà in the town center. Drivers will find the town ringed with easy numbered parking lots (#3 and #5 are free; #3 is most likely to have a place, but comes with a steeper hike into town). The most central lots are the pay lots at Porta Fiorentina and underground at Piazza Martiri della Libertà (€1.50/hour, €11/24 hours).

Helpful Hints

Market Day: Market day is Saturday morning near the Roman Theater (8:00–13:00, in Piazza dei Priori in winter).

Festivals: Volterra's Medieval Festival takes place the third and fourth Sundays of August (Aug 21 and 28 in 2011). Fall is a popular time for food festivals—check with the TI for dates and events planned.

Internet Access: Web & Wine has a few terminals and fine wine by the glass (€3/hour, no minimum, summer daily 9:30–1:00 in the morning, off-season closed Thu, Via Porta all'Arco 11–15, tel. 0588-81531, www.webandwine.com, Lallo speaks English). **Enjoy Café Internet Point** has a couple of terminals in their basement (€3/hour, daily 6:30–1:00 in the morning, Piazza dei Martiri 3, tel. 0588-80530).

Local Guide: American **Annie Adair** married into the local community; she organizes American weddings in Tuscany, is an excellent private guide, and can organize wine and food tours (€125/half-day, €250/day, tel. 0588-87774, mobile 347-143-5004, www.tuscantour.com, info@tuscantour.com).

Sights in Volterra

▲▲**Guided Volterra Walk**—Annie Adair and her colleagues offer a great one-hour English-only introductory walking tour of Volterra for €5. The walk touches on Volterra's Etruscan, Roman, and medieval history, as well as the contemporary cultural scene (April–Sept daily, rain or shine, at 18:00; depart from Piazza Martiri della Libertà, at the bus terminal above the underground parking lot; no need to reserve—just show up, they need a minimum of 4 people—or €20—to make the tour go, www.volterrawalkingtour.com or www.tuscantour.com, info@volterrawalkingtour.com). There's no better way to spend €5 and one hour in this city.

▲▲**Self-Guided Historic Town Walk**—You can easily lace the town's top sights and my descriptions together to make your own handy little town walk. Here's the spine of the walk (all described

Volterra

in this order below): Start with the Etruscan Arch, browse up what I call "Artisan Lane," follow my tour of Via Matteotti, side-trip to the main square and Duomo, detour (if you like) to the Pinacoteca and Roman Theater, head over to the Etruscan Museum and Alabaster Workshop, and finish with a drink under all the bras with Bruno and Lucio at La Vena di Vino. The town's other sights are easily grafted onto this route.

▲"Porta all'Arco" Etruscan Arch—Volterra's most famous sight is its Etruscan arch, built of massive volcanic tuff stones in the fourth century B.C. Volterra's original wall was four miles around—twice the size of the wall that encircles it today. With 25,000 people, Volterra was a key Etruscan trade center—one of 12 leading towns that made up the Etruscan *Dodecapolis* (a league of Etruscan cities). The three seriously eroded heads, dating from the first century B.C., show what happens when you leave something outside for 2,000 years. The newer stones are

Legend:

- ⊼ VIEW
- **P** PARKING
- ★ PIAZZA DEI PRIORI
- ‖‖‖ STAIRS

1. To Park Hotel Le Fonti
2. Albergo Etruria
3. Hotel La Locanda
4. To Albergo Villa Nencini
5. Albergo Nazionale
6. Seminario Vescovile Sant'Andrea
7. To Volterra Youth Hostel & Trattoria da Bado
8. To Podere Marcampo
9. Rist. Enoteca del Duca
10. Trattoria Don Beta
11. La Vecchia Lira
12. Rist. Il Sacco Fiorentino
13. La Vena di Vino Wine Bar
14. Ombra della Sera & Pizzeria Tavernetta
15. Despar Market
16. Alab'Arte Alabaster Showroom
17. Alab'Arte Alabaster Workshop
18. "Artisan Lane"
19. Internet Cafés (2)

Map labels: V. D'ANNUNZIO, PORTA DI DOCCIOLA, V. FILOSOFI, PORTA MARCOLI, VIA DI PORTA, ETRUSCAN MUSEUM, ROCCA NUOVA, V. DON MINZONI, MEDICI FORTRESS, V. CARDUCCI, PORTA A SELCI, TO SAN GIMIGNANO, SIENA

part of the 13th-century city wall, which incorporated parts of the much older Etruscan wall.

A plaque just outside remembers June 30, 1944. That night, Nazi forces were planning to blow up the arch to slow the Allied advance. To save their treasured landmark, Volterrans ripped up the stones that pave Via Porta all'Arco and plugged the gate,

managing to convince the Nazi commander that there was no need to blow up the arch. Today, all the stones are back in their places, and, like silent heroes, they welcome you through the oldest standing Etruscan gate into Volterra. Locals claim this as the only surviving round arch of the Etruscan age, and believe this is where Romans got the idea for using a keystone in their arches.

"Artisan Lane"—Via Porta all'Arco (which leads to and from the Etruscan arch) is lined with interesting shops featuring the work of artisans and producers. Because of its alabaster heritage, Volterra attracted artisans and artists, who brought with them a rich variety of crafts (shops generally open Mon–Sat 10:00–13:00 & 16:00–19:00, closed Sun; the TI produces a free booklet called *Handicraft in Volterra*).

From the Etruscan Arch, browse your way up the hill, checking out these shops (listed from bottom to top): La Mia Fattoria, a co-op of producers of cheese, salami, and oil, letting you buy direct at farm prices (#52); alabaster shops (#57 and #45); book bindery and papery (#26); jewelry (#25); etchings and silk screening (#23); leather (#16); Web & Wine (Internet access; #11-15); and bronze work (#6).

▲**Via Matteotti**—The town's main drag, named after the popular Socialist leader killed by the Fascists in 1924, provides a good cultural scavenger hunt. The street starts 30 yards from Palazzo dei Priori (City Hall and cathedral, described later).

At #1 is a typical Italian bank security door. (Step in and say, "Beam me up, Scotty.") Look up and all around. Find the medieval griffin torch holder—symbol of Volterra—and imagine it holding a lit torch. The pharmacy sports the symbol of its medieval guild. As you head down Via Matteotti, notice how the doors show centuries of refitting work.

At #2, look up and imagine heavy beams cantilevered out, supporting extra wooden rooms and balconies crowding out over the street. Throughout Tuscany, today's stark and stony old building fronts once supported a tangle of wooden extensions. Doors that once led to these extra rooms are now partially bricked up to make windows. Contemplate urban density in the 14th century, before the plague thinned out the population. Be careful: There's a wild boar (a local delicacy) at #10.

At #12, notice how the typical palace, once the home of a single rich family, is now occupied by many middle-class families (judging from the line of doorbells). After the social revolution in the 18th century and the rise of the middle class, former palaces were condominium-ized. Even so, like in *Dr. Zhivago*, the original family still lives here. Apartment #1 is the home of Count Guidi.

At #16, pop in to an alabaster showroom. Alabaster, mined nearby, has long been a big industry here. Volterra alabaster—softer and more porous than marble—was sliced thin to serve as windows for Italy's medieval churches.

At #19, the recommended La Vecchia Lira is a lively cafeteria. The Bar L'Incontro across the street is a favorite for homemade gelato and pastries.

Vampire Volterra

Sitting on its stony main square at midnight, watching bats dart about as if they own the place, I realize there really is something supernatural about Volterra. The cliffs of Volterra inspired Dante's "cliffs of hell." In the winter, the town's vibrancy is smothered under a deadening cloak of clouds. The name Volterra means "land that floats"—referring to the clouds that often seem to cut it off from the rest of the world below.

The people of Volterra live in a cloud of mystery, too. Their favorite cookie, crunchy with almonds, is called Ossi di Morta ("bones of the dead"). The town's first disco was named Catacombs. And in the 1970s, when Volterra was the set of a wildly popular TV horror series called *Ritratto di Donna Velata (Portrait of a Veiled Woman),* all of Italy tuned in to Volterra every week for a good scare.

Lately the town is attracting international attention for its connection to the bestselling *Twilight* series of vampire romance novels and movies. Part of the second movie, *New Moon* (2009), is set in Volterra. Even though most of it was actually filmed in Montepulciano, the TI plays a video clip of *New Moon* continuously and is proud of Volterra's Hollywood connection.

As a result, the town is seeing lots of "Twihards," who come not for the Etruscan Museum, but to run across the sun-drenched square at noon and retrace the footsteps of Edward and Bella down dark alleyways. The movie has definitely stirred up vampire tourism—it's in their blood.

Across the way, up Vicolo delle Prigioni, is a fun bakery *(panificio).* They're happy to sell small quantities if you want to try the local *cantuccini* (almond biscotti) or munch a cannoli.

At #51, a bit of Etruscan wall is artfully used to display more alabaster art. And #56B is the alabaster art gallery of Paolo Sabatini.

Locals gather early each evening at Osteria dei Poeti (at #57) for the best cocktails in town—served with free munchies. The cinema is across the street. Movies in Italy are rarely in *versione originale*. Italians are used to getting their movies dubbed into Italian.

At #66, the end of the street is marked by another Tuscan tower. This noble house has a ground floor with no interior access to the safe upper floors. Rope ladders were used to get upstairs. The tiny door was wide enough to let in your skinny friends...but definitely not anyone wearing armor and carrying big weapons.

Across the street stands the ancient Church of St. Michael. After long years of barbarian chaos, the Lombards moved in from the north and asserted law and order in places like Volterra. That generally included building a Christian church on the old Roman forum to symbolically claim and tame the center of town. The church standing here today is Romanesque, dating from the 12th century. Find the crude little guys under its eaves—they've been making faces at the passing crowds for 800 years.

Palazzo dei Priori—Volterra's City Hall (c. 1209) claims to be the oldest of any Tuscan city-state. It clearly inspired the more famous Palazzo Vecchio in Florence. Town halls like this were emblematic of an era when city-states were powerful. They were architectural exclamation points declaring that, around here, no pope or emperor called the shots. Towns such as Volterra were truly city-states—proudly independent and relatively democratic. They had their own armies, taxes, and even weights and measures. Notice the horizontal "cane" cut into the City Hall wall. For a thousand years, this square hosted a market, and the "cane" was the local yardstick. When not in use for meetings or weddings, the city council chambers—lavishly painted and lit with fun dragon lamps as they have been for centuries of town meetings—are open to visitors.

   Cost and Hours: €1, April–Oct daily 10:30–17:30, Nov–March Sat–Sun only 10:00–17:00.

Duomo—A common arrangement in the Middle Ages was for the church to face the baptistery (you couldn't enter the church until you were baptized)...and for the hospital to face the cemetery. All of these overlooked the same square. That's how it is in Pisa. And that's how it is here.

   This 12th-century church is not as elaborate as its cousin in Pisa, but the simple facade and central nave flanked by monolithic stone columns are beautiful examples of the Pisan Romanesque style. The chapel to the left of the entry has painted terra-cotta statue groups. The interior was decorated mostly in the late 16th century, during Florentine rule under the Medici family. You'll see a lot of the Medici coat of arms (with the six pills, representing the family's first trade—as doctors, or *medici*). The 12th-century marble pulpit is beautifully carved. All of the apostles are together except Judas, who's under the table with the evil dragon (his name is the only one not carved onto the relief).

   Just before the pulpit (in the Rosary Chapel, on the left), check out the *Annunciation* by Fra Bartolomeo (who was a student of Fra Angelico and painted this in 1497). Bartolomeo delicately gives worshippers a way to see Mary "conceived by the Holy Spirit." Note the vibrant colors, exaggerated perspective, and Mary's *contrapposto* pose—all attributes of the Renaissance.

   To the right of the main altar is a dreamy painted-and-gilded-wood *Deposition* (Jesus being taken down from the cross), restored to its original form. Painted in 1228, a generation before Giotto, it shows emotion and motion way ahead of its time.

The glowing windows in the transept and behind the altar are sheets of alabaster. These, along with the recorded Gregorian chants, add to the church's wonderful ambience.

Cost and Hours: Free, daily 8:00–12:30 & 15:00–17:00.

Sacred Art Museum—This humble four-room museum collects sacred art from deconsecrated churches and small, unguarded churches from nearby villages.

Cost and Hours: €9 combo-ticket includes Etruscan Museum and Pinacoteca, daily 9:00–13:00 & 15:00–18:00, morning only in winter, well-explained in English, next to the Duomo at Via Roma 1, tel. 0588-86290.

Pinacoteca—This museum fills a 14th-century palace with fine paintings that feel more Florentine than Sienese—a reminder of whose domain this town was in. Its highlights are Luca Signorelli's beautifully lit *Annunciation,* an example of classic High Renaissance (from the town cathedral), and (to the right) *Deposition from the Cross,* the groundbreaking Mannerist work by Rosso Fiorentino (note the elongated bodies and harsh emotional lighting and colors). Notice also Ghirlandaio's *Christ in Glory.* The two devout-looking kneeling women are actually pagan, pre-Christian Etruscan demigoddesses, Attinea and Greciniana, but the church identified them as obscure saints to make the painting acceptable.

Cost and Hours: €9 combo-ticket includes Etruscan and Sacred Art museums, daily 9:00–19:00, Nov–mid-March until 13:45, Via dei Sarti 1, tel. 0588-87580.

Palazzo Viti—Go behind the rustic, heavy stone walls of the city and see how the nobility lived (in this case, rich from 19th-century alabaster wealth). One of the finest private residential buildings in Italy, with 12 rooms open to the public, Palazzo Viti feels remarkably lived in because it is. You'll also find Senora Viti herself selling admission tickets. It's no wonder this time warp is so popular with Italian movie directors. While exquisite, it's pricey. But remember, you're helping keep a noble family in leotards.

Cost and Hours: €5, pick up the loaner English description, April–Oct daily 10:00–13:00 & 14:30–18:30, closed Nov–March, Via dei Sarti 41, tel. 0588-84047, www.palazzoviti.it.

Roman Theater—Built in about 10 B.C., this well-preserved theater is considered to have some of the best acoustics of its kind. Because of the fine aerial view you get from the city wall promenade, you may find it unnecessary to pay admission to enter. Belly up to the 13th-century wall and look down. The wall that you're standing on divided the theater from the town center...so, naturally, the theater became the town dump. Over time, the theater

Under the Etruscan Sun
(c. 900 B.C.–A.D. 1)

About 550 B.C.—just before the Golden Age of Greece—the Etruscan people of central Italy had their own Golden Age. Though their origins are mysterious, their mix of Greek-style art with Roman-style customs helped lay a civilized foundation for the rise of Rome. As you travel through Italy—particularly in Tuscany (from "Etruscan"), Umbria, and North Latium—you'll find traces of the long-lost Etruscans.

The Etruscans first appeared in the ninth century B.C., when a number of cities sprouted up in sparsely populated Tuscany and Umbria, including today's hill towns of Cortona, Chiusi, and Volterra. Perhaps they were immigrants from Western Turkey, but more likely they were just the local farmers who moved to the city, became traders and craftsmen, and welcomed new ideas from Greece.

More technologically advanced than their neighbors, they mined metal, exporting it around the Mediterranean, both as crude ingots and as some of the finest-crafted jewelry in the known world. The Etruscans drained and irrigated large tracts of land, creating the fertile farmland of central Italy's breadbasket. With their disciplined army, warships, merchant vessels, and (from the Greek perspective) pirate galleys, they ruled central Italy and the major ports along the Tyrrhenian Sea. For nearly two centuries (c. 700–500 B.C.), much of Italy lived a golden age of peace and prosperity under the Etruscan sun.

Judging from the many luxury items that have survived, the Etruscans enjoyed the good life. Frescoes show men and women looking remarkably like how the Greeks and Romans described them: healthy, vibrant, and well-dressed, playing flutes, dancing with birds, or playing party games. Etruscan artists celebrated individual people, showing their wrinkles, crooked noses, silly smiles, and funny haircuts.

Thousands upon thousands of surviving ceramic plates, cups, and vases attest to the importance of food. Hosting a banquet was a symbol that you'd arrived. Men and women ate together, propped on their elbows on dining couches, surrounded by colorful frescoes and terra-cotta tiles. According to contemporary accounts, the Etruscans (and even their slaves) were Europe's best-dressed people. They ate off dinnerware either imported from Greece or made in the Greek style—red and black ceramics, decorated with warriors, nymphs, sphinxes, and gods. The banqueters were entertained with music and dancing and served by elegant and well-treated slaves.

Scholars today have deciphered the Etruscans' Greek-style alphabet and some individual words, but they've yet to fully master the grammar or crack the code. Virtually no long-enough Etruscan documents survive.

Much of what we know of the Etruscans comes from their tombs, often clustered in a necropolis. The tomb was your home

The Etruscan Empire

in the hereafter, fully furnished for the afterlife, complete with all your belongings. The lid of the sarcophagus might have a statue of the deceased at a banquet—lying across a dining couch, spooning with his wife, smiles on their faces, living the good life for all eternity.

Seven decades of wars with Greeks (545–474 B.C.) disrupted the trade routes and drained the Etruscan League, just as a new Mediterranean power was emerging: Rome. In 509 B.C., the Romans overthrew their Etruscan king, and Rome expanded, capturing Etruscan cities one by one (the last in 264 B.C.). Etruscan resisters were killed, the survivors intermarried with Romans, their kids grew up speaking Latin, and the culture became Romanized. By Julius Caesar's time, the only remnants of Etruscan culture were Etruscan priests, who became Rome's professional soothsayers. The shape a flock of birds made, the bend in a lightning flash, or a scar on a goat's liver could tell a priest how a client's business might fare next year. Interestingly, the Etruscan prophets had foreseen their own demise, having predicted that Etruscan civilization would last 10 centuries.

But Etruscan culture lived on in Roman religion (pantheon of gods, household gods, and divination rituals), art (realism), lifestyle (the banquet), and in a taste for Greek styles—the mix that became our "Western civilization."

Etruscan Sights in Italy
Here are some of the more important and more accessible Etruscan sights (all are mentioned in this book):
Rome: Traces of original Etruscan engineering projects (e.g., Circus Maximus), Vatican Museum artifacts, and Villa Giulia Museum, with the famous "husband and wife sarcophagus."
Orvieto: Archaeological Museum (coins, dinnerware, and a sarcophagus), necropolis, and underground tunnels and caves.
Volterra: Etruscan gate (Porta dell'Arco, from fourth century B.C.) and Etruscan Museum (funerary urns).
Chiusi: Museum, tombs, and tunnels.
Cortona: Museum and dome-shaped tombs.

was forgotten—covered in the garbage of Volterra. Luckily, it was rediscovered in the 1950s.

The stage wall was standard Roman design—with three levels from which actors would appear: one for mortals, one for heroes, and the top one for gods. Parts of two levels still stand. Gods leaped out onto the third level for the last time in the fourth century A.D., when the town decided to abandon the theater and to use its stones to build fancy baths instead. You can see the remains of the baths behind the theater, including the round sauna with brick supports to raise the heated floor.

Cost and Hours: €3, but you can view the theater free from Via Lungo le Mure, April–Oct daily 10:30–17:30, Nov–March Sat–Sun only 10:00–16:00.

View from Promenade: From the vantage point on the city wall promenade, you can trace Volterra's vast Etruscan wall. Find the church in the distance, on the left, and notice the stones just below. They are from the Etruscan wall that followed the ridge into the valley and defined Volterra five centuries before Christ.

▲▲**Etruscan Museum (Museo Etrusco Guarnacci)**—Filled top to bottom with rare Etruscan artifacts, this museum—even with few English explanations and its dusty, almost neglectful, old-school style—makes it easy to appreciate how advanced this pre-Roman culture was.

The collection starts with pre-Etruscan Villanovian artifacts (c. 1500 B.C.), but its highlight is a seemingly endless collection of Etruscan funerary urns (designed to contain the ashes of cremated loved ones).

Each urn is tenderly carved with a unique scene, offering a peek into the still-mysterious Etruscan society. While contemporaries of the Greeks, the Etruscans were more libertine. Their religion was less demanding, and their women were a respected part of both the social and public spheres. Women and men alike are depicted lounging on Etruscan urns. While they seem to be just hanging out, the lounging dead were actually offering the gods a banquet—in  order to gain their favor in the transition to the next life. The outcome of the banquet had eternal consequences.

On urns dating from the seventh to the first century B.C., the dearly departed are often depicted holding scrolls, blank wax tablets (symbolizing blank new lives in the next world), and libation cups—offering wine to the gods. Realistic scenes show the fabled horseback-and-carriage ride to the underworld, where the dead are greeted by Caron, with his hammer and pointy ears. While the finer urns are carved of alabaster, most are made of volcanic tuff. Most lids are mismatched—casualties of reckless 18th- and 19th-century archaeology. Look at the faces, and imagine the lives they lived and the loved ones they left behind.

On the top floor is a re-created grave site, with several urns and artifacts that would have been buried with the deceased. Some of these were funeral dowry (called *corredo*) that the dead would pack along. You'll see artifacts such as mirrors, coins, hardware for vases, votive statues, pots, pans, and jewelry.

Fans of Alberto Giacometti will be amazed at how the tall, skinny figure called *The Shadow of Night (L'Ombra della Sera)* looks just like the modern Swiss sculptor's work—but is 2,500 years older.

Cost and Hours: €9 combo-ticket includes—like it or not—the Pinacoteca and Sacred Art Museum, daily 9:00–19:00, Nov–March until 13:45, ask at the ticket window for mildly interesting English pamphlet, €3 audioguide fleshes out your visit well, Via Don Minzoni 15, tel. 0588-86347, www.comune.volterra.pi.it /english.

After your visit, duck across the street to the alabaster showroom and the wine bar (both described next).

▲Alabaster Workshop—Alab'Arte offers a fun peek into the art of alabaster. Their showroom is across from the Etruscan Museum.

A block downhill, in front of Porta Marcoli, is their powdery workshop, where you can watch Roberto Chiti and Giorgio Finazzo at work. They are delighted to share their art with visitors. Lighting shows off the translucent quality of the stone and the expertise of these artists For more artisans in action, visit the "Artisan Lane" described earlier, or ask the TI for their list of the town's many workshops open to the public.

Cost and Hours: Showroom—daily 10:30–13:00 & 15:30–19:00, Via Don Minzoni 18; workshop—Mon–Sat 9:30–13:00 & 15:00–19:00, closed Sun, Via Orti Sant'Agostino 28; tel. 0588-87968, www.alabarte.com.

▲La Vena di Vino (Wine-Tasting with Bruno and Lucio)—La Vena di Vino, also just across from the Etruscan Museum, is a fun *enoteca* where two guys have devoted themselves to the wonders of wine and share it with a fun-loving passion. Each day Bruno and Lucio open six or eight bottles, serve your choice by the glass, pair it with characteristic munchies, and offer fine music (guitars available for patrons) and an unusual decor (the place is strewn with bras). Hang out here with the local characters. This is your chance to try the Super Tuscan—a creative mix of international grapes grown in Tuscany. According to Bruno, "While the Brunello (€7/glass) is just right for wild boar, the Super Tuscan (€6) is just right for meditation." Food is served all day, including some hot dishes or a plate of meats and cheeses (Wed–Mon 11:00–1:00 in the morning, closed Tue, 3- and 5-glass wine-tastings, Via Don Minzoni 30, tel. 0588-81491, www.lavenadivino.com). While Volterra is

famously quiet late at night, this place is full of action. There's a vintage dentist chair attached to the karaoke machine downstairs.

Medici Fortress and Archaeological Park—The Parco Archeologico marks what was the acropolis of Volterra from 1500 B.C. until A.D. 1472, when Florence conquered the pesky city and burned its political and historic center, turning it into a grassy commons (park closes at 20:00 in summer, 17:00 in winter) and building the adjacent Medici Fortezza. The old fortress—a symbol of Florentine dominance—now keeps people in rather than out. It's a maximum-security prison housing only about 60 special prisoners. (Note that when you're driving from San Gimignano to Volterra, you pass another big, modern prison—almost surreal in the midst of all the Tuscan wonder.) Authorities prefer to keep organized-crime figures locked up far away from their family ties in Sicily.

Sleeping in Volterra

(€1 = about $1.25, country code: 39)

$$$ Park Hotel Le Fonti, a 10-minute walk downhill from Porta al Arco, is a spacious, family-run hotel in an imposing building with 67 rooms, many with views. In addition to the swimming pool, guests can use a small spa with sauna, hot tub, and an intriguing "emotional shower" (Db-€89–165 but prices vary wildly depending on season, elevator, on-site restaurant, wine bar, free parking, Via di Fontecorrenti 5, tel. 0588-85219, fax 0588-92728, www.parkhotellefonti.com, info@parkhotellefonti.com, Pedro, Paola, and Ghebo Bessi).

$$ Albergo Etruria, on Volterra's main drag, rents 21 fresh, modern, and spacious rooms within an ancient stone structure. They have a welcoming TV lounge and a peaceful garden out back. Request a quiet room off the street (Sb-€75, Db-€95, Tb-€115, 10 percent discount with cash and this book, fans, Wi-Fi, Via

Matteotti 32, tel. 0588-87377, fax 0588-92784, www.albergoetruria
.it, info@albergoetruria.it, Lisa and Giuseppina are fine hosts).

$$ Hotel La Locanda is well-located and rents 18 decent
rooms (Db-€93–125, air-con, Wi-Fi, Via Guarnacci 24/28, tel.
0588-81547, www.hotel-lalocanda.com, staff@hotel-lalocanda
.com, Jenny, Stefania, and Irina).

$$ Albergo Villa Nencini, just outside of town, is big,
modern, and professional, with 36 fine rooms. A few rooms have
terraces and many have views. There's also a large pool and free
parking (Sb-€67, Db-€88, Tb-€115, 10 percent discount with cash
and this book, Borgo Santo Stefano 55, a 15-minute uphill walk to
main square, tel. 0588-86386, fax 0588-80601, www.villanencini
.it, info@villanencini.it, Nencini family).

$$ Albergo Nazionale, with 38 big rooms, is simple, a little
musty, short on smiles, popular with school groups, and steps from
the bus stop (Sb-€65–70, Db-€80–90, Tb-€105, less off-season,
Via dei Marchesi 11, tel. 0588-86284, fax 0588-84097, www.hotel
nazionale-volterra.it, info@hotelnazionale-volterra.it).

$ Seminario Vescovile Sant'Andrea has been training
priests for more than 500 years. Today, the remaining eight priests
still train students, but when classes are over, their 16 rooms—
separated by vast and holy halls in an echoing old mansion—are
rented very cheaply. Look for the 15th-century Ascension ceramic
by Andrea della Robbia, tucked away in a corner upstairs (S-€15,
Sb-€20, D-€28, Db-€36, T-€42, Tb-€54, breakfast-€3, elevator,
closes at 24:00, groups welcome, free parking, easy 7-minute walk
from Etruscan Museum, Viale Vittorio Veneto 2, tel. 0588-86028,
semvescovile@diocesivolterra.it, Alberto or Angela).

$ Volterra Youth Hostel fills a wing of the restored Convent
of San Girolamo with 85 beds. It's spacious and has lots of ser-
vices, but it's a 15-minute hike out of town, in a boring area, and
no cheaper than the more memorable seminary option closer to
town (bed in 6-bed dorm-€17, Db-€60, breakfast-€3, lockers, tel.
0588-86613, www.ostellovolterra.it, info@ostellovolterra.it).

Near Volterra

$$ Podere Marcampo is a new *agriturismo* about four miles outside
Volterra on the road to Pisa. Run by Genuino (owner of the recom-
mended Ristorante Enoteca del Duca) and his wife, this peaceful
spot has three well-appointed rooms and three apartments, plus a
swimming pool with panoramic views. Genuino produces his award-
winning merlot on-site and offers €15 wine-tastings with cheese
and homemade salami. Cooking classes are also available (Db-
€90, apartment-€125–160, includes breakfast, air-con, Wi-Fi, free
parking, tel. 0588-85393, mobile 348-514-9782, www.agriturismo
-marcampo.com, info@agriturismo-marcampo.com).

Eating in Volterra

Menus feature a Volterran take on regional dishes. *Zuppa alla Volterrana* is a fresh vegetable-and-bread soup, similar to *ribollita* (except that it isn't made from leftovers). *Torta di ceci,* also known as *cecina,* is a savory pancake–like dish made with garbanzo beans. Those with more adventurous palates dive into *trippa* (tripe; comes in a bowl like stew), the traditional breakfast of the alabaster carvers.

Ristorante Enoteca del Duca, with a locally respected chef named Genuino, serves well-presented and creative Tuscan cuisine. You can dine under a medieval arch with walls lined with wine bottles, in a stark dining room (with an Etruscan statuette at each table), or on a nice little patio out back. It's a good place for truffles, and has a fine wine list (which includes Genuino's own merlot) and friendly staff. The spacious seating, dressy clientele, and calm atmosphere make this a good choice for a romantic meal (€42 food-sampler fixed-price meal, €10 pastas, €17 *secondi,* Wed–Mon 12:30–15:00 & 19:30–22:00, closed Tue, near City Hall at Via di Castello 2, tel. 0588-81510).

Trattoria da Bado, a 10-minute hike out of town, is every local's favorite for its *tipica cucina Volterrana.* Giacomo and family offer a rustic atmosphere and serve food with no pretense—"the way you wish your mamma cooks" (meals Thu–Tue from 12:30 and 19:30, closed Wed, Borgo San Lazzero 9, tel. 0588-86477, reserve before you go as it's often full).

Don Beta is a family-run trattoria on the main drag, popular with trendy Volterrans for its stylish home cooking. Mirko supervises the lively young team as they whisk out steaming plates of seafood pasta and homemade desserts (€10 pastas, €15 *secondi,* reservations smart, Via Matteotti 39, tel. 0588-86730, Paolo, Azzura, and Mamica).

La Vecchia Lira, bright and cheery, is a classy self-serve eatery that's a hit with locals as a quick and cheap lunch spot by day, and a fancier restaurant at night (Fri–Wed 12:00–14:30 & 19:00–22:30, closed Thu, Via Matteotti 19, tel. 0588-86180, Lamberto and Massimo).

Ristorante il Sacco Fiorentino is a local favorite for traditional cuisine and seasonal seafood specials (€8 pastas, €15 *secondi,* Thu–Tue 12:00–14:30 & 19:00–21:30, closed Wed, Piazza XX Settembre 18, tel. 0588-88537).

La Vena di Vino is an *enoteca* serving up simple and traditional dishes and the best of Tuscan wine in a fun atmosphere (Wed–Mon 11:00–1:00 in the morning, closed Tue, Via Don Minzoni 30, tel. 0588-81491, www.lavenadivino.com).

Pizzerias: **Ombra della Sera** dishes out what local kids consider the best pizza in town. At €6 and big enough to split, they make for a cheap date (Tue–Sun 12:00–15:00 & 19:00–22:00, closed Mon, Via Guarnacci 16, tel. 0588-85274).

Pizzeria Tavernetta, next door, is more romantic, with delightful indoor and on-the-street seating. Marco, who looks like Billy Joel, serves splittable €7 pizzas (Thu–Tue, closed Wed, Via Guarnacci 14, tel. 0588-87630).

Picnics: You can assemble a picnic at the few *alimentari* around town (try Despar Market at Via Gramsci 12, Wed 7:30–13:00, Thu–Tue 7:30–13:00 & 17:00–20:00) and eat in the breezy Archaeological Park.

Volterra Connections

The nearest train station is in **Saline di Volterra,** a 15-minute bus ride away (7/day, 4/day Sun). In Volterra, buses come and go from Piazza Martiri della Libertà (buy tickets at any *tabacchi* shop).

From Volterra by Bus to: Florence (4/day, 2/day Sun, 2 hours, change in Colle Val d'Elsa), **Siena** (4/day, 1/day Sun, 2 hours, change in Colle Val d'Elsa), **San Gimignano** (4/day, 2/day Sun, 2 hours, change in Colle Val d'Elsa), **Pisa** (9/day, 2 hours, change in Pontedera). For Siena, Florence, and San Gimignano, C.P.T. bus tickets get you only as far as Colle Val d'Elsa (4/day, 50 minutes, €2.50); you must then buy another ticket (from another bus company) at the newsstand near the bus stop.

Montalcino

On a hill overlooking vineyards and valleys, Montalcino—famous for its delicious and pricey Brunello di Montalcino red wines—is a must for wine-lovers. Everyone touring this area seems to be relaxed and in an easy groove...as if enjoying a little wine buzz.

In the Middle Ages, Montalcino (mohn-tahl-CHEE-noh) was considered Siena's biggest ally. Originally allied with Florence, the town switched sides after the Sienese beat up Florence in the Battle of Montaperti in 1260. The Sienese persuaded the Montalcini to join their side by forcing them to sleep one night in the bloody Florentine-strewn battlefield.

Montalcino prospered under Siena, but like its ally, it waned after the Medici family took control of the region. The village became a humble place. Then, in the late 19th century, the Biondi Santi family created a fine, dark red wine, calling it "the brunette" (Brunello). Today's affluence is due to the town's much-sought-after wine.

Non–wine–lovers may find Montalcino a bit too focused on *vino,* but one sip of Brunello makes even wine skeptics believe that Bacchus was onto something. Note that Rosso di Montalcino (a younger version of Brunello) is also very good, at half the price. Those with a sweet tooth will enjoy crunching the Ossi di Morta ("bones of the dead") cookies popular in Tuscany.

Orientation to Montalcino

Sitting atop a hill amidst a sea of vineyards, Montalcino is surrounded by walls and dominated by the Fortezza (a.k.a. "La Rocca"). From here, roads lead down into the two main squares: Piazza Garibaldi and Piazza del Popolo.

Tourist Information: The TI, just off Piazza Garibaldi in the City Hall, can find you a room (Db-€50–80) for no fee. They have information on taxi service to nearby towns, abbeys, and monasteries (daily 10:00–13:00 & 14:00–17:30, tel. & fax 0577-849-331, www.prolocomontalcino.it).

Arrival in Montalcino: The bus station is on Piazza Cavour, about 300 yards from the town center. Drivers coming in for a short visit should drive right through the old gate under the fortress (follow signs to *Fortezza;* it looks almost forbidden) and grab a spot in the pay lot at the fortress (€1.50/hour, free 20:00–8:00). Otherwise, park for free a short walk away.

Helpful Hints: Market day is Friday (7:00–13:00) on Viale della Libertà. Day-trippers be warned: Montalcino has **no baggage storage.**

Sights in Montalcino

Fortezza—This 14th-century fort, built under the rule of Siena, is now little more than an empty shell. People visit for its *enoteca.* You can climb the ramparts to enjoy a panoramic view of the Asso and Orcia valleys, or enjoy a picnic in the park surrounding the fort.

Cost and Hours: €4 for rampart walk—buy ticket in the

Montalcino

- ❶ Hotel Dei Capitani
- ❷ Palazzina Cesira B&B
- ❸ Albergo Giardino & Osteria al Giardino
- ❹ Affittacamere Mariuccia
- ❺ Taverna il Grappolo Blu
- ❻ Trattoria l'Angolo
- ❼ Ristorante-Pizzeria San Giorgio
- ❽ Co-op Supermarket
- ❾ Enoteca la Fortezza di Montalcino
- ❿ Caffè Fiaschetteria Italiana
- ⓫ Enoteca di Piazza
- ⓬ To Banfi & Argiano Wineries

wine bar, €6 combo-ticket includes Civic Museum—sold only at museum, daily 9:00–20:00.

Piazza del Popolo—All roads in tiny Montalcino seem to lead to the main square, Piazza del Popolo ("People's Square"). Since 1888, the recommended Caffè Fiaschetteria Italiana has been the elegant place to enjoy a drink. Its founder, inspired by Caffè Florian in Venice, brought fine coffee to this humble town of woodcutters.

The City Hall was the fortified seat of government. It's decorated by the coats of arms of judges who, in the interest of fairness, were from outside of town. Like Siena, Montalcino was a republic in the Middle Ages. When Florentines took Siena in 1555, Siena's ruling class retreated here and held out for four more years. The Medici coat of arms (with the six pills) superseding all the others is a reminder that in 1559 Florence finally took Montalcino.

The one-handed clock was the norm until 200 years ago. For five centuries the arcaded loggia hosted the town market. And, of course, it's fun to simply observe the *passeggiata*—these days mostly a parade of tourists here for the wine.

Civic Museum (Museo Civico)—Gothic sacred art is the star of this museum, with works from Montalcino's heyday, the 13th to 16th centuries. Most of the art was created by local artists. Among the museum's highlights are a glazed terra-cotta altarpiece and statue of St. Sebastian by Andrea della Robbia. The ground floor is best, with an impressive collection of crucifixes.

Cost and Hours: €4.50, €6 combo-ticket includes rampart walk at Fortezza, Tue–Sun 10:00–13:00 & 14:00–17:50, closed Mon, Via Ricasoli 31, to the right of Sant'Agostino Church, tel. 0577-846-014.

Sleeping in Montalcino

(€1 = about $1.25, country code: 39)

$$$ Hotel Dei Capitani, at the end of town near the bus station, is well-run and rents 29 rooms. It has plush public spaces, an inviting pool, and a cliffside terrace offering plenty of reasons for lounging (Db-€120 with this book in 2011, extra bed-€30, air-con, half the rooms come with vast Tuscan views for the same price—request a view room when you reserve, Wi-Fi in lounge, free parking, Via Lapini 6, tel. 0577-847-227, www.deicapitani.it, info@deicapitani.it).

$$ Palazzina Cesira, right in the heart of the old town, rents five spacious and tastefully decorated rooms in a fine 13th-century residence with a palatial lounge. You'll enjoy a refined and tranquil ambience, a nice breakfast, and the chance to get to know Lucilla and her American husband Roberto (Db-€95, suites-€115, cash only, 2-night minimum except 3-night minimum on holiday weekends, Wi-Fi, Via Soccorso Saloni 2, tel. & fax 0577-846-055, www.montalcinoitaly.com, p.cesira@tin.it).

$ Albergo Giardino, old and basic, has nine big simple rooms, no public spaces, and a fine locale (Db-€55–60, 10 percent discount with this book, no breakfast, Piazza Cavour 4, tel. & fax 0577-848-257, mobile 338-684-3163, albergoilgiardino@virgilio.it, Roberto and his dad, Mario).

$ Affittacamere Mariuccia has three basic, Ikea-chic rooms on the main drag over a heaven-scented bakery (Db-€50, no breakfast, check-in across the street at Enoteca Pierangioli before 20:00 or let them know arrival time, Piazza del Popolo 16, rooms at #28, tel. 0577-849-113, mobile 348-392-4780, www.affittacamere mariuccia.it, enotecapierangioli@hotmail.com, Alessandro speaks English).

Near Montalcino

$$ La Crociona, an *agriturismo* farm and working vineyard, rents seven fully equipped apartments. Fiorella Vannoni and Roberto and Barbara Nannetti offer cooking classes and tastes of the Brunello wine grown and bottled on the premises (Db-€95, or €65 in Oct–mid-May; Qb-€130, or €95 in Oct–mid-May; lower weekly rates, metered gas heating, laundry-€8/load, pool, La Croce 15, tel. 0577-847-133, fax 0577-846-994, www.lacrociona .com, crociona@tin.it). The farm is two miles south of Montalcino on the road to the Sant'Antimo Monastery (look for big yellow *Piombaia La Crociona* sign on left, then follow directions to Tenuta Crocedimezzo e Crociona). A good restaurant is next door.

Eating in Montalcino

Taverna il Grappolo Blu is unpretentious, friendly, and serious about its wine, serving local specialties and vegetarian options to an enthusiastic crowd (€8.50 pastas, €12.50 *secondi,* daily 12:00–15:00 & 19:00–22:00, reservations smart, near the main square, a few steps off Via Mazzini at Scale di Via Moglio 1, tel. 0577-847-150).

Trattoria l'Angolo, a family-run hole-in-the-wall, has nine small tables and homemade desserts (€7 pastas, €8 meat dishes, Wed–Mon 12:00–14:30 & 19:00–21:30, closed Tue, Via Ricasoli 9, tel. 0577-848-017). The other **l'Angolo,** at the Fortezza end of Via Ricasoli, is mainly a food store with just a couple of tables for munching on plates of cheese and salami (closed Tue).

Osteria al Giardino is small and dressy, serving near-gourmet creative Tuscan cuisine at the bus-station end of town. Owner and chef Giovanni Luca makes everything fresh, from the bread to the desserts, always has a veggie option, and offers a tasting *menu* (€10 pastas, €14 *secondi,* Mon–Sat 12:30–14:30 & 19:30–21:45, closed

Sun, Piazza Cavour 1, tel. 0577-849-076). Giovanni's wife, Paola, runs the dining room.

Ristorante-Pizzeria San Giorgio is a homely trattoria-pizzeria with kitschy decor and great prices, run by the same family as Trattoria l'Angolo (pizza €4.50–7 served evenings only, daily 12:00–15:00 & 19:00–22:30, near recommended hotel Palazzina Cesira at Via S. Saloni 10–14, tel. 0577-848-507, Mara).

Gather ingredients for a picnic at the **Co-op supermarket** on Via Sant'Agostino (just off Via Ricasoli in front of Sant'Agostino Church, closed Sun), then enjoy your feast up at the Madonna del Soccorso Church, with vast territorial views.

Wine-Tasting and Wineries

Enoteca la Fortezza di Montalcino offers a chance to taste top-end wines by the glass, each with an English explanation. While wine snobs turn up their noses, the medieval setting inside Montalcino's fort is a hit for most visitors. Spoil yourself with Brunello in the cozy *enoteca* or at an outdoor table (€12 for 3 tastings; €5–9 sampler plates of cheeses, *salumi*, honeys, and olive oil; daily 9:00–20:00, closes at 18:00 in off-season, inside the Fortezza, tel. 0577-849-211, www.enotecalafortezza.com).

Caffè Fiaschetteria Italiana was founded by Ferruccio Biondi Santi, who created the famous Brunello wine. The wine library in the back of the café boasts many local wine choices. A meeting place since 1888, this grand café also serves light lunches and espresso to tourists and locals alike (€6–15 for a glass of Brunello and plate of snacks; same prices inside, outside, or in back room; Fri–Wed 7:30–23:00, closed Thu, Piazza del Popolo 6, tel. 0577-849-043). And if it's coffee you need, this place—with its classic 1961 espresso machine—is considered the best in town.

Enoteca di Piazza is one of a chain of wine shops with a system of mechanical wine dispensers. You get a card that keeps track of the samples you take, and you'll pay from €1 to €9 for each 50-mililiter taste of 100 different wines kept fresh in the fancy machines. The only nibbles are saltine-type crackers. They hope you'll buy a bottle of the samples you like, and are happy to educate you in English. (Rule of thumb: a bottle costs about 10 times the cost of the sample. If you buy a bottle, the sample of that wine is free.) While the place feels a little formulaic and sterile, it can be fun—and the wine is great (daily 9:00–20:00, near Piazza del Popolo at Via Matteotti 43, tel. 0577-848-104, www.enotecadipiazza.com).

Wineries: While there are plenty of *enoteche,* there are no real wineries inside the city. The nearby countryside, however, is littered with them, and some offer tastings. While some require an appointment, many also are happy to serve a glass to potential buyers and show them around. **Banfi** is run by the Italian-American

Mariani brothers. Huge and the most touristy, it produces well-respected wines (daily 10:00–18:00, tours daily at 16:00, reserve in advance, 10-minute drive south of Montalcino in Sant'Angelo Scalo, tel. 0577-877-500, www.castellobanfi.com, reservations @banfi.it). **Argiano** claims to be the oldest working winery in the region, dating back to 1580. Not far from Banfi at Sant'Angelo in Colle, their one-hour tour in English includes the vineyards, the exterior of a historic villa, and ancient moldy cellars full of wine casks. They also rent on-site apartments—handy for those who have oversampled (€20 tour includes six wine samples, reserve in advance, tel. 0577-844-037, www.argiano.net, argiano@argiano .net, coming by car the last two miles are along a rough-but-drivable track through vineyards). The Montalcino TI can give you a list of more than 150 regional wineries. Or check with the vintners' consortium (tel. 0577-848-246, www.consorziobrunello dimontalcino.it, info@consorziobrunellodimontalcino.it).

Montalcino Connections

The nearest train station is a 30-minute bus ride (running nearly hourly) away in Buonconvento. Montalcino's bus station is on Piazza Cavour, within the town walls. Bus tickets are sold at the bar on Piazza Cavour or at *tabacchi* shops, but not on board. Check schedules at the TI, at the bus station, or at www.sienamobilita.it.

From Montalcino by Bus to: Siena (6/day, 1.5 hours, €3.50), **Pienza** (5/day, none on Sun, change to line #114 in Torrenieri, 1 hour plus changing time), **Sant'Antimo** (3/day, none on Sun, 15 minutes, €1.50, buy tickets on board). Anyone going to Florence changes in Siena—the most convenient route is by bus to Buonconvento, then take the train.

Pienza

Set on a crest, surrounded by green, rolling hills, the small town of Pienza packs a lot of Renaissance punch. In the 1400s, locally born Pope Pius II of the Piccolomini family decided to remodel his birthplace in the style that was all the rage: Renaissance. Propelled by papal clout, the town of Corsignano was transformed—in only five years' time—into a jewel of Renaissance architecture. It was renamed Pienza, after Pope Pius. The plan was to remodel the entire town, but work ended in 1464 when both the pope and his architect, Bernardo Rossellino, died. Their vision—what you see today—was completed a century later. The architectural focal point is the square, Piazza Pio II, surrounded by the Duomo and the pope's family residence, Palazzo Piccolomini. While Piazza Pio II is Pienza's pride and joy, the entire town—a mix of old stonework, potted plants, and grand views— is fun to explore, especially with a camera or sketchpad in hand. You can walk each lane in the tiny town in a few minutes.

Cute as the town is, it also feels a bit greedy and is entirely given over to snaring the tourist dollar. Because of that, I'd recommend popping in to enjoy the setting, and perhaps touring the palace, but not lingering for an overnight.

Nearly every shop sells the town's specialty: Pecorino cheese. This pungent sheep's cheese is available fresh *(fresco)* or aged *(secco)*, and sometimes contains other ingredients, such as truffles or peppers. Look on menus for warm Pecorino *(al forno* or *alla griglia)*, often topped with honey or pears and served with bread. Along with a glass of local wine, this just might lead you to a new understanding of *la dolce vita*.

Orientation to Pienza

Tourist Information: The TI is 10 yards up the street from Piazza Pio II, inside the Diocesan Museum (daily 10:00–13:00 & 15:00–18:00, shorter hours Nov–March, tel. 0578-749-905). Ignore the kiosk just outside the gate, labeled *Informaturista*, which is a private travel agency.

Arrival in Pienza: Free street parking is available—if you can find it. Otherwise you can park at the large lot near Largo Roma outside of the old town (€1.50/hour, often completely full in the morning).

Helpful Hints: Market day is Friday morning. A public **WC**, marked *gabinetto*, is on the right just outside the town gate on Piazza Dante Alighieri.

Sights in Pienza

▲**Piazza Pio II**—One of Italy's classic piazzas, this square is famous for its elegance and artistic unity. The square and the surrounding buildings were all designed by Rossellino to form an "outdoor room." Spinning around clockwise, you'll see the City Hall (13th-century bell tower with a Renaissance facade and a fine loggia), the Bishop's Palace (now an art museum), the Duomo, and the Piccolomini family palace. Just to the left of the church, a lane leads to the best viewpoint in town.

Duomo—Its classic, symmetrical Renaissance facade—dated 1462 with the Piccolomini family coat of arms immodestly front and center—dominates Piazza Pio II. The interior is charming, with several Gothic altarpieces and painted arches. Windows feature the crest of Pius II, with five half-moons advertising the number of crusades that his family funded. The interior art is Sienese Gothic on the cusp of the Renaissance. As the local clay and *tufa* stone were not ideal building material

for the foundation, the church is slouching. See the cracks in the apse walls, and get seasick behind the main altar.

Cost and Hours: Free, generally open daily 7:00–13:00 & 14:30–19:00.

▲▲**Palazzo Piccolomini**—The home of Pius II and the Piccolomini family (until 1962) can be visited with a guided tour. While the 30-minute tour (in English and Italian) visits only six rooms and the loggia, it offers a fascinating slice of 15th-century aristocratic life and is the sightseeing highlight of the town. In fact, it's the most impressive small-town palace experience I've found in Tuscany. You can check out the well-preserved painted courtyard for free. In Renaissance times, most buildings were covered with elaborate paintings like these.

Cost and Hours: €7, Tue–Sun 10:00–13:00 & 14:00–18:30, closed Mon, tel. 0578-748-392, www.palazzopiccolominipienza.it.

Diocesan Museum (Museo Diocesano)—This collection of religious paintings from local churches fills the cardinal's Renaissance palace. The art is provincial Sienese, displayed in chronological order from the 12th through 17th centuries, conveniently all on one floor.

Cost and Hours: €4; mid-March–Dec Wed–Mon 10:00–13:00 & 15:00–18:00, closed Tue; Jan–mid-March Sat–Sun only 10:00–13:00 & 15:00–18:00; Corso il Rossellino 30.

View Terrace—As you face the church, the upper lane leading left brings you to the panoramic promenade. Views from the terrace include the Tuscan countryside and Monte Amiata, the largest mountain in southern Tuscany, in the distance.

Pienza Connections

Bus tickets are sold at the *edicola/libreria* just outside Pienza's town gate and at some *tabacchi* (or pay a little extra and buy tickets from the driver). Montepulciano is the nearest transportation hub to other points.

From Pienza by Bus to: Siena (5/day, none on Sun, 1.5 hours), **Montepulciano** (8/day, 30 minutes).

Montepulciano

Curving its way along a ridge, Montepulciano (mohn-teh-pull-cheeAH-noh) delights visitors with *vino* and views. Alternately under Sienese and Florentine rule, the city still retains its medieval *contrade* districts, each with a mascot and flag. The neighborhoods compete the last Sunday of August in the Bravio delle Botti, where teams of men push large wine casks uphill from Piazza Marzocco to Piazza Grande, all hoping to win a banner and bragging rights. The entire last week of  August is a festival: Each *contrada* arranges musical entertainment and prepares food at outdoor eateries that offer generous tastings of the local *vino*.

The city is a collage of architectural styles, but the elegant San Biagio Church, at the base of the hill, is its most impressive Renaissance building. Most visitors ignore the architecture and focus more on the city's other creative accomplishment, Vino Nobile di Montepulciano, a tasty red wine.

Orientation to Montepulciano

The commercial action in Montepulciano centers in the lower town, mostly along Via di Gracciano nel Corso (nicknamed Corso). Strolling here, you'll find cheap eateries, gift shops, and tourist traps. The back streets are worth exploring. The main square at the top of town is Piazza Grande. Standing proudly above all the touristy sales energy, it has a more noble, Florentine feel.

Tourist Information: The TI is near the bus station, in Piazza Don Minzoni. It books hotels and rooms for no fee, sells train tickets, has an Internet terminal (€3.50/hour), and can book one of the town's two taxis (Mon–Sat 9:30–12:30 & 15:00–18:00, Sun 9:30–12:30, daily until 19:00 in summer except until 20:00 in Aug, tel. 0578-757-341, www.prolocomontepulciano.it).

Note that there's a more central office that looks like a TI, but is actually a privately run "Strada del Vino" (Wine Road) agency. They don't have city info, but provide wine-road maps

and organize **wine tours** in the city, and minibus winery tours
farther afield. They also offer other tours (olive oil, cheese, and
slow food), cooking classes, and more, depending on season and
demand (Mon–Sat 10:00–13:00 & 15:00–18:00, closed Sun, closed
Sat off-season, Piazza Grande 7, tel. 0578-717-484, www.strada
vinonobile.it).

Arrival in Montepulciano: Most visits begin at the fortified Porta al Prato gate, near the bus station. From the gate, it's
a 15-minute walk uphill along the Corso, the bustling main drag
(note the Etruscan reliefs on the foundation of Palazzo Bucelli—
see photo on previous page), to the main square, Piazza Grande. If
you arrive at the bus station, an orange shuttle bus can take you to
Piazza Grande (2/hour); it's a good strategy to take the bus up and
walk back down.

Drivers arriving by car should park outside the walls (don't
try to tackle the tiny roads inside the city), either at the bus station
or the numerous lots on the edge of town. For a free spot near the
top of the hill, follow signs for lots #7 and #8. If you're sleeping
in town, your hotelier will give you a permit to park within the
walls.

Helpful Hints: Market day is Thursday. There's no official
baggage storage in town, but the TI might let you leave bags with
them if they have space. Public **WCs** are located at the TI, to the
right of Palazzo Comunale, and at the Sant'Agostino Church. A
self-service **laundry** is at Via del Paolino 2 (€4 wash, €4 dry, daily
8:00–22:00, tel. 0578-717-544). For a **taxi,** call 335-617-7126.

Sights in Montepulciano

Piazza Grande—This pleasant, lively piazza is surrounded by a
grab bag of architectural sights. If the medieval Palazzo Comunale
reminds you of Palazzo Vecchio in Florence, it's because Florence

dominated this town in the 15th and
16th centuries. The crenellations
along the roof were never intended
to hide soldiers—they're meant just
to symbolize power. A cistern system fed by rainwater draining from
surrounding palaces supplied the
courtyard's fine well. Check out its
19th-century pulleys, the grills to
keep animals from contaminating
the water supply, and the Medici
coat of arms (with lions symbolizing political power of Florence).

Climbing the **tower** rewards you with a windy but commanding view from the terrace below the clock. Go into the Palazzo

Montepulciano

1. Mueblè il Riccio Rooms
2. Albergo Duomo
3. Camere Bellavista Rooms
4. To Agriturismo Cretaiole
5. Ai Quattro Venti
6. Osteria dell'Aquacheta
7. Osteria del Conte
8. Launderette
9. Ramaio Cesare
   Coppersmith Workshop

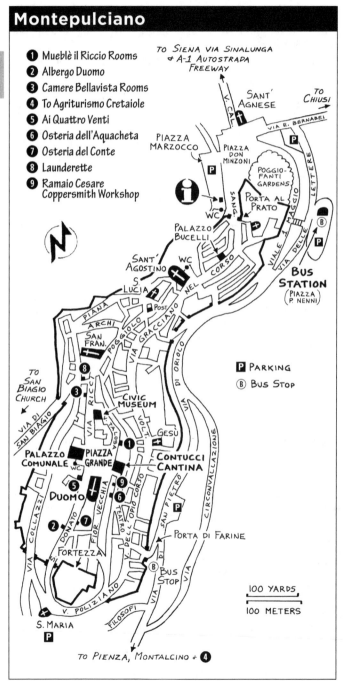

Comunale, head up the stairs to your left, and pay on the second floor (€2, daily 10:00–18:00, closed in winter). The Palazzo de' Nobili-Tarugi is a Renaissance arcaded confection; meanwhile, the unfinished Duomo looks glumly on, wishing the city hadn't run out of money for its facade. The Contucci Palace (left of the church) is lucky enough to have a 16th-century Renaissance facade. The Contucci family still lives in their palace, producing and selling their own wine. The town is fortunate to be graced with so many bold and noble palazzos—Florentine nobility favored Montepulciano as a breezy and relaxed place for a secondary residence.

Duomo—This church's unfinished facade—rough stonework left waiting for the final marble veneer—is not that unusual. Many churches were built just to the point where they had a functional interior, and then, for various practical reasons, the facades were left unfinished. But step inside and you'll be rewarded with some fine art. A beautiful Andrea della Robbia glazed-terra-cotta *Altar of the Lilies* is behind the baptismal font (on the left as you enter). The high altar features a luminous early-Renaissance Assumption triptych by the Sienese artist Taddeo di Bartolo. Showing Mary in her dreamy eternal sleep as she ascends to be crowned by Jesus, it illustrates how Siena clung to the Gothic aesthetic—elaborate gold leaf and lacy pointed arches—to show heavenly grandeur at the expense of realism.

Cost and Hours: Free, daily 9:00–13:00 & 15:00–18:00.

▲▲**Contucci Cantina**—Montepulciano's most popular attraction isn't made of stone...it's the famous wine, Vino Nobile. This robust red can be tasted in any of the cantinas lining Via Ricci and Via di Gracciano nel Corso, but the cantina in the base-

ment of the Contucci Palace is both historic and fun. While the palace has a formal wine-tasting showroom facing the square, head down the lane on the right to the actual cellars, where you'll meet lively Adamo, who has been making wine since 1953 and welcomes tourists into his cellar. While at the palace, you may meet Andrea Contucci, whose family has lived here since the 11th century. He loves to share his family's products with the public. Adamo and Signor Contucci usually have a dozen bottles open (free drop-in tasting, daily 8:30–12:30 & 14:30–18:30, Piazza Grande 7, tel. 0578-757-006, www.contucci.it).

After sipping a little wine with Adamo, explore the palace basement, with its 13th-century vaults. Originally part of the town's wall, these chambers have been filled since the 1500s with huge barrels of wine. Dozens of barrels of Croatian, Italian, and French oak (1,000–2,500 liters each) cradle the wine through a two-year in-the-barrel aging process, while the wine picks up the personality of the wood. After about 35 years, an exhausted barrel has nothing left to offer its wine, so it's retired. Adamo explains that the French oak gives the wine "pure elegance," the Croatian is more masculine, and the Italian oak is a marriage of the two. Each barrel is labeled with the size in liters, the year the wine was barreled, and the percentage of alcohol (determined by how much sun shone in that year). "Nobile"-grade wine needs a minimum of 13 percent alcohol.

Civic Museum (Museo Civico)—The highlight of this small, eclectic, and forgettable museum is its colorful Andrea della Robbia ceramic altarpieces and Etruscan artifacts.

Cost and Hours: €4.20, Tue–Sun 10:00–13:00 & 15:00–18:00, closed Mon, no English, Via Ricci 10, tel. 0578-717-300.

Ramaio Cesare—Cesare the coppersmith is an institution in Montepulciano, carrying on his grandfather's trade by hammering into existence an immense selection of copper objects in his cavern-like workshop. Though his English is limited, he's happy to show you photos of his work—including the copper top of the Duomo in Siena (Via dell'Opio nel Corso 64, tel. 0578-758-753, www.rameria.com).

San Biagio Church—Just outside of town, down a picturesque driveway lined with cypresses, this church—designed by Antonio da Sangallo and built of locally quarried travertine—is Renaissance perfection. The proportions of the Greek cross floor plan give the building a pleasing rhythmic quality. Bramante, who designed St. Peter's at the Vatican in 1516, was inspired by this dome. Walk around the building to study the freestanding towers. The lone tower was supposed to have a twin, but it was never built. The soaring interior, with a high dome and lantern, creates a fine Renaissance space.

Cost and Hours: Free, normally open daily 8:30–18:30. Consider a picnic or snooze on the grass in back. The street called Via di San Biagio, leading from the church up into town, makes for an enjoyable, if challenging, walk.

Sleeping in Montepulciano

(€1 = about $1.25, country code: 39)

$$$ Mueblè il Riccio ("Hedgehog") is medieval-elegant, with six modern and spotless rooms, an awesome roof terrace, and friendly owners (Sb-€80, Db-€100, Tb-€116, breakfast-€8, air-con, Internet access and Wi-Fi, limited free parking—request when you reserve, a block below the main square at Via Talosa 21, tel. & fax 0578-757-713, www.ilriccio.net, info@ilriccio.net, Gió and Ivana speak English). Gió and his son Iacopo give country tours (€30/hour) in one of their classic Italian cars; for tour details, see their website. Ivana makes wonderful breakfast tarts.

$$ Albergo Duomo, renting 13 rooms, is big, fairly modern, and newly decorated, with a comfortable lounge downstairs and a decent breakfast (small Db-€70, standard Db-€90, Tb-€115, family deals, Wi-Fi in lounge, free parking nearby, Via di San Donato 14, tel. 0578-757-473, www.albergoduomo.it, albergoduomo @libero.it, Elisa and Saverio).

$ Camere Bellavista has 10 basic rooms, some with better views than others. Room 6 has a view terrace worth reserving (Db-€70, terrace Db-€80, optional breakfast at a bar in the piazza-€3, cash only, no elevator, Via Ricci 25, no reception—call before arriving or ring bell, mobile 347-823-2314, fax 0578-716-341, bellavista@bccmp.com, Gabriella, little English spoken).

Between Montepulciano and Montalcino: A Green Acres *Agriturismo* Holiday

$$ Agriturismo Cretaiole, in pristine farmland on the Montalcino–Pienza road, is warmly run by Isabella and her husband, Carlo. This family-friendly farm, deeply rooted in the culture, welcomes visitors for weeklong stays (generally Sat–Sat)

in six comfortable apartments. Eager to share their local traditions, they create a community of about 14–20 travelers who are looking for a rich cultural education. Isabella offers pasta-making classes, guided walks and hikes, visits to local wineries, and the chance to help with truffle-hunting and/or grape and olive harvesting. Carlo is a professional olive-oil taster (a class is included as part of your weekly stay). Carlo's father, Luciano, is in charge of the grappa and tending the vegetable garden (take your pick of the free veggies). While there's no swimming pool—for philosophical reasons—many thoughtful touches and extras, such as Wi-Fi, mountain bikes, and loaner mobile phones, are provided (Db-€750/week, small Db apartment-€890/week, large Db apartment-€1,190/week, same apartment for four-€1,390/week, prices soft mid-Nov–mid-March, non-included activities are fairly priced, tel. & fax 0578-748-083, Isabella's mobile 338-740-9245, www.cretaiole.it, info@cretaiole. it). It's on the Montalcino–Pienza road (S-146), about 11 miles out of Montalcino, and about three miles out of Pienza. While they prefer weeklong stays, when things are slow they may accept guests for as few as three nights (for this you must book less than a month in advance, Db-€110, 3-night minimum).

Eating in Montepulciano

Ai Quattro Venti is fresh, flavorful, fun, and right on Piazza Grande, offering good indoor and outdoor seating (€8.50 pastas, Fri–Wed 12:30–14:30 & 19:30–22:30, closed Thu, next to City Hall on Piazza Grande, tel. 0578-717-231, Chiara).

Osteria dell'Aquacheta is a carnivore's dream come true, famous among locals for its excellent beef steaks. Its long, narrow room is jammed with shared tables and tight seating, with an open fire in back and a big hunk of red beef lying on the counter like a corpse on a gurney. Giulio, with a pen tucked into his ponytail, whacks off slabs with a cleaver, confirms the weight and price with the diner, and tosses them on the grill—seven minutes per side. Steaks are sold by the weight (€3/100 grams, or *etto*, one kilo is about the smallest they serve, two can split it for €30). They also serve hearty €6 pastas and salads and a fine house wine (Wed–Mon 12:30–15:00 & 19:30–22:30, closed Tue, Via del Teatro 22, tel. 0578-758-443). In

the tradition of old trattorias, they serve one glass, which you use alternately for wine and water.

Osteria del Conte, an attractive but humble family-run bistro, offers a €30 *menù del Conte*—a four-course dinner of local specialties including wine—as well as à la carte options and cooking like mom's (€7 pastas, €12 *secondi*, indoor and outdoor seating, Thu–Tue 12:30–14:30 & 19:30–21:30, closed Wed, Via S. Donato 19, tel. 0578-756-062).

Montepulciano Connections

All buses leave from Piazza Pietro Nenni. Check www.siena mobilita.it for schedules.

From Montepulciano by Bus to: Florence (3/day with a change in Bettole), **Siena** (8/day, 1.25 hours, none on Sun), **Pienza** (8/day, 30 minutes). There are hourly bus connections to **Chiusi,** a town on the main Florence–Rome rail line; Chiusi is a much better bet than the distant Montepulciano station (5 miles away), which is served only by milk-run trains. Buses connect Montepulciano's bus station and its train station (8/day, none on Sun).

To Montalcino: This connection is problematic by public transportation—consider asking at the TI for a taxi. Although expensive (about €50), a taxi could make sense for two or more people. Otherwise you can take a bus to Buonconvento, then change to get to Montalcino (2 hours). **Drivers** find route S-146 to Montalcino particularly scenic.

Cortona

Cortona blankets a 1,700-foot hill surrounded by dramatic Tuscan and Umbrian views. Frances Mayes' books, such as *Under the Tuscan Sun,* placed this town in the touristic limelight, just as Peter Mayle's books popularized the Luberon region in France. But long before Mayes ever published a book, Cortona was popular with

Romantics and considered one of the classic Tuscan hill towns. Unlike San Gimignano, Cortona maintains a rustic and gritty personality—even with its long history of foreigners who, enamored with its Tuscan charm, made this their adopted home.

The city began as one of the largest Etruscan settlements, the remains of which can be seen at the base of the city walls, as well as in the nearby tombs. It grew to its present size in the 13th to 16th centuries, when it was a colorful and crowded city, eventually allied with Florence. The farmland that fills almost every view from the city was marshy and uninhabitable until about 200 years ago, when it was drained and turned into some of Tuscany's most fertile land.

Art-lovers know Cortona as the home of Renaissance painter Luca Signorelli, Baroque master Pietro da Cortona (Berretini), and the 20th-century Futurist artist Gino Severini. The city's museums and churches reveal many of the works of these native sons.

Orientation to Cortona

Most of the main sights, shops, and restaurants cluster around the level streets on the Piazza Garibaldi–Piazza del Duomo axis, but Cortona will have you huffing and puffing up some steep hills.

Tourist Information: The helpful TI is on the main drag at Via Nazionale 42 (April–Oct daily 9:00–13:00 & 15:00–19:00, shorter hours and closed Sun off-season, sells train and bus tickets, tel. 0575-630-352, www.apt.arezzo.it).

Cortona

TO ETRUSCAN TOMBS
+ AREZZO

TUSCAN
SUN

PIAZZA
DEL DUOMO

DIOCESAN
MUSEUM

PORTA
SANTA
MARIA

DUOMO

PORTA
COLONIA

THEATER
& PIAZZA
SIGNORELLI

VIA DARDANO

VIA

VIA BERRETINI

ETRUSCAN
MUSEUM IN
CASALI PALACE

VIA CASALI

P.
SIG.

POST

13

VIA

S. FRAN.

V. S. INC.

ETRUSC.
GATE

VIA ROMA

12

11

CITY
HALL

9

PZZA.
REPUB.

15

16

10

3

VIA MAFFEI

6

14

VIA NAZIONALE

VIA GUELFA

i

1

B

SAN
DOMEN-
ICO

VIA MERCATO

VIALE C. BATTISTI

P

VIA SEVE

PORTA
SANT'
AGOSTINO

SANTO
SPIRITO

BUS STOP
PIAZZA
GARIBALDI

7

2

DCH

START

Arrival in Cortona: Train travelers arrive at Camucia-Cortona train station, a long, strenuous walk from the town on roads with no sidewalks. Fortunately, buses are generally timed with the arrival of the train and zip you right up to town in 10 minutes (2/hour, €1.10, buy tickets at newsstand 200 yards from station). Buses stop at Piazza Garibaldi. From here, it's a level five-minute walk down bustling shop-lined Via Nazionale (stop by the TI) to Piazza della Repubblica, the heart of the town, dominated by City Hall (Palazzo del Comune). From this square, a two-minute stroll leads you past the interesting Etruscan Museum and theater to Piazza del Duomo, where you'll find the recommended Diocesan Museum. Steep streets, many of them stepped, go from Piazza della Repubblica up to the San Niccolò and Santa Margherita churches and the Medici Fortress (a 30-minute climb from Piazza della Repubblica).

Drivers will find several free lots right outside the walls. Viale Cesare Battisti may be your best bet. A free lot just after the big

❶ Hotel San Luca & Parking
❷ Hotel Villa Marsili
❸ Rugapiana Vacanze B&B
❹ Casa Betania
❺ Istituto Santa Margherita
❻ San Marco Hostel
❼ Casa Kita
❽ To Casa San Martino,
   La Villetta di San Martino B&B
   & Castello di Montegualandro
❾ Trattoria la Grotta
❿ Ristorante La Loggetta
⓫ Ristorante La Bucaccia
⓬ Fufluns Tavern Pizzeria
⓭ Osteria del Teatro
⓮ Enoteca la Saletta
⓯ Despar Market Molesini
⓰ Foto Lamentini
   (Internet Access)

Santo Spirito Church has an escalator leading to Piazza Garibaldi. Piazza Garibaldi itself has a handful of pay spots (marked by blue lines, pay & display, cheap, free 20:00–8:00). The small town is actually very long, and it can be smart to drive to the top for sightseeing up there (parking at Santa Margherita Basilica).

Helpful Hints: Market day is Saturday on Piazza Signorelli (from early morning until 14:00). The town has **no baggage storage,** so try asking nicely at a hotel or museum to store your bag there. The best public **WC** is located in Piazza del Duomo, under Santa Margherita's statue. There are several **Internet** terminals at Foto Lamentini (€3/hour, daily April–Oct 10:00–20:00, Oct–March 10:30–13:00 & 14:00–19:00, Via Nazionale 33, tel. 0575-62588).

Local Guide: Giovanni Adreani exudes energy and a love of his city and Tuscan high culture. He is great at bringing the fine points of the city to life and can take visitors around in his car for no extra price. As this region is speckled with underappreciated charms, having Giovanni for a day as your driver/guide promises to be a fascinating experience (€110/half-day, €200/day, tel. 0575-630-665, mobile 347-176-2830, www.adreanigiovanni .com, adreanigiovanni@alice.it).

Cooking Classes: Husband-and-wife team Romano and Agostina hold morning hands-on cooking and cheesemaking classes in the kitchen of their Ristorante La Bucaccia (described later, under "Eating in Cortona"). In the three-hour class, you'll prepare two *antipasti,* two types of pasta, an entrée, and a dessert, which you then get to eat (€70/person, price includes wine, 5 percent discount with this book, classes start at 9:30, book in advance, personalized classes available, Via Ghibellina 17, tel. 0575-606-039, www.labucaccia.it).

Self-Guided Walk

Welcome to Cortona

This introductory walking tour will take you from Piazza Garibaldi up the main strip to the town center, its piazzas, and the Duomo.

• *Start at the bus stop in...*

Piazza Garibaldi: Many visits start and finish in this square, thanks to its bus stop. While the piazza, bulging out from the town fortifications like a big turret, looks like part of an old rampart, it's really a souvenir of those early French and English Romantics—the ones who first created the notion of a dreamy, idyllic Tuscany. During the Napoleonic Age, the French built this balcony (and the scenic little park behind the adjacent San Domenico Church) simply to enjoy a commanding view of the Tuscan countryside.

With Umbria about a mile away, Cortona marks the end of Tuscany. This is a major cultural divide, as Cortona was the last town in Charlemagne's empire and the last under Medici rule. Umbria, just to the south, was papal territory for centuries. These deep-seated cultural disparities were a great challenge for the visionaries who unified the fractured region to create the modern nation of Italy during the 1860s. A statue in the center of this square honors one of the heroes of the struggle for Italian unification—the brilliant revolutionary general Giuseppe Garibaldi.

Enjoy the commanding view from here. Assisi is just over the ridge on the left. Lake Trasimeno peeks from behind the hill, looking quite normal today. But, according to legend, it was blood-red after Hannibal defeated the Romans here in 217 B.C., and 15,000 died in the battle. The only sizable town you can see, on the right, is Montepulciano. Cortona is still defined by its Etruscan walls—remnants of these walls, with stones laid 2,500 years ago, stretch from here in both directions.

Frances Mayes put Cortona on the map for many Americans

with her book (and later movie) *Under the Tuscan Sun*. The book describes her real-life experience buying, fixing up, and living in a run-down villa in Cortona with her husband, Ed. The movie romanticized the story, turning Frances into a single, recently

divorced writer who restores the villa and her peace of mind. Frances' villa isn't "under the Tuscan sun" very often; it's named "Bramasole"—literally, "craving sun." On the wrong side of the hill, it's in the shade after 15:00. She and her husband still live there part of each year and are respected members of their adopted community (outside the walls, behind the hill on the left).

• *From this square, head into town along...*

Via Nazionale: The only level road in town, locals have nicknamed Via Nazionale the *ruga piana* (flat wrinkle). This is the main commercial street in this town of 2,500, and it's been that way for a long time. Every shop seems to have a medieval cellar or an Etruscan well. Notice the crumbling sandstone door frames. The entire town is constructed out of this grainy, eroding rock.

• *Via Nazionale leads to...*

Piazza della Repubblica: The City Hall faces Cortona's main square. Note how the City Hall is a clever hodgepodge of twin medieval towers, with a bell tower added to connect them, and a grand staircase to lend some gravitas. Notice also the fine wood balconies on the left. In the Middle Ages, wooden extensions such as balconies were common features on the region's stone buildings. These balconies (not original, but rebuilt in the 19th century) would have fit right into the medieval cityscape. These days, you usually see only the holes that once supported the long-gone wooden beams.

This spot has been the town center since Etruscan times. Four centuries before Christ, an important street led from here up to the hill-capping temple. Later, the square became the Roman forum. Opposite the City Hall is the handy, recommended Despar Market Molesini, good for cheap sandwiches. Above that is the loggia—once a fish market, now a recommended restaurant.

• *The second half of the square, to the right of the City Hall, is...*

Piazza Signorelli: Dominated by Casali Palace, this square was the headquarters of the Florentine captains who used to control the city. Peek into the palace entrance for a look at the coats of arms. Every six months, Florence would send a new captain to Cortona, who would help establish his rule by inserting his family coat of arms into the palace's wall. These date from the 15th to the 17th century, and were once painted with bright colors.

Cortona's fine Etruscan Museum (described below, under "Sights in Cortona") is in the Casali Palace courtyard, which is lined with many more of these family coats of arms. The inviting Caffè del Teatro fills the loggia of the theater that is named for the town's most famous artist, Luca Signorelli.

• *Head down the street just to the right of the museum to...*

Piazza del Duomo: Here you'll find the Diocesan Museum (listed under "Sights in Cortona"), cathedral, and a statue of Santa Margherita. If the cathedral seems a little underwhelming and tucked away, that's because it is. Cortona loves its hometown saint, Margherita, and put the energy it would normally invest in its cathedral into the Santa Margherita Basilica, at the top of the hill. Margherita was a 13th-century rich girl who took good care of the poor and was an early follower of St. Francis and St. Clare. Many locals believe that Margherita protected Cortona from WWII bombs.

The Piazza del Duomo terrace comes with a commanding view of the Tuscan countryside. Find the town cemetery in the distance. If you were standing here before the time of Napoleon, you'd be surrounded by tombstones. But Cortona's graveyards—like other urban graveyards throughout Napoleon's realm—were cleaned out in the early 1800s to reclaim land and improve hygiene.

• *Next, enter the...*

Duomo: The Cortona cathedral is not—strictly speaking—a cathedral, because it no longer has a bishop. The white-and-gray Florentine Renaissance–style interior is mucked up with lots of Baroque chapels filling once-spacious side niches. In the rear (on the right) is an altar cluttered with relics. Technically, any Catholic altar, in order to be consecrated, needs a relic embedded in it. Go ahead—gently lift up the tablecloth. The priest here doesn't mind. You'll see a little marble patch that holds a bit of a saint (daily 7:30–13:00 & 15:00–18:30, shorter hours in winter, closed during Mass).

• *From here, you can visit the nearby Diocesan Museum or head back toward Piazza della Repubblica to visit the Etruscan Museum in Piazza Signorelli (both listed next), or to get a bite to eat (see "Eating in Cortona," later).*

Sights in Cortona

▲Etruscan Museum (Museo dell'Accademia Etrusca)— Located in the 13th-century Casali Palace, this fine gallery (established in 1727) is one of the first dedicated to artifacts from the Etruscan civilization. You'll see an exhibit on the Roman settlement and take a virtual tour of the Etruscan "Il Sodo" tombs. The Cortona Tablet (*Tabula Cortonensis,* second century B.C.), a 200-

word contract inscribed in bronze, contains dozens of Etruscan words archaeologists had never seen before its discovery in 1992. Along with lots of gold and jewelry, you'll find a seventh-century B.C. grater (for some *very* aged Parmesan cheese) and a magnificent fourth-century B.C. bronze oil lamp with 16 spouts, set in a small four-pillared temple. The library of the Etruscan Academy, founded in 1727 to promote an understanding of the city through the study of archaeology, is upstairs. This eclectic museum also has an Egyptian section, fine Roman mosaics, and a room dedicated to modern abstract works by Severini, all lovingly described in English.

Cost and Hours: €8, €10 combo-ticket includes Diocesan Museum; April–Oct daily 10:00–19:00; Nov–March Tue–Sun 10:00–17:00, closed Mon; Casali Palace on Piazza Signorelli, tel. 0575-637-235, www.cortonamaec.org.

▲**Diocesan Museum (Museo Diocesano)**—This collection of art from the town's many churches has works by Fra Angelico and Pietro Lorenzetti, and masterpieces by hometown hero and Renaissance master Luca Signorelli.

Don't miss Fra Angelico's sumptuous *Annunciation*. In this scene, Mary says "Yes," consenting to bear God's son. Notice how the house sits on a pillow of flowers...the new Eden. The old Eden, featuring the expulsion of Adam and Eve from Paradise, is in the upper left. The painting comes with comic strip–like narration of scenes from Mary's life: The angel's words are top and bottom, while Mary's answer is upside down (logically, since it's directed to God, who would be reading while looking down from heaven).

The crucifix (by Pietro Lorenzetti, c. 1325, just to the right of the Fra Angelico) is impressive in its severity. Notice the gripping realism—even the tendons in Jesus' arms are pulled tight. Another highlight is Luca Signorelli's *Mourning of the Dead Christ (Compianto sul Cristo Morto)*. Signorelli was a generation ahead of Michelangelo and, with his passion for painting ideas, was an inspiration for the young artist. Everything in his painting has a meaning: The skull of Adam sits under the sacrifice of Jesus; the hammer represents the Passion (the Crucifixion leading to the Resurrection); the lake is blood; and so on. I don't understand all of the medieval symbolism, but it is intense.

Cost and Hours: €5, €10 combo-ticket includes Etruscan Museum, helpful audioguide-€3; April–Oct daily 10:00–19:00; Nov–March Tue–Sun 10:00–17:00, closed Mon; Piazza del Duomo 1, tel. 0575-62-830.

Church of St. Francis—Established by St. Francis' best friend, Brother Elias, this church dates from the 13th century. The wooden beams of the ceiling are original. While the place was redecorated in the Baroque age, some of the original frescoes that once wall-papered the church peek through the whitewash in a chapel on the left. Francis fans visit for its precious Franciscan relics. To the left of the altar, you'll find one of Francis' tunics, his pillow (inside a fancy cover), and his gospel book. Behind the altar is Elias' very simple tomb. It reads "Frate Elia da Cortona." Notice how the entire high altar seems designed to frame its precious relic—a piece of the cross Elias brought back from his visit to the patriarch in Constantinople. You're welcome to climb the altar for a close-up look (daily 9:00–18:30).

San Niccolò Church—Signorelli enthusiasts will want to make the pilgrimage up to this tiny church, a steep 10-minute walk beyond the Church of St. Francis. Ring the bell on the left side of the church and the caretaker might give you a short tour in Italian. The highlight of this humble church is an altarpiece painted on both sides by Signorelli. The caretaker activates a tricky arm mechanism that moves the picture away from the wall to reveal the painting behind it.

   Cost and Hours: €1 donation, daily in summer 9:00–12:00 & 15:00–19:00, off-season until 17:00. Even if you can't get in, it's still worth the walk just to explore the picturesque neighborhood.

Santa Margherita Basilica—From San Niccolò Church, another steep path leads uphill 10 minutes to this basilica, which houses the remains of Margherita, the town's favorite saint. Santa Margherita, an unwed mother from Montepulciano, found her calling with the Franciscans in Cortona, tending to the sick and poor. The well-preserved and remarkably emotional 13th-century crucifix on the right is the cross that, according to legend, talked to Margherita.

   Cost and Hours: Free, daily 9:00–12:00 & 15:00–19:00, tel. 0575-603-116.

   Nearby: Still need more altitude? Head uphill five more minutes to the Medici Fortezza (€3, usually open daily April–Sept 9:00–12:00 & 15:00–18:00, July–Aug until 19:00, closed Oct–March). The views are stunning, stretching all the way to distant Lago Trasimeno.

Etruscan Tombs near Cortona—Guided tours to nearby "Il Sodo" tombs (called *melone* for their melon-like shape) are complicated to arrange. But the excavation site and bits of the ruins are easy to visit and can be seen from outside the fence in the morning. It's just a couple miles out of Cortona on the Arezzo road (R-71), at the edge of Camucia at the foot of the Cortona hill; ask anyone for "Il Sodo."

Sleeping in Cortona

(€1 = about $1.25, country code: 39)

$$$ Hotel San Luca, perched on the side of a cliff, has 57 modern, impersonal business-class rooms, half with stunning views of Lago Trasimeno. While tired and a bit run-down, it's friendly and conveniently located right at the bus stop (Sb-€85, Db-€120, Tb-€150, request a view room when you reserve, popular with Americans and groups, Piazza Garibaldi 1, tel. 0575-630-460, fax 0575-630-105, www.sanlucacortona.com, info@sanlucacortona.com). If driving, you might find a spot at the small public parking lot at the hotel (cheap and easy meters).

$$$ Hotel Villa Marsili is a comfortable splurge just below town. It was originally a 15th-century church, then an elegant 18th-century home. Today its 25 rooms and public areas have been recently redecorated and restored. Guests enjoy a complimentary aperitif every evening on the panoramic terrace (Db-€130–250, Db suite-€230–350, Jacuzzi in some rooms, air-con, Wi-Fi and Internet access, Viale Cesare Battisti 13, tel. 0575-605-252, fax 0575-605-618, www.villamarsili.net, info@villamarsili.net, Stefano).

$$ Rugapiana Vacanze B&B rents four doubles and four apartments, each described separately on their website. Located on Cortona's main drag, it's beautifully furnished with all the thoughtful touches (apartment-€100–115 or Db-€95 with breakfast at a nearby bar, 10 percent discount with this book, family suites, Wi-Fi, Via Nazionale 63, tel. & fax 0575-630-712, mobile 340-808-6879, www.rugapianavacanze.com, info@rugapianavacanze.com, Massimo).

$ Casa Betania, a big, wistful convent with an inviting view terrace, rents 27 fine rooms (mostly twin beds) for the best price in town. While it's primarily for "thoughtful travelers," anyone looking for a peaceful place to call home will feel welcome in this pilgrims' resort (S-€32, D-€44, Db-€48, Tb-€66, extra bed-€20, breakfast-€4, parking, about a third of a mile out of town, a few minutes' walk below Piazza Garibaldi at Via Gino Severini 50, tel. & fax 0575-630-423, www.casaperferiebetania.com, info@casaperferiebetania.com).

$ Istituto Santa Margherita, run by the Serve di Maria Riparatrici sisters, rents 22 cheap and simple rooms in a smaller and more institutional-feeling convent across the street (Sb-€42, Db-€58, Tb-€75, Qb-€86, breakfast-€5, elevator, free parking, Viale Cesare Battisti 15, tel. 0575-178-7203 or 0575-630-336, fax 0575-630-549, comunitacortona@smr.it).

$ San Marco Hostel, at the top of town, is housed in a remodeled 13th-century palace (bed in dorm-€16, in 2-bed and

4-bed rooms-€20, includes breakfast, dinner-€10.50, lockout 10:00–13:00, Via Maffei 57, tel. & fax 0575-601-392, www.cortona hostel.com, ostellocortona@libero.it).

$ Casa Kita, renting four fine rooms, is a homely place at the edge of town with breathtaking views from its terrace (Db-€60, 100 yards below Piazza Garibaldi at Vicolo degli Orti 7, tel. 389-557-9893, www.casakita.com, info@casakita.com, Lorenzini family).

Near Cortona

$$$ Casa San Martino, a 30-minute drive east of Cortona near the isolated village of Lisciano Niccone, is a 250-year-old countryside farmhouse run as a B&B by American Italophile Lois Martin. While Lois reserves the summer (June–Aug) for people staying at least one week, she'll take guests staying a minimum of three nights the rest of the year (Db-€140, 10 percent discount for my readers—mention this book when you reserve, pool, Casa San Martino 19, Lisciano Niccone, tel. 075-844-288, fax 075-844-422, www.tuscanyvacation.com, csm@tuscanyvacation.com).

$$$ Castello di Montegualandro, a well-preserved castle on a hill opposite Cortona, overlooks the lake and countryside. The Marti family rents four charming medieval apartments, formerly peasants' quarters, inside the peaceful castle walls. Each one is unique and named for its former use; for example, the Fornaci's sunken living room used to be a kiln (apartments range from €400–450 for 3-night minimum stay, €700–800/week, cash only; for a 5-night stay, mention this book for a 7 percent discount; 10 percent discount for longer stays; 10 minutes southeast of Cortona in Tuoro sul Trasimeno, tel. & fax 075-823-0267, www.monte gualandro.com, info@montegualandro.com, Claudio and Franca).

$$ La Villetta di San Martino B&B is a tidy place run by Lois' neighbors, Ernestine and Gisbert Schwanke (Db-€80, 2-night minimum, cash only, common kitchen and sitting room, San Martino 36, tel. & fax 075-844-309, www.tuscanyvacation .com, erni@netemedia.net).

Eating in Cortona

Trattoria la Grotta, just off Piazza della Repubblica, is a traditional place serving daily specials to an enthusiastic clientele under grotto-like vaults (€7 pastas, €8 meat dishes, good wine by the glass, Wed–Mon 12:00–14:30 & 19:00–22:00, closed Tue, Piazza Baldelli 3, tel. 0575-630-271).

Ristorante La Loggetta serves up big portions of well-presented Tuscan cuisine on the loggia overlooking Piazza della Repubblica. While they have fine indoor seating, I'd eat here for the chance to gaze at the square over a meal (€8 pastas, €7–15 meat dishes, Thu–Tue 12:30–15:00 & 19:30–23:00, closed Wed, Piazza Pescheria 3, tel. 0575-630-575).

Ristorante La Bucaccia is a family-run eatery set in a rustic medieval wine cellar. It's dressy and romantic. They take great pride in their Chianina beef entrées and homemade pastas. With an evangelical pride in their food, Romano hosts and his wife Agostina cooks (€9 pastas, €14 entrées, daily 12:00–15:30 & 19:00–24:00, show this book for a 5 percent discount and a small free antipasto, Via Ghibellina 17, tel. 0575-606-039).

Fufluns Tavern Pizzeria (that's the Etruscan name for Dionysus) is easy-going, friendly, and remarkably unpretentious for its location in the town center. It's popular with locals for its good, inexpensive Tuscan cooking and friendly staff (cheap, lots of €6 pizza and pasta plus big salads, good house wine, Wed–Mon 12:15–14:30 & 19:15–22:30, closed Tue, a block below Piazza della Repubblica at Via Ghibellina 3, tel. 0575-604-140).

Osteria del Teatro tries very hard to create a romantic Old World atmosphere, and does it well. Chef Emiliano serves nicely presented and tasty international and local cuisine (taking creative liberties with traditions). There's good outdoor seating, too (Thu–Tue 12:30–14:30 & 19:30–21:30, closed Wed, 2 blocks uphill from the main square at Via Maffei 2, tel. 0575-630-556).

Enoteca la Saletta, dark and classy, is good for fine wine and a light meal. You can sit inside surrounded by wine bottles or outside to people-watch on the town's main drag (daily 7:30–24:00, meals served 12:00–24:00, Via Nazionale 26, tel. 0575-603-366).

For a Picnic: On the main square, the chic little **Despar Market Molesini** makes tasty sandwiches (see list on counter and order by number) and sells whatever you might want for a picnic (Mon–Sat 7:00–13:30 & 16:00–19:30, closed Sun, Piazza della Repubblica 23). Munch your picnic across the square on the steps of the City Hall, or just past Piazza Garibaldi in the public gardens behind San Domenico Church.

Cortona Connections

Cortona has good train connections with the rest of Italy through its Camucia-Cortona station. To get to the train station at the foot of the hill, take a taxi or hop the bus (€1.10, 2/hour between Piazza Garibaldi and station, buy tickets at newsstand, TI, or *tabacchi* shop, or buy from driver at double the price). Note that some only take you as far as the newsstand *(edicola)* 200 yards in front of the station.

From Cortona by Train to: Rome (9/day, 2.5 hours), **Florence** (hourly, 1.5 hours), **Assisi** (every 2 hours, 70 minutes), **Montepulciano** (10/day, 1–1.25 hours, change in Chiusi—because few buses serve Montepulciano's town center from its distant train station, it's better to go by train to Chiusi, then by hourly bus to Montepulciano), **Chiusi** (hourly, 30 minutes). Most trains stop at the Camucia-Cortona train station, but some trains to/from Rome and Florence stop at Terontola, 10 miles away (bus to/from Cortona runs hourly during the week, 4/day on Sun, €2, tel. 800-115-605 or call the TI to confirm times).

More Sights in Tuscany

▲San Galgano Monastery

Of southern Tuscany's several evocative monasteries, San Galgano is the best. Set in a forested area called the Montagnolo (medium-size mountains), the isolated abbey and chapel are postcard-perfect.

St. Galgano was a 12th-century saint who renounced his past as a knight to become a hermit. Lacking a cross to display, he created his own by miraculously burying his sword up to its hilt in a stone, à la King Arthur, but in reverse. After his death, a large Cistercian monastery complex grew. Today, all you'll see is the roofless ruined abbey and, on a nearby hill, the Chapel of San Galgano with its fascinating dome and sword in the stone.

Getting There: Although a bus reportedly comes here from Siena, this sight is realistically accessible only for drivers. It's just outside of Monticiano (not Montalcino), about an hour south of Siena. A warning to the queasy: These roads are curvy.

The Abbey: This picturesque Cistercian abbey was once a powerful institution in Tuscany. Known for their skill as builders, the Cistercians oversaw the construction of Siena's cathedral. But after losing most of its population in the plague of 1348, the abbey never really recovered and was eventually deconsecrated.

The Cistercian order was centered in France, and the architecture of the abbey shows a heavy French influence. Notice the large, high windows and the pointy, delicate arches. This is pure French Gothic, a style that never fully caught on in Italy (compare it with the chunky, elaborately decorated cathedral in Siena, built about the same time).

As you enter the church, notice the small section of the cloister wall to the left. This used to surround the garden, and was the only place where the monks were allowed to talk, for one hour each day. From inside the church, the empty windows frame the view of the chapel up on the hill.

The Chapel: A path from the abbey leads up the hill to the Chapel of San Galgano. The unique beehive-like interior houses St. Galgano's sword and stone, recently confirmed to date back to the 12th century. Don't try and pull the sword from the stone—the small chapel to the left displays the severed arms of the last guy who tried. The chapel also contains some deteriorated frescoes and more interesting *sinopie* (fresco sketches). The adjacent gift shop sells a little bit of everything, from wine to postcards to herbs, some of it monk-made.

Cost and Hours: Free, summer daily 9:00–20:00, shoulder season until 18:30, erratic hours Nov–Dec, closed Jan–Feb, tel. 0577-756-738, www.sangalgano.org; concerts sometimes held here in summer—ticket info tel. 0555-978-308. For a quick snack, a small, touristy bar at the end of the driveway is your only option.

Nearby: Other, more accessible Tuscan monasteries worth visiting include Sant'Antimo (6 miles south of Montalcino) and Monte Oliveto Maggiore (15 miles south of Siena, mentioned in "Crete Senese Drives," later).

▲Chiusi

This small hill town (rated ▲▲ for Etruscan fans) was once one of the most important Etruscan cities. Today, it's a key train junction

and a pleasant, workaday Italian village with an enjoyable historic center and few tourists.

The region's trains (to Florence, Siena, Orvieto, and Assisi) go through or change at this hub, making Chiusi an easy day trip. Buses link the train station with the town center two miles away (depart every 40 minutes, tickets at *tabacchi* shop). Easy and free parking lots are a five-minute walk from the center. If you want to rent a car, there's a Hertz office near the train station (Via M. Buonarroti 21, tel. 057-822-3000).

The **TI** is on the main square (May–Sept Tue–Sun 10:00–13:00 & 15:00–17:00, closed Mon; Oct–April Tue–Sun 9:30–12:30, closed Mon; tel. 0578-227-667).

The **Archaeological Museum,** just off the main square, thoughtfully presents a high-quality collection with plenty of explanations in English. The collection of funerary urns, some in painted terra-cotta and some in *pietra fetida* ("stinky stone"), are remarkably intact (€4, July–Sept daily 9:00–20:00, Via Porsenna 93, tel. 0578-20177, www.archeotoscana.beniculturali.it). The museum also arranges tours to visit tombs outside of town. One of the tombs is multichambered, with several sarcophagi. Another, the **Tomba della Scimmia** (Tomb of the Monkey), has some well-preserved frescoes. Visiting the tombs requires a guide, a car, and an advance reservation (€2, Tue, Thu, and Sat only, March–Oct at 11:00 and 16:00, Nov–Feb at 11:00 and 14:30, 25 visitors per tour).

Troglodyte alert! The **Cathedral Museum** on the main square has a dark, underground labyrinth of Etruscan tunnels. The mandatory guided tour of the tunnels ends in a large Roman cistern from which you can climb the church bell tower for an expansive view of the countryside (museum-€2, labyrinth-€3, combo-ticket-€4, daily June–Oct 9:30–12:30 & 16:00–19:00, Nov–May 9:30–12:30 only, 30-minute tunnel tours run every 40 minutes during museum hours, Piazza Duomo 1, tel. 0578-226-490).

Craving more underground fun? The **Museo Civico** provides hourly tours of the Etruscan water system, which includes an underground lake (€3; May–Oct Tue–Sun at 10:15, 11:30, 12:45, 15:15, 16:30, and 17:45; closed Mon, fewer tours off-season, call to confirm times, Via II Ciminia 1, tel. 0578-227-667, mobile 334-626-6851).

▲Florence American Cemetery and Memorial

The compelling sight of endless rows of white marble crosses and Stars of David recalls the heroism of the young Americans who fought so valiantly to free Italy (and ultimately Europe) from the grip of fascism. This particular cemetery is the final resting place of more than 4,000 Americans who died in the liberation of Italy during World War II. Climb the hill, past the perfectly manicured lawn lined with grave markers, to  the memorial, where maps and a history of the Italian campaign detail the Allied advance.

Cost and Hours: Free, daily 9:00–17:00; 7.5 miles south of Florence, off Via Cassia, which parallels the *superstrada* between Florence and Siena, 2 miles south of Florence Certosa exit on A-1 autostrada; tel. 055-202-0020, www.abmc.gov. Buses from Florence stop just outside the cemetery.

▲▲Crete Senese Drives

South of Siena, the hilly area known as the "Sienese Crests" is full of colorful fields and curvy, scenic roads. You'll see an endless parade of classic Tuscan scenes, rolling hills topped with medieval towns, olive groves, rustic stone farmhouses, and a skyline punctuated with cypress trees. You won't find many wineries here, since the clay soil is better for wheat and sunflowers, but you will find the same pristine, panoramic Tuscan countryside that you see on calendars and postcards.

During the spring, the fields are painted in yellow and green with fava beans and broom, dotted by red poppies on the fringes. Sunflowers decorate the area during June and July, and expanses of windblown grass fill the landscape almost all year.

Most roads to the southeast of Siena will give you a taste of this area, but one of the most scenic stretches is the Lauretan road (Siena–Asciano–San Giovanni d'Asso, #438 on road maps; you can also take S-2—Via Cassia—toward Rome and turn off at *Asciano* sign, either way allows you to easily continue to Montalcino). You'll come across plenty of turnouts for panoramic photo opportunities on this road, as well as a few roadside picnic areas.

For a break from the winding road, about 15 miles from Siena, you'll find the quaint and non-touristy village of **Asciano.** With a medieval town center and several interesting churches and museums, this town offers a rare look at everyday Tuscan living—and a great place for lunch (TI open Tue–Fri 10:30–13:00 & 15:00–18:00, Sat–Sun 10:30–13:00, closed Mon, at Corso Matteotti 18, tel. 0577-719-510). If you're in town on Saturday, gather a picnic at the outdoor market (Via Amendola, 8:00–13:00).

Five miles south of Asciano, the **Abbey of Monte Oliveto Maggiore** houses a famous fresco cycle of the life of St. Benedict, painted by Renaissance masters Il Sodoma and Luca Signorelli (free, daily 9:15–12:00 & 15:15–18:00, Nov–March until 17:00, Gregorian chanting Sun at 11:00 and Mon–Sat at 18:15, call to confirm, tel. 0577-707-611, www.monteolivetomaggiore.it). Once you reach the town of **San Giovanni d'Asso,** it's only another 12 miles southwest to Montalcino.

Another scenic drive is the lovely stretch between Montalcino and Montepulciano (S-146 on road maps). This route alternates between the grassy hills of the Crete Senese and sunbathed vineyards of the Orcia River valley. Stop by Pienza en route.

Sleeping in the Crete Senese: **$$ Agriturismo il Molinello** rents five apartments, two built over a medieval mill. Hardworking Alessandro and Elisa share their organic produce and offer weekly wine-tastings for a minimum of four people. From May through October, they offer free guided tours of Siena on Tuesday afternoons. With children, friendly dogs, toys, and a swimming pool, this is ideal for families (Qb-€70–100, apartment for up to 8-€150–180, optional organic breakfast-€9.50, one-week stay required in summer, discounts and no minimum stay off-season, free Internet access, mountain-bike rentals, biking maps and guided bike tours, near Asciano, 30 minutes southeast of Siena, tel. 0577-704-791, mobile 335-692-5720, fax 0577-705-605, www.molinello.com, info@molinello.com).

Urbino

If you're driving through central Italy, Urbino is worth a stop for its sprawling, fascinating Ducal Palace. Although Urbino is the hometown of the artist Raphael and architect Donato Bramante, it's better known for the Duke of Montefeltro, a mercenary general who built the palace and turned Urbino into an important Renaissance center. For my expanded coverage of Urbino, see www.ricksteves.com/urbino.

A classic hill town, Urbino has a medieval wall with four gates, and two main roads that crisscross at the town's main square, Piazza della Repubblica. The tiny **TI** is just across from the Ducal Palace (Tue–Fri 9:00–13:00 & 15:00–18:00, Mon and Sat 9:00–13:00 only, closed Sun, Piazza Duca Federico 35, tel. 0722-2613, www.urbinoculturaturismo.it).

The **Ducal Palace** (Palazzo Ducale), which has more than 300 rooms, was built in the mid-1400s. While the rooms are fairly bare, the palace holds a few very special paintings, as well as exquisite inlaid-wood decorations. It's a monument to how one man—the Duke of Montefeltro—brought the Renaissance to his small town (€4, but sometimes €8 for special exhibits; Mon 8:30–14:00, last entry at 12:30; Tue–Sun 8:30–19:15, last entry at 18:00; tel. 072-232-2625).

The highlights of the palace include great paintings such as Raphael's *Portrait of a Gentlewoman* (a.k.a. *La Muta*); the Renaissance **courtyard** patterned after the trendsetting Medici-Riccardi Palace in Florence; the richly paneled and inlaid-wood walls of the duke's **study;** and the vast **cellars** that include a giant stable with a clever horse-pie disposal system.

Stop by the **Oratory of St. John** to see its remarkable frescoed interior that tells the story of the life of St. John the Baptist (€2.50, Mon–Sat 10:00–12:30 & 15:00–17:30, Sun 10:00–12:30, 5-minute walk from main square—follow signs, Piazza Baricci 31; if no one's there, find attendant at the Oratory of San Giuseppe a few steps away; mobile 347-671-1181).

Finally, for the ultimate Urbino view, climb up to the grassy park surrounding the **fortress** (interior closed, but grounds open to the public). The Franciscan church spire, on the left, marks the main square.

Getting There: Urbino is easier for drivers, but public transportation is an option. Buses link Urbino with Pesaro, on the Ravenna-Pescara train line (buses run hourly, 1-hour trip). From Venice, Florence, or Rome, trains leave for Pesaro almost hourly (taking 3–5 hours). In Urbino, buses come and go from the Piazza Mercatale parking lot below the town, where an elevator lifts you up to the base of the Ducal Palace (or take a 5-minute steep walk up Via Mazzini to Piazza della Repubblica).

Sleeping in Urbino: The hotel scene is limited to a few comfortable, expensive places, including **Albergo San Domenico** (www.viphotels.it), **Hotel Raffaello** (www.albergoraffaello.com), and **Albergo Italia** (www.albergo-italia-urbino.it). The TI has a line on lots of families renting rooms.

Eating in Urbino: Try **Taverna degli Artisti** (Via Bramante 52) and **Il Coppiere** (Via Santa Margherita 1), or **Ristorante/ Pizzeria Tre Piante** (Via Voltaccia della Vecchia 1).

Orvieto

Just off the freeway and the main train line, Umbria's grand hill town entices those heading to and from Rome. While no secret, it's well worth a visit.

The town sits majestically a thousand feet above the valley floor on a big chunk of tuff *(tufa)*, an easy-to-dig volcanic rock. While a regional power in the Middle Ages, it was also one of the dozen major Etruscan cities centuries before Christ. Some historians believe Orvieto may have been a kind of Etruscan Mecca (locals are looking for archaeological proof—the town and surrounding countryside are dotted with Etruscan ruins).

Orvieto, which has three popular claims to fame (cathedral, Classico wine, and ceramics), is loaded with tourists by day and quiet by night. Drinking a shot of the local white wine in a ceramic cup as you gaze up at the cathedral lets you experience Orvieto's three C's all at once. (Is the cathedral best in the afternoon, when the facade basks in golden light, or early in the morning, when it rises above the hilltop mist? You decide.) And a visit to Orvieto comes with a wonderful bonus: an easy bus connection with my favorite hill town, Civita di Bagnoregio (covered later in this chapter).

Orientation to Orvieto

Orvieto has two distinct parts: the old-town hilltop and the new town below. Whether coming by train or car, you first arrive in the forgettable, modern lower part of town. From there you can drive or take the funicular up to the medieval upper town, an atmospheric labyrinth of streets and squares where all the sight-seeing action is.

Tourist Information

A seasonal TI is at the top of the funicular, to your right as you exit into Piazza Cahen, the start of the upper town (daily May–mid-Aug 10:00–18:00, March–April and mid-Aug–Sept 10:00–13:00 & 15:00–18:00, closed Oct–Feb). The main TI is on the cathedral square at Piazza del Duomo 24 (Mon–Fri 8:15–13:50 & 16:00–19:00, Sat–Sun 10:00–13:00 & 15:00–18:00, tel. 076-334-1772, www.comune.orvieto.tr.it). Pick up the free city map and their green city guide, and ask about train and bus schedules. The ticket office (next to the main TI) sells combo-tickets, and books reservations for the underground tours (tel. 0763-340-688).

Combo-Ticket: The €18 **Carta Unica** combo-ticket covers Orvieto's top sights (virtually every sight recommended here, including Underground Orvieto Tours) and includes either five hours of parking (at *parcheggio* Campo della Fiera) or one round-trip on the bus and/or funicular (www.cartaunica.it). To cover your funicular ride into the upper town, you can buy the combo-ticket at the bar at the train station upon arrival (if they haven't run out), or at a seasonal ticket office in the train station parking lot (tel. 0763-302-378). It's also available at the ticket office on Piazza del Duomo, as well as at most of the sights it covers.

Arrival in Orvieto

By Train: From the train station at the foot of the hill town, a funicular carries you to the top. Buy your ticket at the entrance to the *funiculare;* look for the *biglietteria* sign (€1, €0.80 with same-day train ticket, good for 70 minutes, includes minibus from Piazza Cahen to Piazza del Duomo, Mon–Sat 7:20–20:30, Sun 8:00–20:30, every 10 minutes). Or buy a Carta Unica combo-ticket (described earlier) to cover your funicular ride. If you arrive outside the funicular's operating hours, you can take a bus or taxi to the upper town. Note that there's no baggage storage at the train station (the nearest place for day-trippers to store bags is the recommended Hotel Picchio, €4/bag).

As you exit the funicular at the top, you're in Piazza Cahen, located at the east end of the upper town. To your left is a ruined fortress with a garden, WC, and a commanding view. To your right is the seasonal TI (closed Oct–Feb) and, down a steep road, St. Patrick's Well. Farther to the right is a park with Etruscan ruins and another sweeping view. Just in front of you is the orange shuttle bus, waiting to take you to Piazza del Duomo. The bus fills up fast, but the views from the ruined fortress are worth pausing for—if you miss the bus, you can wait for the next one, or just walk to the cathedral (head uphill on Corso Cavour; after about 10 minutes take a left onto Via del Duomo). The bus drops you in Piazza del Duomo just steps from the main TI and within easy walking distance of most of my recommended sights. If you forgot to check at the station for the train schedule to your next destination, no problem—the train schedule is posted at the top of the funicular and is also available at the TI.

By Car: You can park for free at the base of the hill at the huge lot behind the train station (5 minutes off the autostrada, follow the *P funiculare* signs); in Piazza Cahen (north half, with white lines); or inside the Ex-Caserma (just as you arrive at the top of Orvieto, turn right and follow signs). Otherwise go to the small pay lot to the right of Orvieto's cathedral (€1.50 for first hour, €1/hour thereafter) or the blue-lined half of Piazza Cahen (€1/hour). Generally, white lines indicate free parking, and blue lines require that you must buy a "pay and display" slip from a nearby machine. While you can drive up Via Postierla and Via Roma to get to central parking lots, Corso Cavour and other streets in the old center are closed to traffic and monitored by cameras (look for red lights).

If arriving from the southwest, Campo della Fiera is your most convenient parking lot (€0.80/hour). From its top level, it's still a steep climb up; you can avoid it by taking an escalator (7:00–24:00) or an elevator (7:00–21:00) to the upper town (both free).

By Taxi: Taxis line up in front of the station and charge about €12 for a ride to the cathedral (a ridiculous price considering the fun and ease of the €1 funicular/shuttle-bus ride to the cathedral square, tel. 360-433-057).

Helpful Hints

Market Days: On Thursday and Saturday mornings, Piazza del Popolo becomes a busy farmers market.

Internet Access: Caffè Montanucci has four terminals (€2.50/30 minutes, Corso Cavour 21, daily 7:00–24:00), **Copisteria ESPA** has three (€3/30 minutes, Via Felice Cavallotti 9, Mon–Fri 9:00–13:00 & 16:00–19:40, Sat 9:00–13:00, closed Sun), and the **library** on Piazza Febei offers free Internet access during its limited hours (Mon–Fri 8:30–13:30; Sept–June also Mon, Wed, and Fri 15:30–18:30; closed Sat–Sun).

Driver: For a private car hire, consider Giuliotaxi, enthusiastically run by charming and English-speaking Giulio and his sister Maria Serena. They charge about €50 for a ride to Bagnoregio, and provide a good way to explore the region (mobile 360-433-057, www.umbria-transfer.com).

Local Guide: Manuela Del Turco is good (€100/2.5-hour tour, mobile 333-221-9879, manueladel@virgilio.it).

Orvieto

- **1** Hotel Maitani
- **2** Hotel Duomo
- **3** Grand Hotel Italia
- **4** Hotel Corso
- **5** Hotel Posta
- **6** Villa Mercede
- **7** Istituto S.S. Salvatore
- **8** Valentina's Rooms
- **9** La Magnolia B&B
- **10** Casa Sèlita B&B
- **11** Hotel Picchio
- **12** Picchio II B&B
- **13** La Palomba Restaurant
- **14** Antico Bucchero
- **15** L'Antica Trattoria dell'Orso
- **16** Trattoria la Grotta & Sidis Supermarket

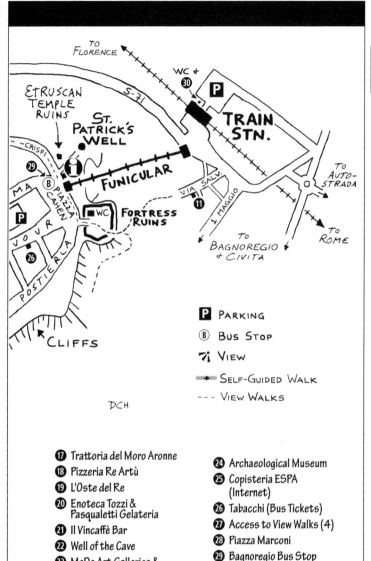

P PARKING
B BUS STOP
⫘ VIEW
➡ SELF-GUIDED WALK
--- VIEW WALKS

DCH

⑰ Trattoria del Moro Aronne
⑱ Pizzeria Re Artù
⑲ L'Oste del Re
⑳ Enoteca Tozzi &
   Pasqualetti Gelateria
㉑ Il Vincaffè Bar
㉒ Well of the Cave
㉓ MoDo Art Galleries &
   Nat'l Arch. Museum

㉔ Archaeological Museum
㉕ Copisteria ESPA
   (Internet)
㉖ Tabacchi (Bus Tickets)
㉗ Access to View Walks (4)
㉘ Piazza Marconi
㉙ Bagnoregio Bus Stop
㉚ Combo-Ticket Kiosk

After Dark: In the evening, there's little going on other than strolling and eating. The big *passeggiata* scene is down Via del Duomo and Corso Cavour. **Il Vincaffè** is *the* place for the classy young crowd late at night, with lots of good wines by the glass (Via Filippeschi 39).

Self-Guided Walk

Welcome to Orvieto

A quickie L-shaped walk takes you through Orvieto's historic center. Each evening, this route is the scene of the local *passeggiata*. Facing the cathedral, head left. Stroll under the clock tower (first put here in 1347 for the workers building the cathedral), which marks the start of Via del Duomo, lined with shops selling ceramics. Via dei Magoni (first left) has several artisan shops and the crazy little Il Mago di Oz ("Wizard of Oz") shop, a wondrous toyland created by eccentric Giuseppe Rosella (Via dei Magoni 4, tel. 076-334-2063; he runs another store nearby at Via Pedota 9). Have Giuseppe push a few buttons, and you're far from Kansas (no photos allowed).

Via del Duomo continues to Orvieto's main intersection, where it meets Corso Cavour and a tall, stark tower—the Torre del Moro. The tower marks the center of town, serves as a handy orientation tool, and is decorated by the coats of arms of past governors. The elevator leaves you with 173 steps still to go to earn a commanding view (€3, daily March–Oct 10:00–19:00, May–Aug until 20:00, shorter hours off-season).

This crossroads divides the town into four quarters (notice the *Quartiere* signs on the corners). Residents of these four districts compete in a lively equestrian competition on Piazza del Popolo during the annual Corpus Christi celebration. Historically, the four streets led from here to the market and the fine palazzo on Piazza del Popolo, the well, the Duomo, and City Hall.

Before heading left down Corso Cavour, side-trip a block farther ahead, behind the tower, for a look at the striking Palazzo del Popolo. Built of local *tufa*, this is a textbook example of a fortified medieval public palace: a fortress designed to house the city leadership and military, with a market at its base, fancy meeting rooms upstairs, and aristocratic living quarters on the top level.

Return to the tower and head down Corso Cavour (turning right) past classic storefronts to Piazza della Repubblica and City Hall. The original vision—though it never came to fruition—was for City Hall to have five arches flanking the main central arch (marked by the flags today). The Church of Sant'Andrea (left of City Hall) sits atop an Etruscan temple that was likely the birthplace of Orvieto centuries before Christ. Inside is an interesting architectural progression: Romanesque (with scant frescoes surviving), Gothic, and a Renaissance barrel vault in the apse (behind the altar)—all lit by fine alabaster windows.

From City Hall, you can continue to the far end of town to the Church of San Giovenale—where, if you have the MoDo ticket, you can see the statues of apostles that once stood in the Duomo (warning: these statues may be moved back inside the Duomo in 2011). From here you can take a left and walk the cliffside ramparts (see "View Walks," later).

Sights in Orvieto

▲▲Duomo

The cathedral has Italy's liveliest facade (from 1330, by Lorenzo Maitani and others). This colorful, prickly Gothic facade, divided

by four pillars, has been compared to a medieval altarpiece. Grab a gelato (buy it to the left of the church) and study this gleaming mass of mosaics, stained glass, and sculpture.

At the base of the cathedral, the four broad marble pillars carved with biblical scenes tell the story of the world from left to right in four acts: Genesis, Old Testament, New Testament, and Revelation. The relief on the far left shows the Creation (see God performing surgery as he extracts Adam's rib, and the snake tempting Eve). Next is the Tree of Jesse (Jesus' family tree—with Mary, then Jesus on top) flanked by Old Testament stories, then the New Testament (look for the unique manger scene and other famous scenes from the life of Christ). On the far right is the Last Judgment (Christ judging on top, with a commotion of sarcophagi popping open and all hell breaking loose at the bottom).

Each pillar is topped by a bronze symbol of one of the Evangelists: angel (Matthew), lion (Mark), eagle (John), and ox (Luke). The bronze doors are modern, by the Sicilian sculptor Emilio Greco. (A gallery devoted to Greco's work is to the immediate right of the church.) In the mosaic below the rose window, Mary is transported to heaven. In the uppermost mosaic, Mary is crowned.

Step inside. The nave feels spacious and less cluttered than most Italian churches. Until 1877 it was much busier, with statues of the apostles at each column and fancy chapels. Then the people decided they wanted to "un-Baroque" their church. More recently, however, there's been talk of returning the apostles to their original locations—perhaps in time for your visit.

Orvieto's Duomo

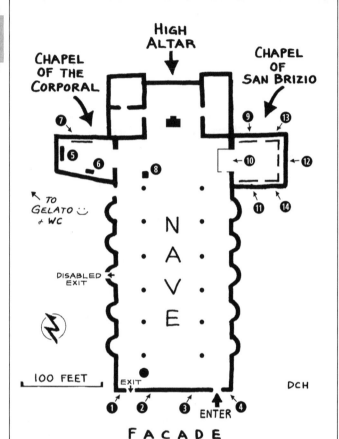

1. Creation
2. Tree of Jesse & Old Testament Stories
3. New Testament Stories
4. Last Judgment
5. "Corporal" (Linen Cloth)
6. Reliquary
7. Miracle of Bolsena Fresco
8. Pietà
9. Sermon of the Antichrist
10. End of the World (above doorway)
11. Resurrection of the Bodies
12. Last Judgment
13. Elect in Heaven
14. Damned in Hell

The interior is warmly lit by alabaster windows, highlighting the black-and-white striped stonework. Why such a big and impressive church in such a little town? Well, first of all, it's not as big as it looks. The architect created an illusion—the nave is wider at the back and narrower at the altar so that from the back, it looks like it's a longer distance to the front. Still, it's a big and rich church. That's because of a famous blood-stained cloth, kept in a silver-gilt reliquary in the Chapel of the Corporal.

Visit the church in three parts: Chapel of the Corporal (north transept, left of altar, in front), high altar (center front), and Chapel of San Brizio (left front, paid entry).

Cost and Hours: The Duomo is open daily April–Sept 7:30–19:30, March and Oct until 18:30, Nov–Feb until 17:30. Admission is €2, or €3 if you want to see the Chapel of San Brizio, which has shorter hours than the Duomo. The Chapel of San Brizio is open Mon–Sat 9:00–19:00, Sun 13:30–18:30 (closes one hour earlier in winter). A €5 combo-ticket includes the Duomo, the chapel, and the Museo dell'Opera del Duomo—the "MoDo" (available at the chapel; MoDo alone costs €4). Admission is also covered by the €18 Carta Unica combo-ticket.

Chapel of the Corporal: In 1263, or so the story goes, a skeptical priest named Peter of Prague passed through Bolsena (a few miles from Orvieto) while on a pilgrimage to Rome. He had doubts that the bread used in Communion could really be transformed into the body of Christ. But during Mass, as he held the host aloft and blessed it, the bread began to bleed, running down his arms and dripping onto a linen cloth (a "corporal") on the altar. The bloody cloth (in the turquoise frame above the main altar) was brought to Orvieto, where Pope Urban IV happened to be visiting. The amazed pope proclaimed a new holiday, Corpus Christi (Body of Christ), and the Orvieto cathedral was built (begun in 1290) to display the miraculous relic. Find the fine gilded enamel **reliquary** (which no longer holds the blood-stained relic) in a glass case on the left. Until the 1970s, this silver-and-blue enamel reliquary (c. 1358)—considered one of the finest medieval jewels in Italy—held the linen relic as if in a frame. Notice how it evokes the facade of this cathedral. For centuries, the precious linen was paraded through the streets of Orvieto in this ornate reliquary.

The room was frescoed in the 14th century with scenes attesting to Christ's presence in the communion wafer (for example, the panel above the glass case to the left illustrates how the wafer bleeds if you cook it). You can see the **Miracle of Bolsena** depicted in the fresco on the chapel's right wall (light it with a €0.50 coin in the box).

The new cathedral put Orvieto (then known as "Urbs Vetus") on the map, and with lots of pilgrims came lots of wealth. Two future popes used the town as a refuge when their enemies forced them to flee Rome.

Now leave the Chapel of the Corporal and walk to the middle front of the church, where you'll see a patch in the marble floor, a fine marble statue, and the highly decorated high altar.

The High Altar: The brilliant stained glass from the 14th century is original and painstakingly restored. The fine organ has more than 5,000 pipes. The marble *pietà* (statue of Mary holding Jesus' just-crucified body) was carved in 1579 by local artist Ippolito Scalza. Clearly inspired by Michelangelo's *Pietà*, this exceptional piece with four figures was sculpted from one piece of marble. Notice the texture Scalza gave this wonderful work. Look at the alabaster rose window. Also note from here how the architect's trick, making the church look bigger from the rear, works in reverse from here. If you look to the back, the church feels stubbier than it actually is.

As the Roman church countered the Reformation, it made reforms of its own. For instance, altars were moved back to let people get closer to the religious action. The confused patching on the marble floor is evidence that, prior to the Counter-Reformation, the altar stood here.

Chapel of San Brizio: This chapel, to the right of the altar, is Orvieto's one must-see artistic sight. It features Luca Signorelli's

brilliantly lit frescoes of the Apocalypse (painted 1499–1504). Step into the chapel and you're surrounded by vivid scenes crammed with figures. The frescoes depict events at the end of the world, but they also reflect the turbulent political and religious atmosphere of late 15th-century Italy.

The chapel is decorated in one big and cohesive story. Follow the plot (counterclockwise): Antichrist, end of world (above the arch facing the nave), Resurrection, hell, Judgment Day (Fra Angelico's Jesus above the window), and finally heaven. Now the story: In the **Sermon of the Antichrist** (left wall), a crowd gathers around a man preaching from a pedestal. It's the Antichrist, who comes posing as Jesus to mislead the faithful. This befuddled Antichrist forgets his lines mid-speech, but the Devil is on hand to whisper what to say next. His words sow wickedness through the world, including executions (upper right). The worried woman in red and white (foreground, left of pedestal) gets money from a man for something she's not proud of (perhaps receiving funds from a Jewish moneylender—notice the Stars of David on his purse).

Most likely, the Antichrist himself is a veiled reference to Savonarola (1452–1498), the charismatic Florentine monk who defied the pope, drove the Medici family from power, and riled the populace with apocalyptic sermons. Many Italians—including the painter Signorelli—viewed Savonarola as a tyrant and heretic, the Antichrist who was ushering in the Last Days.

In the upper left, notice the hardworking angel. He looks as if he's at batting practice, hitting followers of the Antichrist back to earth as they try to get through the pearly gates. In the bottom left corner of the scene is a self-portrait of the artist, **Luca Signorelli** (c. 1450–1523), well-dressed in black with long golden hair. Signorelli, from nearby Cortona, was at the peak of his powers, and this chapel was his masterpiece. He looks out proudly as if to say, "I did all this in just five years, on time and on budget," confirming his reputation as a speedy, businesslike painter. Next to him is the artist Fra Angelico, who started the chapel decoration five decades earlier, but completed only a small part of it.

Around the arch, opposite the windows, are signs of the **end of the world:** eclipse, tsunami, falling stars, earthquakes, violence in the streets, and a laser-wielding gray angel.

On the right wall (opposite the Antichrist) is the **Resurrection of the Bodies.** Trumpeting angels blow a wake-up call, and the dead climb dreamily out of the earth to be clothed with new bodies. On the same wall (below the action, at eye level) is a gripping *pietà.* Also by Signorelli, this *pietà* gives an insight into the genius and personality of the artist. Look at the emotion in the faces of the two Marys and consider that Signorelli's son had just died. The Deposition scene (behind Jesus' leg) seems inspired by ancient Greek scenes of a pre-Christian hero's death. In the confident spirit of the Renaissance, the artist incorporates a pagan scene to support a Christian story. This 3-D realism in a 2-D sketch shows the work of a talented master.

The altar wall (with the windows) features the **Last Judgment.** To the left of the altar (and continuing on the left wall) are the **Elect in Heaven.** They spend eternity posing like bodybuilders while listening to celestial Muzak. To the right (and continuing on the right wall) are the **Damned in Hell,** in the scariest mosh pit ever. Devils torment sinners in graphic detail, while winged demons control the airspace overhead. In the center, one lusty demon turns to tell the frightened woman on his back exactly what he's got planned for their date. (According to legend, this was Signorelli's lover, who betrayed him...and ended up here. You'll see this couple all over town.) Signorelli's ability to tell a story through human actions and gestures, rather than symbols, inspired his younger contemporary, Michelangelo, who meticulously studied the elder artist's nudes.

In this chapel, Christian theology sits physically and figuratively upon a foundation of classical logic. Below everything are Greek and Latin philosophers, plus Dante, struggling to reconcile Classic truth with Church doctrine. You can see the intellectual challenge on their faces as they ponder this puzzle. They're immersed in fanciful Grotesque decor. Dating from 1499, this is one of the first uses of the frilly, nubile, and even sexy "wallpaper pattern" so popular in the Renaissance. (It was inspired by the decorations found in Nero's Golden House in Rome, which had been discovered just a few years earlier.)

During the Renaissance, nakedness symbolized purity. When attitudes changed during the Counter-Reformation, the male figures in Signorelli's frescoes were given penis-covering sashes. During a 1982 restoration, most—but not all—of the sashes were removed. A little of that prudishness survives to this day, as those in heaven were left with their sashes modestly in place.

After leaving the cathedral, if you want to visit a **viewpoint park,** exit left and pass the small parking lot and WC.

Near the Duomo: MoDo and Other Museums

▲▲MoDo City Museum (Museo dell'Opera del Duomo)— This museum is a confusing ensemble of several different sights, scattered around town: the cathedral art collections split between two small galleries behind the cathedral; the Emilio Greco collection (next to the cathedral, in Palazzo Soliano); and, at the far end of town, the Church of San Giovenale, which has statues of the 12 apostles that were added to the Duomo in the Baroque Age (c. 1700) and removed in the late 1800s.

Cost and Hours: €4 MoDo ticket covers all MoDo sights (or get the €5 combo-ticket that includes the Duomo and Chapel of San Brizio), open daily 9:30–19:00, shorter hours off-season.

Cathedral Art Collections: Behind the Duomo in Palazzi Papali, a complex of medieval palaces shows off the city's best art. The highlight is just inside the door: the *Sala della Maestà*—a bronze Mary and child with exquisite angels, under a canopy that once filled the niche in the center of the cathedral's facade. This is proto-Renaissance, dating from around 1300.

Other highlights include fine inlaid woodwork from the original choir; a room full of sinopias (wall charts for frescoes with a roughed-up surface so the wet plaster would stick); a *Madonna with Child* from 1322 by Sienese great Simone Martini, who worked in Orvieto; and paintings from the late 1500s that decorated the side chapels with a harsher Counter-Reformation message.

Museo Emilio Greco: Emilio Greco (1913–1995) was a Sicilian artist who designed the modern doors of Orvieto's cathedral. His sketches and about 30 of his bronze statues are on display here, showing his absorption with gently twisting and turning nudes. Greco's sketchy outlines of women are simply beautiful. The artful installation of his work in this palazzo, with walkways and even a spiral staircase up to the ceiling, allows you to view his sculptures from different angles.

National Archaeological Museum of Orvieto—This small four-room collection, immediately behind the cathedral in the ground floor of Palazzi Papali (under MoDo), beautifully shows off a trove of well-preserved Etruscan bronze, terra-cotta, and ceramics—some with painted colors surviving from 500 B.C. The reconstructed Golini tombs (named after the man who discovered them in 1836) show scenes from an Etruscan afterlife banquet.

Cost and Hours: €3, daily 8:30–19:30. The overpriced audioguide gives a virtual visit to the excavation sites (€5, 30 minutes).

Archaeological Museum (Museo Claudio Faina e Museo Civico)—A former palace, across from the entrance to the cathedral, holds an Etruscan collection. The highlights of the first floor are the Roman coins; push the brass buttons and they rotate so you can see both sides. The best of the Etruscan vases and bronzes are on the top floor.

Cost and Hours: €4.50; April–Sept daily 9:30–18:00; Oct–March Tue–Sun 10:00–17:00, closed Mon; English descriptions throughout, tel. 076-334-1511.

Underground Orvieto

If you're short on time and have to choose one means of going underground in Orvieto, I'd recommend Well of the Cave or St. Patrick's Well over Underground Orvieto Tours.

▲**St. Patrick's Well (Pozzo di San Patrizio)**—Modern engineers are impressed by this deep well—175 feet deep and 45 feet

wide—designed in the 16th century with a double-helix pattern. The two spiral stairways allow an efficient one-way traffic flow: intriguing now, but critical then. Imagine if donkeys and people, balancing jugs of water, had to go up and down the same stairway. At the bottom is a bridge that people could walk on to scoop up water.

The well was built because a pope got nervous. After Rome was sacked in 1527 by renegade troops of the Holy Roman Empire, the pope fled to Orvieto. He feared that even this little town (with no water source on top) would be besieged. He commissioned a well, which was started in 1527 and finished 10 years later. It was a huge project. (As it turns out, the town was never besieged, but supporters believe that the well was worth the cost and labor because of its deterrence value—attackers would think twice about besieging a town with a water source.) Even today, when a local is faced with a difficult task, people say, "It's like digging St. Patrick's Well." It's a total of 496 steps up and down—lots of exercise and not much to see other than some amazing 16th-century engineering.

Cost and Hours: €4.50; interesting €1 audioguide, ID required; daily April–Sept 9:00–20:00, shorter hours in winter, the well is to your right as you exit the funicular. Bring a sweater if you plan to descend to the chilly depths.

Well of the Cave (Pozzo della Cava)—While renovating its trattoria, an Orvieto family discovered a vast underground network of Etruscan-era caves, wells, and tunnels. The excavation started in 1984 and continues to this day. It's well-explained in English and makes for a fun subterranean wander.

Cost and Hours: €3, Tue–Sun 9:00–20:00, closed Mon, Via della Cava 28, tel. 076-334-2373.

Underground Orvieto Tours (Parco delle Grotte)—Guides weave a good archaeological history into an hour-long look at about 100 yards of Etruscan and medieval caves. You'll see the remains of an old olive press, an impressive 130-foot-deep Etruscan well shaft, and what's left of a primitive cement quarry.

Cost and Hours: €5.50; 1-hour English tours depart from ticket office next to main TI at 11:15, 12:30, 16:15, and 17:15, with more scheduled according to demand; book tour at ticket office, confirm times at TI or by calling 076-334-0688, www.orvietounder ground.it.

Etruscan Necropolis—Below town, at the base of the cliff, is a

remarkable "city of the dead" that dates back to about five centuries before Christ. The tombs, which are laid out in a kind of street grid, are empty, and there's precious little to see here other than the basic stony construction. But it is both eerie and fascinating to wander the streets of an Etruscan cemetery.

Cost and Hours: €3, daily April–Sept 8:30–19:00, Oct–March 8:30–17:00.

View Walks

▲Hike Around the City on the Rupe—Orvieto's Rupe is a peaceful paved path that completely circles the town at the base

of the cliff upon which it sits. With the help of the TI brochure on "la Rupe," you'll see there are three access points from the town for the three-mile walk. Once on the trail, it's fairly level and easy to follow. On one side you have the cliff, with the town high above. On the other side you have Umbrian views stretching into the distance. I'd leave the town at Piazza Marconi and walk left (counterclockwise) three-quarters of the way around the town (with a fine view down onto the Etruscan Necropolis mid-way) and ride the escalator and elevator back up to the town from the big new Campo della Fiera parking lot. If you're ever confused about the path, follow the *la Rupe* and *Giro dell'Umbria* signs.

▲**Shorter Romantic Rampart Stroll**—Thanks to its dramatic hilltop setting, several fine little walks wind around the edges of Orvieto. My favorite after dark, when it's lamplit and romantic, is along the ramparts of the far west end of town. Start at the Church of San Giovenale. With your back to the church, go a block to the right to the end of town. Then head left along the ramparts, with cypress-dotted Umbria to your right, and follow Vicolo Volsinia to the Church of San Giovanni Evangelista.

Near Orvieto

Wine-Tasting—Orvieto Classico white wine is justly famous. For a short tour of a winery with Etruscan cellars, visit **Tenuta Le Velette,** where English-speaking Corrado and Cecilia (cheh-CHEEL-yah) Bottai will welcome you—if you've called ahead to set up an appointment (€8–18 for tour and tasting, price varies depending on wines, Mon–Fri 8:30–12:00 & 14:00–17:00, Sat 8:30–12:00, closed Sun, also have accommodations, tel. 076-329-090, mobile 348-300-2002, www .levelette.it). From their sign (5-minute drive past Orvieto at top of switchbacks just before Canale, on road to Bagnoregio), cruise down a long tree-lined drive, then park at the striped gate (must call ahead; no drop-ins).

Custodi is another respected family-run winery that produces Orvieto Classico, grappa, and olive oil on their 140-acre estate. Stop by for a tour of their cantina, an explanation of the winemaking process, and a tasting of four of their wines. Reserve ahead for an assortment of *salumi* and local cheeses or lunch to go with your wine-tasting (€7/person, €11–15/person with *antipasti* or lunch, daily 8:30–12:30 & 16:00–18:30, Viale Venere S.N.C. Loc. Canale;

on the road from Orvieto to Civita, a half-mile after Le Velette, it's the first building before Canale; tel. 076-329-053, mobile 338-316-0405, www.cantinacustodi.com, info@cantinacustodi.com). Helpful Chiara and Laura Custodi speak English.

Sleeping in Orvieto

(€1 = about $1.25, country code: 39)

Most of my recommended hotels are in the old town. The exceptions: Casa Sèlita B&B and Picchio II B&B are near the Campo della Fiera elevator, and Hotel Picchio is in a more modern neighborhood near the station.

$$$ Hotel Maitani is an overpriced time warp with antiquated outlets and rotary phones. Still, its grand public spaces and 39 rooms—each elegant and individual—offer a memorable splurge in a venerable centuries-old building half a block from the Duomo (Sb-€79, Db-€130, Db suite-€152 and €175, claim your 8 percent Rick Steves discount if you book direct, I'd skip their €10 breakfast, calls from the room are very expensive, air-con, elevator, 20 yards from the bus stop behind the TI at Via Lorenzo Maitani 5, tel. & fax 076-334-2011, www.hotelmaitani.com, direzione @hotelmaitani.com, Giuseppi and Norma).

$$$ Hotel Duomo is centrally located and modern, with splashy art and 17 sleek rooms. Double-paned windows keep the sound of the church bells well-muffled (Sb-€80, Db-€120, Db suite-€140, Tb-€150, extra bed-€10, 10 percent cash discount with this book, buffet breakfast, air-con, elevator, free Internet access, pay Wi-Fi, sunny terrace, a block from Duomo behind *gelateria* at Vicolo di Maurizio 7, tel. 076-334-1887, fax 076-339-4973, www .orvietohotelduomo.com, hotelduomo@tiscalinet.it, Gianni and Maura Massaccesi don't speak English, daughter Elisa does). The Massaccesi family also owns a three-room B&B 50 yards from the hotel (Sb-€70, Db-€90, Tb-€110, breakfast at the main hotel).

$$$ Grand Hotel Italia, new and top-end, rents 46 modern and spacious rooms farther into the old town (Db-€140, extra bed-€20, air-con, Via di Piazza del Popolo 13, tel. 0763-342-065, www .grandhotelitalia.it, hotelita@libero.it).

$$ Hotel Corso is friendly, with 18 comfy, contemporary rooms—some with balconies and views. Everyone can enjoy their sunlit little terrace (Sb-€70, Db-€95, Tb-€115, 10 percent discount with this book, buffet breakfast-€6.50, ask for quieter room off street, air-con, elevator, pay Wi-Fi, free parking nearby, on main street up from funicular toward Duomo at Corso Cavour 343, tel. 076-334-2020, fax 076-334-0648, www.hotelcorso.net, info@hotel corso.net, Carla).

$ Hotel Posta is a dumpy, long-ago-elegant palazzo renting 20 quirky rooms with vintage furniture—among the cheapest in town (S-€31, Sb-€37, D-€44, Db-€56, breakfast-€6, cash only, Via Luca Signorelli 18, tel. & fax 076-334-1909, www.orvietohotels.it, hotelposta@orvietohotels.it, little English spoken).

$ Villa Mercede, a wonderful value, is a religious institution offering 23 cheap, simple twin-bedded rooms, each with a big modern bathroom and many with glorious Umbrian views (Sb-€50, Db-€70, Tb-€90, free parking, Wi-Fi, a half-block from Duomo at Via Soliana 2, tel. 076-334-1766, fax 076-334-0119, www.argoweb.it/casareligiosa_villamercede, villamercede @orvienet.it).

$ Istituto S.S. Salvatore rents 15 spotless twin rooms and four singles in their convent, which comes with a peaceful terrace and an evening curfew (Sb-€38, Db-€58 April–Sept, Db-€48 Oct–March, cash only, no breakfast, elevator, parking, just off Piazza del Popolo at Via del Popolo 1, tel. & fax 076-334-2910, istitutosuoresansalvatore@tiscali.it, no English spoken).

$ Valentina's Rooms include six clean, airy, well-appointed rooms and two apartments, all with big beds and antique furniture. Her place is located in the heart of Orvieto, behind the palace on Piazza del Popolo (Db-€54 for two or more nights, Db-€60 for one-night stops, Tb-€75, studio with kitchen-€80; bright, spacious family apartment for up to 5 people-€150 for two or more nights, €170 for one night; these special discounted cash-only prices with this book, breakfast-€3, air-con-€5, Wi-Fi, Via Vivaria 7, tel. 076-334-1607, mobile 393-970-5868, www.bandbvalentina.com, valentina.z@tiscalinet.it). Valentina also rents three rooms across the square that share a kitchen (Db-€50, no air-con).

$ La Magnolia B&B has lots of fancy terra-cotta tiles, a couple of rooms with frescoed ceilings, terraces, and other welcoming touches. Its seven unique rooms, some like mini-apartments with kitchens, are cheerfully decorated and *tranquillo* despite being on the town's main drag (Db-€65, plush Db apartment-€70–75, extra person-€15, family deals, book direct and stay at least two nights to get a 10 percent Rick Steves discount, cash only, no elevator, use of washer-€3, Via Duomo 29, tel. 076-334-2808, mobile 338-902-7400, www.bblamagnolia.it, info@bblamagnolia.it, Serena).

$ Casa Sèlita B&B, a peaceful country house, offers easy access to Orvieto for drivers and train trippers. It's nestled in an orchard just below the town cliffs (under the big Campo della Fiera parking lot, with its handy escalator up into town). Its several rooms with terraces are airy and fresh, with dark hardwood floors, fluffy down comforters, and modern baths. Enjoy the views from the relaxing garden. Sèlita, her husband Ennio, and daughter

Elena are gracious hosts (Sb-€50, Db-€70, Tb-€85, €5 more off-season for heat, these prices promised to my readers through 2011 if you book direct, cash only, fans, free Internet access and Wi-Fi, free parking, Strada di Porta Romana 8, tel. 076-334-4218, www .casaselita.com, info@casaselita.com).

$ Hotel Picchio is a hardworking little family-run place with 27 overpriced rooms stuck back in the modern world, in a forgettable zone 300 yards from the train station at the base of the hill. A trail leads from here up to the old town (Sb-€45, Db-€62, superior Db-€85, Tb-€80–95, higher rates are for newer and brighter rooms in annex across street, 10 percent discount with this book when you book direct, air-con-€6, Wi-Fi, free outdoor parking, Via G. Salvatori 17, tel. & fax 076-330-1144, hotelpicchio@tin .it, Alessandra and Giovanna, who speaks English). Alessandra and Giovanna also run **Picchio II B&B,** a classier place on the opposite side of town (works well for drivers but otherwise inconvenient, Db-€70–80, air-con, Wi-Fi, double-paned windows keep out most traffic noise, free parking, small garden, near the base of the Campo della Fiera elevator at Via Adige 3).

Near Orvieto

$$$ Agriturismo Fattoria di Vibio produces olive oil and honey, sells organic products, and offers classes and spa services. In August, its 14 rooms rent at peak prices (and for one week during the month they require a minimum seven-night stay, with arrivals and departures on Saturdays). The rest of the year, no minimum stay is required, although rates drop dramatically for longer visits (Db-€250–320, includes breakfast and dinner). Its three cottages sleep 4–7 people and rent only by the week (€980–1,680/week depending on amenities, see complicated rate table on website, located 20 miles northeast of Orvieto, tel. 075-874-9607, fax 075-878-0014, www.fattoriadivibio.com, info@fattoriadivibio.com).

$$$ Agriturismo La Rocca Orvieto, run by Emiliano and Sabrina, is a fancy spa-type place, located 15 minutes north of Orvieto by car. They produce their own olive oil and wine and have nine rooms and 10 apartments—all with air-conditioning and Wi-Fi (Db-€98–140, 10 percent discount with this book—mention when you reserve, pool, panoramic view restaurant, Wellness Center with Jacuzzi and steam room, gym, mountain bikes, bocce court, hiking paths, tel. 076-334-4210 or 076-339-3437, fax 076-339-5155, mobile 348-640-0845, www.laroccaorvieto.com, info @laroccaorvieto.com).

At **$$$ Agriturismo Locanda Rosati,** you'll be greeted by gracious hosts Cristina and Giampiero Rosati, who rent 10 tastefully decorated rooms in a pleasant, homey atmosphere (Db-€110–140, Tb-€140–160, full traditional dinners for €35 on request with this book, air-con, swimming pool, 5 miles from Orvieto on the road to Viterbo, tel. 076-321-7314, www.locandarosati.it, info @locandarosati.it).

$$ Tenuta Le Velette is a sprawling, family-run farmhouse. Cecilia and Corrado Bottai rent six fully furnished apartments and villas housing 2–14 people in perfect Umbrian rural peace and tranquility (Db apartment-€90–110, see website for details on various villas, 3-night minimum, 20 percent discount for weekly stay, cash only, pool, bocce court, 5 minutes from Orvieto—drive toward Bagnoregio-Canale and follow *Tenuta le Velette* signs, fax 076-329-114, mobile 348-300-2002, www.levelette.it, cecilia levelette@libero.it). They also offer wine-tastings.

$$ Borgo Fontanile is a vacation home with a swimming pool, terrace, and kids' play area. Its five new apartments with rustic wood beams and terra-cotta tile floors sleep 2–4 people (€50–60/night per person, discounts for longer stays, €400–800/ apartment per week, air-con, Vocabolo Fornace 159, Loc. Baschi, tel. & fax 074-495-7342, www.borgofontanile.com, info@borgo fontanile.com).

$ Agriturismo Pomonte Umbria, seven miles east of Orvieto, offers home-cooked meals, lovely vistas, and seven comfortable rooms in a recently built guest house (Db-€58, includes breakfast, €92-half-pension, €115-full pension, Loc. Canino di Orvieto 1, Corbara, tel. 076-330-4041, fax 076-330-4080, www.pomonte.it, info@pomonte.it).

Eating in Orvieto

La Palomba features game and truffle specialties in a wood-paneled dining room. Gianpiero, Enrica, and the Cinti family take care of their regulars and visiting travelers alike, offering both a fine value and a classy conviviality. Seating is comfortable and not too crowded. Truffles are ground right at your table—try the *ombricelli al tartufo* (homemade pasta with truffles). As firm believers in the slow-food movement, they use ingredients that are mostly organic and locally produced (€8 pastas, €12 *secondi,* Thu–Tue 12:30–14:15 & 19:30–22:00, closed Wed, reservations smart, just off Piazza della Repubblica at Via Cipriano Manente 16, tel. 076-334-3395).

Antico Bucchero, a bit mod under a big white vault, makes a nice splurge with its candlelit ambience and delicious food (€8 pastas, €12 *secondi,* Thu–Tue 12:00–15:00 & 19:00–23:00, closed Wed, indoor/outdoor seating, a half-block south of Corso Cavour, between Torre del Moro and Piazza della Repubblica at Via de Cartari 4, tel. 076-334-1725, Piero and Silvana).

L'Antica Trattoria dell'Orso offers well-prepared Umbrian cuisine paired with fine wines in a homey and peaceful atmosphere. Ciro and chef Gabriele enjoy getting to know their diners, and will steer you toward the freshest seasonal plates of their famous pastas and passionately prepared vegetables. Or just trust Gabriele, and go for their €30 complete tasting meal—including wine (Wed–Sun 12:00–14:00 & 19:30–22:00, closed Mon–Tue, just off Piazza della Repubblica at Via della Misericordia 18/20, tel. 076-334-1642).

Trattoria la Grotta, pricey and chic, prides itself on serving only the freshest food and finest wine. The decor is Signorelli mod and the ambience is quiet, with courteous service. Owner-chef Franco has been at it for 50 years, and promises diners a free coffee, grappa, *limoncello,* or *vin santo* with this book (Wed–Mon opens at 12:00 for lunch and at 19:00 for dinner, closed Tue, Via Luca Signorelli 5, tel. 076-334-1348).

Trattoria del Moro Aronne is a long-established family bistro run by Cristian and his mother Rolanda, who lovingly prepare homemade pasta and market-fresh meats and produce for their typical Umbrian specialties. Be sure to sample the *nidi*—folds of fresh pasta enveloping warm, gooey Pecorino cheese sweetened with honey. The crème brûlée is a winner for dessert. Three small and separate dining areas make the interior feel intimate. This place is known locally as a good value (Wed–Mon 12:00–15:00 & 19:00–22:00, closed Tue, Via S. Leonardo 7, tel. 076-334-2763).

Pizzeria Re Artù is a local favorite open only in the evenings. It's popular with families and students for casual dinners of wood-fired €7 pizzas, big salads, homemade pasta, or grilled meat. In a quiet courtyard guarded by a medieval tower, it's centrally located a block southwest of Piazza della Repubblica (Thu–Tue 18:30–22:30, closed Wed, Via Loggia dei Mercanti 14, tel. 076-339-3438).

At **L'Oste del Re,** a simple trattoria on Corso Cavour, the Re Artù team serves lunch, with a focus on local cheeses and meats (Thu–Tue 11:00–15:30, closed Wed, Corso Cavour 58, tel. 0763-343-846).

Enoteca Tozzi, to the left of the Duomo, serves up rustic *panini*—try the roast suckling pig *(porchetta)* if it's available (daily 9:00–19:00, open sporadically in winter, Piazza del Duomo 13, tel. 076-334-4393).

Sidis supermarket, tucked away two minutes from the Duomo, has what you need to put together a functional picnic or stock your hotel room pantry (daily 8:00–13:00 & 16:30–19:30, next to recommended Trattoria la Grotta at Via Luca Signorelli 23).

Gelato: For dessert, try the deservedly popular *gelateria* **Pasqualetti** (daily 11:30–21:00, open later June–Aug, closed in winter, next to left transept of church, Piazza del Duomo 14; another branch is at Corso Cavour 56, open daily 11:00–23:00).

Italy Is Made of Tuff Stuff

Tuff (or *tufa* in Italian) is a light-colored volcanic rock that is common in Italy. A part of Tuscany is even called the "Tuff Area." The seven hills of Rome are made of tuff, and quarried blocks of this stone can be seen in the Colosseum, Pantheon, and Castel Sant'Angelo. Just outside of Rome, the catacombs were carved from tuff. Sorrento rises above the sea

on a tuff outcrop. Orvieto, Civita di Bagnoregio (pictured), and many other hill towns perch on bluffs of tuff.

Italy's early inhabitants, including the Etruscans and Romans, carved caves, tunnels, burial niches, and even roads out of tuff. Blocks of this rock were quarried to make houses and walls. Tuff is soft and easy to carve when it's first exposed to air, but hardens later, which makes it a good building stone.

Italy's tuff-producing volcanoes resulted from a lot of tectonic-plate bumping and grinding. This violent geologic history is reflected in Italy's volcanoes, like Vesuvius and Etna, and earthquakes such as the 2009 quake in the L'Aquila area northeast of Rome.

Tuff is actually just a big hardened pile of old volcanic ash. When volcanoes hold magma that contains a lot of water, they erupt explosively (think heat + water = steam = POW!). The exploded rock material gets blasted out as hot volcanic ash, which settles on the surrounding landscape, piles up, and over time welds together into the rock called tuff.

So when you're visiting an area in Italy of ancient caves or catacombs built out of this material, you'll know that at least once (and maybe more) upon a time, it was a site of a lot of volcanic activity.

Orvieto Connections

From Orvieto by Train to: Rome (hourly, 70 minutes), **Florence** (hourly, 2 hours, use Firenze S.M.N. train station), **Siena** (12/day, 2.5 hours, change in Chiusi, all Florence-bound trains stop in Chiusi), **Assisi** (roughly hourly, 2.5 hours, 1 or 2 transfers). The train station's Buffet della Stazione is surprisingly good if you need a quick *focaccia* sandwich or pizza picnic for the train ride.

By Bus to Bagnoregio (30-minute walk from Civita di Bagnoregio, described next): It's a one-hour trip (€2 one-way or

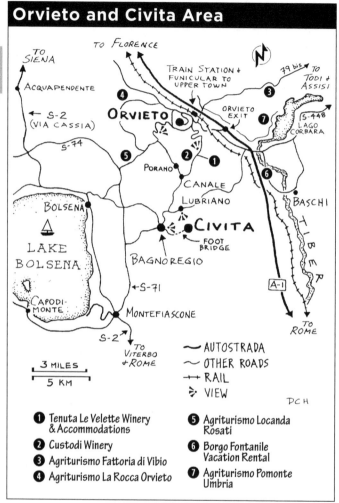

Orvieto and Civita Area

TO SIENA

TO FLORENCE

ACQUAPENDENTE

TRAIN STATION & FUNICULAR TO UPPER TOWN

79 bis TO TODI & ASSISI

← S-2 (VIA CASSIA)

❹

ORVIETO

ORVIETO EXIT

❸

❼

S-448 LAGO CORBARA

S-74

❺

❷

❶

PORANO

CANALE

❻

BASCHI

BOLSENA

LUBRIANO

TIBER

LAKE BOLSENA

CIVITA

FOOT BRIDGE

BAGNOREGIO

A-1

←S-71

CAPODI-MONTE

MONTEFIASCONE

S-2 ↙ TO VITERBO & ROME

TO ROME

⌒ AUTOSTRADA
⌒ OTHER ROADS
⊷ RAIL
⋟ VIEW

3 MILES
5 KM

DCH

❶ Tenuta Le Velette Winery & Accommodations

❷ Custodi Winery

❸ Agriturismo Fattoria di Vibio

❹ Agriturismo La Rocca Orvieto

❺ Agriturismo Locanda Rosati

❻ Borgo Fontanile Vacation Rental

❼ Agriturismo Pomonte Umbria

€4 round-trip if bought in advance from bar or *tabacchi*, €7 one-way or €14 round-trip if purchased from driver). Here are likely departure times (but confirm) from Orvieto's Piazza Cahen on the blue Cotral bus, daily except Sunday: 6:15, 12:45, 15:45, 17:40, and 18:20 (buses stop at Orvieto's train station 5 minutes later). During the school year (roughly Sept–June), there are additional departures at 7:20, 7:50, and 13:55. Confirm the schedule and buy your round-trip ticket at the train-station bar or at the *tabacchi* shop on Corso Cavour, a block up from the funicular (remember, if you wait to buy your ticket from the driver, you'll pay much more).

The schedule is also posted across the street from the bus parking lot (look for sign saying *A.Co.Tral Capolinea*). To find the bus stop, face the funicular. The bus stop is at the far left end of Piazza Cahen. Remember to confirm departure and return times with the driver—the bus you want says *Bagnoregio* in the window. The last bus back from Bagnoregio usually leaves at 17:45. If you catch the bus down below at Orvieto's train station, wait to the left of the funicular station (as you're facing it). For schedule and tickets, visit the *tabacchi*/bar in the train station, see www.cotralspa.it, or call 0761-760-049 (may be Italian-only).

Tip for Drivers: If you're thinking of driving to Rome, consider stashing your car here instead. You can easily park the car, safe and free, behind the Orvieto train station (even for a week or more), and zip effortlessly into Rome by train (70 minutes).

Civita di Bagnoregio

Perched on a pinnacle in a grand canyon, the traffic-free village of Civita di Bagnoregio is Italy's ultimate hill town. In the last decade, the real Civita (chee-VEE-tah) has died—the last of its lifelong residents have moved away. But relatives and newcomers are moving in and revitalizing the village, and it remains an amazing place to visit. (It's even become popular as a movie backdrop—most recently for a 2008 made-for-TV version of *Pinocchio*.) Civita is connected to the world and the town of Bagnoregio by a long pedestrian bridge—and a website (www.civitadibagnoregio.it, run by B&B owner Franco).

Civita's history goes back to Etruscan and ancient Roman times. In the early Middle Ages, Bagnoregio was a suburb of Civita, which had a population of about 4,000. Later, Bagnoregio surpassed Civita in size—especially following a 1695 earthquake, after which many residents fled Civita to live in Bagnoregio, fearing their houses would be shaken off the edge into the valley below. You'll notice Bagnoregio is dominated by Renaissance-style buildings while, architecturally, Civita remains stuck in the Middle Ages.

While Bagnoregio lacks the pinnacle-town romance of Civita, it's actually a healthy, vibrant community (unlike Civita, the suburb now nicknamed "the dead city"). In Bagnoregio, get a haircut, sip a coffee on the square, and walk down to the old laundry (ask, *"Dov'è la lavanderia vecchia?"*). Off-season, when Civita and Bagnoregio are deadly quiet—and cold—I'd side-trip in quickly from Orvieto rather than spend the night.

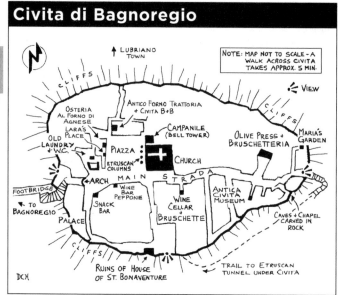

Orientation to Civita

Arrival in Bagnoregio, near Civita

If you're taking the **bus** from Orvieto, you'll get off at the bus stop in Bagnoregio. Look at the posted bus schedule and write down the return times to Orvieto, or check with the driver.

From Bagnoregio to Civita: Civita sits at the opposite end of Bagnoregio, about a mile away. From Bagnoregio, you can walk (allow around 30 minutes) or take a little **shuttle bus**—yellow, orange, or white—to the base of the bridge to Civita (hourly, 10-minute ride, €1 round-trip, pay driver, first bus runs Mon–Sat at about 7:30, Sun at 8:50, last at 18:45, no buses 13:00–15:30, fewer buses June–Aug, catch bus across from gas station). From the base of the bridge, you have to walk the rest of the way (a 10-minute hike up a pedestrian bridge). If you want to return to Bagnoregio by bus, check the schedule posted near the bridge (at edge of parking lot, where bus let you off) before heading up to Civita, or ask at the recommended Trattoria Antico Forno.

To **walk** from the Bagnoregio bus stop to the base of Civita's bridge (at least 20 minutes, fairly level), take the road going uphill, Via Garibaldi (overlooking the big parking lot). Once on the road, take the first right and an immediate left onto the main drag, Via Roma. Follow this straight out to the belvedere for a superb viewpoint. From the viewpoint, backtrack a few steps (staircase at end of viewpoint is a dead end) and take the stairs down to the road leading to the bridge.

Drivers coming from Orvieto or elsewhere can avoid a long walk by driving through Bagnoregio and parking under the bridge at the base of Civita.

Helpful Hints

Market Day: A lively market fills the Bagnoregio bus-station parking lot each Monday.

Baggage Storage: While there's no official baggage-check service in Bagnoregio, I've arranged with Mauro Laurenti, who runs the **Bar/Enoteca/Caffè Gianfu** and **Cinema Alberto Sordi,** to let you leave your bags there (€1/bag, Fri–Wed 6:00–13:00 & 13:30–23:00, closed Thu). As you get off the bus, go back 50 yards or so in the direction that the Orvieto bus just came from, and go right around corner.

Food near Bagnoregio Bus Stop: About 100 yards from the bus stop, within a few steps of the Porta Albana (old gate to the town), you'll find both a small grocery store and a great little bakery (**L'Arte del Pane**—with fresh pizza by the slice, Via Matteotti 5).

Bus Tickets: To save money on bus fare to Orvieto, buy a ticket before boarding from the newsstand near the Bagnoregio bus stop, across from the gas station (€2 one-way or €4 round-trip; otherwise €7 one-way or €14 round-trip if purchased from driver).

Self-Guided Walk

Welcome to Civita

Civita was once connected to Bagnoregio, before the saddle between the separate towns eroded away. Photographs around town show the old donkey path, the original bridge. It was bombed in World War II and replaced in 1966 with the new footbridge that you're climbing today. The town's hearty old folks hang on to the bridge's handrail when fierce winter weather rolls through.

• *Entering the town, you'll pass through a cut in the rock and a 12th-century Romanesque...*

Arch: This was the main Etruscan road leading to the Tiber Valley and Rome. The stone passageway was cut by the Etruscans 2,500 years ago.

• *Inside the town gate, to the left, is an unmarked WC, behind the Bottega souvenir store. It faces the town's old laundry, which dates from just after World War II, when water was finally piped into the town. Until recently, this was a lively village gossip center. Nearby, inside the entry arch and on the right, are the remains of a...*

Renaissance Palace: The wooden door and windows (above the door) lead only to thin air. They were part of the facade of one of five palaces that once graced Civita. Much of the palace fell into the valley, riding a chunk of the ever-eroding rock pinnacle. Today, the door leads to a remaining section of the palace—complete with Civita's first hot tub, as it was once owned by the "Marchesa," a countess who married into Italy's biggest industrialist family. Check out the canyon viewpoint a few steps to the left of the palace. Lean over the banister and listen to the sounds of the birds and the bees. Just beyond that is the site of the long-gone home of Civita's one famous son, St. Bonaventure, known as the "second founder of the Franciscans" (look for the small plaque on the wall to your right).

• *Now wander to the main square and Civita's church.*

Piazza: Here in the town square is Wine Bar Peppone (if it's chilly, go inside for the inviting fire), two restaurants, and wild donkey races on the first Sunday of June and the second Sunday of September. At Christmastime, a living nativity scene is enacted in this square, and if you're here at the end of July or beginning of August, you might catch a play here. The pillars that stand like giants' bar stools are ancient Etruscan. The church with its *campanile*

(bell tower) marks the spot where an Etruscan temple, and then a Roman temple, once stood.

• *Go into the church.*

Church: A cathedral until 1699, the church houses records of about 60 bishops that date back to the seventh century. Inside you'll see frescoes and statues from "the school of Donatello." The central altar is built upon the relics of the Roman martyr St. Victoria, who once was the patron saint of the town. St. Marlonbrando served as a bishop here in the ninth century; an altar dedicated to him is on the right.

The fine crucifix, carved out of pear wood in the 15th century, is from the school of Donatello. It's remarkably expressive and greatly venerated by locals. Jesus' gaze is almost haunting. Some say his appearance changes based on what angle you view him from: looking alive from the front, in agony from the left, and dead from the right. Regardless, his eyes follow you from side to side. On Good Friday, this crucifix goes out and is the focus of the midnight procession.

On the left side of the nave above an altar is an intimate fresco of the Madonna of the Earthquake, given this name because—in the shake of 1695—the whitewash fell off and revealed this tender fresco of Mary and her child. (During the Baroque era, a white-and-bright interior was in vogue, and churches such as these—which were covered with precious and historic frescoes—were simply whitewashed over.) On the same wall—toward the front—find a faded portrait of Santa Apollonia, the patron saint of your teeth; notice the scary-looking pincers. Say hello to Annarita, the church attendant (daily 9:30–13:00 & 15:00–18:00). Drop a coin into the offering box.

• *Just around the corner from the church, on the main street, are several...*

Eateries: At Rossana and Antonio's cool **Bruschette con Prodotti Locali,** pull up a chair and let them or their daughters, Arianna and Antonella, serve you *panini* (sandwiches), bruschetta (garlic toast with optional tomato topping), *salumi*, grilled sausages, wine, and a local cake called *ciambella*. After eating, wander down to see their cellar with its traditional winemaking gear and provisions for rolling huge kegs up the stairs. Tap on the kegs in the bottom level to see which are full (daily 11:00–17:00, in summer until 20:00, tel. 0761-793-270).

The rock below Civita is honeycombed with ancient cellars like this (for keeping wine at the same temperature all year) and cisterns (for collecting rainwater, since there was no well in town). Many date from Etruscan times.

Farther down on the left, you'll find **Antico Frantoio Bruschetteria,** a rustic, super-atmospheric place for a bite to eat. Vittoria's sons Sandro and Felice, and her grandsons Maurizio and Fabrizio, toast delicious bruschetta (roughly 10:00–20:00 in summer, off-season open weekends only 10:00–19:00, tel. 076-194-8429, mobile 328-689-9375). Peruse the menu, choose

your topping (chopped tomato is super), and get a glass of wine for a fun, affordable snack.

While waiting for your bruschetta, take a look around to see Vittoria's mill *(mulino),* an interesting collection of old olive presses. The huge **olive press** in the entry is about 1,500 years old. Until the 1960s, blindfolded donkeys trudged in the circle here, crushing olives and creating paste that filled the circular filters and was put into a second press. Notice the 2,500-year-old sarcophagus niche. The hole in the floor (with the glass top) was a garbage hole. In ancient times, residents would toss their jewels down when under attack; excavations uncovered a windfall of treasures (if you're not eating here, a €1 donation is requested).

• *Across the street and down a tiny lane, find...*

Antica Civita: This is the closest thing the town has to a museum. The new collection is the brainchild of Felice, Vittoria's husband, who has hung farm tools, olive presses, and local artifacts in a series of old caves. Felice wants to give visitors a feeling for life in Civita when it had its traditional economy. He promised me he'd be adding old black-and-white photos and English explanations to his humble exhibits (€1).

• *On the left 20 yards farther down is...*

Maria's Garden (Maria's Giardino): Maria is too frail to live in Civita these days, but you can peek into her garden and enjoy her view. She and her husband, Peppone (who passed away in 2009), used to carry goods on a donkey back and forth 40 times a day on the path between the old town and Bagnoregio. She's now the last native Civita resident still living. As you view the canyon in which Civita is stranded, imagine the work the two rivers did—in the same style as the Colorado River—to carve all this. Listen to the roosters and voices from distant farms.

• *At the end of town, the main drag winds downhill. On your right are small...*

Etruscan Caves: The first two caves were used as stables until a few years ago. The third cave is an unusual chapel, cut deep into the rock, with a barred door; this is the **Chapel of the Incarcerated** (Cappella del Carcere). In Etruscan times, the chapel—with a painted tile depicting the Madonna and child—may have originally been a tomb, and in medieval times, it was used as a jail. When Civita's few residents have a religious procession, they come here in honor of the Madonna of the Incarcerated.

• *After the chapel, the paving-stone path peters out into a dirt trail leading down and around to the right to an...*

Etruscan Tunnel: This tunnel dates from the Etruscan era. Tall enough for a woman with a jug on her head to pass through, it may have served as a shortcut to the river below. It was widened in the 1930s so that farmers could get between their scattered fields more easily. Think of the scared villagers who huddled here for refuge during WWII bombing raids.

• *Backtrack to return to the...*

Piazza: Evenings on Civita's town square are a bite of Italy. The same people sat on the same church steps under the same moon, night after night, year after year. I love my cool, late eve-nings in Civita. If you visit in the morning, have cappuccino and rolls at the small café/wine bar on the town square.

Whenever you visit, stop halfway up the donkey path and listen to the sounds of rural Italy. Reach out and touch one of the Monopoly houses. If you know how to turn the volume up on the crickets, do so.

Sleeping in Civita or Bagnoregio

(€1 = about $1.25, country code: 39)

In Civita and Bagnoregio, there are 15 B&B rooms up for grabs and one newly remodeled hotel. Outside the town there are plenty of *agriturismi;* otherwise, there's always Orvieto.

$$ Romantica Pucci B&B in Bagnoregio is a haven for city-weary travelers. Its eight spacious rooms are indeed romantic, with canopied beds and flowing veils. Both homey and elegant, it's like sleeping at Katharine Hepburn's place. Pucci and Lamberto take special care of their guests (Db-€80, air-con, free time-limited Internet access, free parking, her "Trust Pucci" €20 special fam-ily-style dinner is popular with guests—non-guests are also wel-come for dinner, Piazza Cavour 1, tel. 076-179-2121, www.hotel romanticapucci.it, hotelromanticapucci@libero.it). It's just above the parking lot you see when you arrive in Bagnoregio—look for a sign marking its private parking place. From the Orvieto bus stop, take Via Garibaldi uphill above the parking lot, at the *tabacchi* bear right onto Via Roma, then look for the hotel sign straight ahead.

$$ Laura's Place has four rooms decorated medieval-rustic-mod, filling the old mayor's house and overlooking Civita's piazza. The local-products shop just across the square functions as the reception (Db-€80–100 depending on demand, breakfast at nearby café, mobile 347-627-5628, raffaele_rocchi@libero.it, Laura).

$ Hotel Divino Amore, in Bagnoregio, has 23 bright, mod-ern rooms (Db-€70, Tb-€80, Via Fidanza 25–27, tel. & fax 076-178-0882, mobile 328-071-7244, www.hoteldivinoamore.com, info @hoteldivinoamore.com). From the bus stop, follow Via Garibaldi uphill above the parking lot, where it becomes Via Fidanza, and continue straight along for about 200 yards; #25 is on the left.

$ Civita B&B, run by Franco Sala (who also owns Trattoria Antico Forno and the only dog in Civita—17-year-old Birillo), has three fine little rooms, each overlooking Civita's main square (D-€65, Db-€70, T-€90, continental breakfast, Wi-Fi, Piazza del Duomo Vecchio, tel. 076-176-0016, mobile 347-611-5426, www .civitadibagnoregio.it, fsala@pelagus.it).

Eating in Civita

Osteria Al Forno di Agnese is a delightful spot where Manuela and her friends serve visitors simple yet delicious meals on a covered patio just off Civita's main square (€8 pastas, €8 *secondi*, €1.50 cover, Wed–Mon opens at 12:30 for lunch and at 19:30 for dinner, closed Tue, tel. 340-1259-721).

Trattoria Antico Forno cooks up rustic dishes, homemade pasta, and salads at affordable prices (€7 pastas, €8 *secondi*, daily for lunch 12:30–15:30 and sporadically for dinner 19:30–22:00, on main square, also rents rooms, tel. 076-176-0016, Franco and his assistants Gina and Nina).

Hostaria del Ponte is *the* place for serious cooking. It offers light, creative, and traditional cuisine with a great view terrace at the parking lot at the base of the bridge to Civita. Big space heaters make it comfortable to enjoy the wonderful view as you dine from their rooftop terrace, even in spring and fall (€7 pastas, €10 *secondi*, reservations often essential, Tue–Sun 12:30–14:30 & 19:30–21:30, closed Mon; Nov–April also closed Sun eve, tel. 076-179-3565, Lorena).

Bagnoregio Connections

From Bagnoregio to Orvieto: Public buses (6/day, 1 hour, €2 one-way or €4 round-trip if purchased in advance, €7 one-way or €14 round-trip from driver) connect Bagnoregio to the rest of the world via Orvieto. Departures from Bagnoregio—daily except Sunday and some holidays—are likely to be (but confirm): 5:30, 9:55, 10:10, 13:00, 14:25, and 17:25. During the school year (roughly Sept–June), buses also run at 6:35, 6:50, and 13:35. Remember to save money by buying your ticket in Bagnoregio before boarding the bus—purchase one from the newsstand near the bus stop, across from the gas station.

Driving from Orvieto to Bagnoregio: Orvieto overlooks the autostrada (and has its own exit). The shortest way to Civita from the freeway exit is to turn left (below Orvieto) and then simply follow the signs to *Lubriano* and *Bagnoregio*.

A more winding and scenic route takes 20 minutes longer: From the freeway, pass under hill-capping Orvieto (on your right, signs to *Lago di Bolsena*, on Viale I Maggio), then take the first left (direction: Bagnoregio), winding up past great Orvieto views through Canale, and through farms and fields of giant shredded wheat to Bagnoregio.

Either way, just before Bagnoregio, follow the signs left to *Lubriano* and pull into the first little square by the church on your right for a breathtaking view of Civita. You'll find an even better view farther inside the town, from the tiny square at the next church (San Giovanni Battista). Then return to the Bagnoregio road.

Drive through the town of Bagnoregio (following yellow *Civita* signs) to the lot at the base of the steep pedestrian bridge. Park for free in spaces with no blue lines (plenty under the bridge). The €1 fee for parking in the blue-lined spaces is loosely enforced. While you're supposed to pay at the restaurant or shop opposite (same family), if no one's there, just park and don't worry. The bridge at this parking lot leads up to the traffic-free 2,500-year-old canyon-swamped pinnacle town of Civita di Bagnoregio.

More Hill Towns

If you haven't gotten your fill of hill towns, here are more to check out.

▲Gubbio

This handsome town climbs Monte Ingino in northeast Umbria. Tuesday is market day, when Piazza 40 Martiri (named for 40

local martyrs shot by Nazis) bustles. Nearby are the ruins of the Roman amphitheater, and a park close by that's perfect for a picnic. Head up Via della Repubblica to the main square with the imposing Palazzo dei Consoli. Farther up, Via San Gerolamo leads to the funky lift that will carry you up the hill, in two-person "baskets," for a stunning view from the top, where the Basilica of San Ubaldo is worth a look. The **TI** is at Via della Repubblica 15 (April–Sept 8:30–13:45 & 15:30–18:30, Oct–March closes at 18:00 daily; tel. 075-922-0693, www.gubbio -altochiascio.umbria2000.it). Buses from Gubbio run directly to Rome and Perugia (where you can transfer to Florence).

▲Bevagna

This sleeper of a town south of Assisi has Roman ruins, interesting churches, and more. Locals offer their guiding services for free (usually Italian-speaking only) and are excited to show visitors their town. Get a map at the **TI** at Piazza Silvestri 1 (daily 9:30–13:00 & 15:00–19:00, tel. 074-236-1667) and wander. Highlights

HILL TOWNS

are the Roman mosaics, remains of the arena, a paper-making workshop, the Romanesque Church of San Silvestro, and a gem of a 19th-century theater. Bevagna has all the elements of a hill town except one: a hill. You can see the main sights easily in a couple of hours. For an overnight stay, consider the fancy **$$ Hotel Palazzo Brunamonti** (Sb-€55, Db-€80–100, Tb-€110, air-con, Corso Giacomo Matteotti 79, tel. 074-236-1932, fax 074-236-1948, www.brunamonti.com, hotel@brunamonti.com). Buses connect Bevagna with Foligno (except on Sun).

▲Spello

Umbrian hill town aficionados always include Spello on their list. Just six miles south of Assisi, this town is much less touristy than its neighbor to the north. Spello will give your legs a workout. Via Consolare goes up, up, up to the top of town. Views from the terrace of the **Il Trombone** restaurant (closed Tue, tel. 074-230-1006) will have you singing a tune. The **TI** is on Piazza Giacomo Matteotti 3 (daily 9:30–12:30 & 15:30–18:30, afternoons 15:00–17:00 in winter, tel. 074-230-1009, www.prospello.it). Spello is on the Perugia–Assisi–Foligno train line.

SIENA

Siena was medieval Florence's archrival. And while Florence ultimately won the battle for political and economic superiority, Siena still competes for the tourists. Sure, Florence has the heavyweight sights. But Siena seems to be every Italy connoisseur's favorite pet town. In my office, whenever Siena is mentioned, someone moans, "Siena? I looove Siena!"

Once upon a time (about 1260–1348), Siena was a major banking and trade center, and a military power in a class with Florence, Venice, and Genoa. With a population of 60,000, it was even bigger than Paris. Situated on the north–south road to Rome (the Via Francigena), Siena traded with all of Europe. Then, in 1348, the Black Death (bubonic plague) that swept through Europe hit Siena and cut the population by more than a third. Siena never recovered. In the 1550s, Florence, with the help of Philip II's Spanish army, conquered the flailing city-state, forever rendering Siena a non-threatening backwater. Siena's loss became our sightseeing gain, as its political and economic irrelevance pickled the city in a purely medieval brine. Today, Siena's population is still 60,000, compared with Florence's 420,000.

Siena's thriving historic center, with red-brick lanes cascading every which way, offers Italy's best medieval city experience. Most people do Siena, just 35 miles south of Florence, as a day trip, but it's best experienced at twilight. While Florence has the blockbuster museums, Siena has an easy-to-enjoy soul: Courtyards sport flower-decked wells, alleys dead-end at rooftop views, and the sky is a rich blue dome.

For those who dream of a Fiat-free Italy, Siena is a haven. Pedestrians rule in the old center of Siena. Sit at a café on the main square. Wander narrow streets lined with colorful flags and iron rings to tether horses. Take time to savor the first European city to eliminate automobile traffic from its main square (1966) and then, just to be silly, wonder what would happen if they did it in your hometown.

Planning Your Time

On a quick trip, consider spending two nights in Siena (or three nights with a whole-day side trip into Florence). Whatever you do, enjoy a sleepy medieval evening in Siena. The next morning, you can see the city's major sights in half a day.

Orientation to Siena

Siena lounges atop a hill, stretching its three legs out from Il Campo. This main square, the historic meeting point of Siena's

neighborhoods, is pedestrian-only. And most of those pedestrians are students from the local university.

Just about everything mentioned in this chapter is within a 15-minute walk of the square. Navigate by three major landmarks (Il Campo, Duomo, and Church of San Domenico), following the excellent system of street-corner signs. The typical visitor sticks to the Il Campo–San Domenico axis. Make a point to stray from the current of this main artery.

Siena itself is one big sight. Its individual sights come in two little clusters: the square (Civic Museum and City Tower) and the cathedral (Baptistery and Duomo Museum with its surprise viewpoint). Check these sights off, and then you're free to wander.

Tourist Information

The TI on Il Campo can be an exasperating place, but you can pick up some good handouts and buy a €0.50 map (daily 9:00–19:00, on Il Campo at #56, tel. 0577-280-551, www.terresiena.it, incoming @terresiena.it). The helpful booklet *Siena* from their *Terre di Siena* series lists current hours and prices for sights in Siena and outlying towns. The TI organizes walking tours of the old town and San Gimignano (€20, daily April–Sept).

There's also a little TI, which is primarily for hotel promotion, across the street from the Church of San Domenico, and a TI at the train station (daily 9:30–13:30, tel. 0577-270-600).

Greater Siena

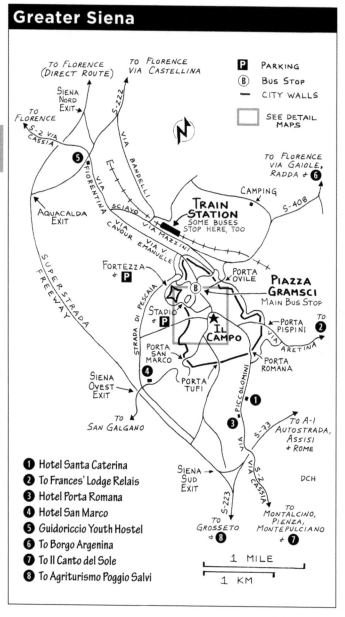

SIENA

P PARKING
B BUS STOP
— CITY WALLS
☐ SEE DETAIL MAPS

TO FLORENCE (DIRECT ROUTE)
TO FLORENCE VIA CASTELLINA
S-222
SIENA NORD EXIT
TO FLORENCE
S-2 VIA CASSIA
VIA FIORENTINA
VIA BANDELLI
N
5
TO FLORENCE VIA GAIOLE, RADDA & **6**
CAMPING
S-408
AQUACALDA EXIT
SCIAVO
TRAIN STATION
SOME BUSES STOP HERE, TOO
VIA CAVOUR
VIA MAZZINI
VIA V. EMANUELE
SUPERSTRADA FREEWAY
FORTEZZA & **P**
PORTA OVILE
PIAZZA GRAMSCI
MAIN BUS STOP
B
STRADA DI PESCAIA
STADIO & **P**
IL CAMPO
PORTA PISPINI
TO **2**
VIA ARETINA
PORTA SAN MARCO
PORTA ROMANA
VIA PICCOLOMINI
4
PORTA TUFI
SIENA OVEST EXIT
1
TO SAN GALGANO
3
S-73
TO A-1 AUTOSTRADA, ASSISI & ROME
SIENA SUD EXIT
VIA CASSIA S-2
DCH
S-223
TO GROSSETO & **8**
TO MONTALCINO, PIENZA, MONTEPULCIANO & **7**

1 Hotel Santa Caterina
2 To Frances' Lodge Relais
3 Hotel Porta Romana
4 Hotel San Marco
5 Guidoriccio Youth Hostel
6 To Borgo Argenina
7 To Il Canto del Sole
8 To Agriturismo Poggio Salvi

1 MILE
1 KM

Arrival in Siena

By Train: The small train station, located on the edge of town, has a bar, a TI (daily 9:30–13:30), a bus office (Mon–Sat 6:15–20:15, Sun 7:30–12:30 & 14:30–18:30), and a newsstand (which sells bus tickets—buy one now if you're taking the city bus into town), but no baggage check or lockers (check bags at Piazza Gramsci—see "By Intercity Bus," below). A shopping mall is right in front of the station.

To get from the station to the city center by **city bus,** exit the station, go left 15 yards, and head across the road to the shopping mall, a brick-and-glass building labeled *Galleria Porta Siena.* Enter the right-hand glass door and use the elevator to go down one floor. If you didn't buy bus tickets in the train station, you can get tickets (€1) from the blue machine (touch the screen for English and select "urban" for type of ticket). Most orange or red-and-silver buses go to the city center (6/hour, fewer on Sun and after 22:00). Double-check the destination with the driver by asking *"Centro?"* Punch your ticket in the machine onboard to validate it. Ride the last stop, Piazza Gramsci (or nearby Piazza del Sale).

If you're leaving Siena and you need to get to the train station, catch an orange or red-and-silver city bus from Piazza Gramsci. Confirm with the driver that the bus is going to the *stazione* (stat-zee-OH-nay); remember to purchase your ticket in advance from a *tabacchi* shop, then validate it on board.

The **taxi stand** is to your far right as you exit the train station, but as the city is chronically short on cabs, getting one here can take forever (about €9 to Il Campo, taxi tel. 0577-49222).

By Intercity Bus: Some buses arrive in Siena at Piazza Gramsci (a few blocks from the city center), though most arrive at the train station. (Some go first to the train station, then continue to Piazza Gramsci.) The main bus companies are Sena and the confusingly named Tra-In (pronounced TRAH-in). Day-trippers can store baggage underneath Piazza Gramsci in Sottopassaggio la Lizza (€5.50/day, open daily 7:00–19:00, carry-on-sized luggage no more than 33 pounds, no overnight storage). For more on buses, see the very end of this chapter.

By Car: Drivers coming from the autostrada take the *Siena Ovest* exit and follow signs for *Centro,* then *Stadio* (stadium). The soccer-ball signs take you to the stadium lot (Parcheggio Stadio, €1.60/hour, pay when you leave) near the huge bare-brick Church of San Domenico. The Fortezza lot nearby charges the same amount. For the Il Campo parking lot, take exit *Siena Sud,* follow *Direzione Roma,* then turn immediately left and follow the sign for *Il Campo* (special €25/day rate, ask at your hotel).

On parking spots, blue stripes mean "pay and display"; white stripes mean free parking. You can park for free in the lot west of

Siena at a Glance

▲▲▲**Il Campo** Best square in Italy. **Hours:** Always open. See page 102.

▲▲▲**Duomo** Art-packed cathedral with mosaic floors and statues by Michelangelo and Bernini. **Hours:** March–Sept Mon–Sat 10:30–19:30, June–Aug until 20:00, Sun 13:30–17:30; Oct–Feb Mon–Sat 10:30–18:00, Sun 13:30–17:30. See page 106.

▲▲**Duomo Museum** Displays cathedral art (including Duccio's *Maestà*) and offers sweeping Tuscan view. **Hours:** Daily March–Sept 9:30–20:00, Oct–Feb 10:00–17:00. See page 109.

▲**Civic Museum** City museum in City Hall with Sienese frescoes of Good and Bad Government. **Hours:** Daily March–Oct 10:00–19:00, Nov–Feb 10:00–17:15. May be open later in summer. See page 103.

▲**City Tower** 330-foot tower climb. **Hours:** Daily March–Oct 10:00–19:00, Nov–Feb 10:00–16:00. See page 105.

▲**Pinacoteca** Fine Sienese paintings. **Hours:** Sun–Mon 9:00–13:00, Tue–Sat 10:00–18:00. See page 106.

▲**Baptistery** Cave-like building has baptismal font decorated by Ghiberti and Donatello. **Hours:** Daily 9:30–19:00. See page 110.

▲**Santa Maria della Scala** Museum with vibrant ceiling and wall frescoes depicting day-to-day life in a medieval hospital, much of the original *Fountain of Joy,* and an Etruscan artifact exhibit. **Hours:** Daily 10:30–18:30. See page 110.

Church of San Domenico Huge brick church with St. Catherine's head and thumb. **Hours:** Daily March–Oct 7:00–18:30, Nov–Feb 9:00–18:30. See page 111.

Sanctuary of St. Catherine Home of St. Catherine. **Hours:** Daily 9:30–19:00. See page 112.

the Fortezza; in white-striped spots behind the Hotel Villa Liberty (behind the Fortezza); and overnight in most city lots from 20:00 to 8:00. Watch for signs showing a street cleaner and a day of the week—that's when the street is closed to cars for cleaning.

Driving within Siena's city center is restricted to local cars, and policed by automatic cameras. If you drive or park anywhere marked *Zona Traffico Limitato (ZTL)*, you'll likely have a hefty ticket waiting for you in the mail back home.

Technically, hotel customers are allowed to drop off bags at their hotel before finding a place to park overnight, but getting permission to do so isn't worth the trouble.

SIENA

Helpful Hints

Combo-Tickets: A deranged person cobbled together a pile of illogically paired combo-tickets for the sights in Siena— nothing covers everything, and the meager savings are just not worth the brainpower it takes to figure out the system. Only three of these combo-tickets are really worth considering: The best is the **"My Name is Duccio"** (DOO-choh) ticket, which covers the Duomo, Duomo Museum, Crypt, and Baptistery (€10, buy ticket at museum to skip line at Duomo). The **Civic Museum** offers two different combo-tickets (€12 combined with City Tower, €11 combined with Santa Maria della Scala—but no ticket combines all three).

Wednesday-Morning Market: The weekly market (clothes, knickknacks, and food) sprawls between the Fortezza and Piazza Gramsci along Viale Cesare Maccari and the adjacent Viale XXV Aprile.

Internet Access: In this university town, there are lots of places to get plugged in. **Cheap Phone Center** is hidden in a small shopping mall at Via Angiolieri Cecco 16 (€2/hour to use terminals, €1/hour to access Wi-Fi with your laptop, Mon–Sat 10:00–22:00, Sun 11:00–23:00; coming from Il Campo, go uphill past recommended Albergo Tre Donzelle, turn left, and after 20 yards, look for the *Buffet Restaurant* sign on your left). **Internet Point** is located upstairs at Via di Città 80, with the entrance around the corner on Via delle Campane (€3/hour, daily 9:00–21:00).

Post Office: It's on Piazza Matteotti (Mon–Fri 8:15–19:00, Sat 8:15–13:30, closed Sun).

Books: Libreria Senese sells books (including my guidebooks), newspapers, and magazines in English, with an emphasis on Italian-related topics (daily 9:00–20:00, Via di Città 62, tel. 0577-280-845). The **Feltrinelli** bookstore at Banchi di Sopra 52 also sells books and magazines in English (Mon–Sat 9:00– 19:30, closed Sun, tel. 0577-271-104).

Laundry: Two modern self-service launderettes are **Express Wash** (near Logge del Papa at Via di Pantaneto 38) and **Onda Blu** (50 yards from Il Campo at Via del Casato di Sotto 17). Both are open daily 8:00–22:00 with last loads at 21:00.

Travel Agency: Palio Viaggi, on Piazza Gramsci, sells train tickets (downstairs under the arch) and plane tickets (upstairs), but no bus tickets (Mon–Fri 9:00–12:45 & 15:00–18:30, Sat 9:00–12:30, closed Sun, opposite the columns of NH Excelsior Hotel at La Lizza 12, tel. 0577-280-828, info@palio viaggi.it).

Wine Classes: The Tuscan Wine School gives two-hour classes in English on Italian wines and includes samples of five vintages (a one-hour "crash course" may also be available). Rebecca and her fellow sommeliers keep things entertaining. They also have an outlet store that sells wine from local producers at cost (€40/person, daily, 2-hour classes at 11:00 and 16:00, later class specializes in Tuscan wines, Via Stalloreggi 26, 30 yards from recommended Hotel Duomo, tel. 0577-221-704, mobile 333-722-9716, www.tuscanwineschool.com, info@tuscanwines chool.com).

Tours in Siena

Local Guides—Roberto Bechi, a hardworking Sienese guide, specializes in off-the-beaten-path tours of the surrounding countryside by minibus (up to eight passengers, convenient pickup at hotel). Married to an American (Patti) and having run restaurants in Siena and the US, Roberto communicates well with Americans. His passions are Sienese culture, Tuscan history, and local cuisine. It's ideal to book well in advance, but you might be able to schedule a tour if you call the day before (seven different tours, full-day tours are €90/person—mention this book for a free gift, off-season 4-hour tours are €60/person, entry fees are extra; assistant Anna can schedule city tours as well as other guides if Roberto is booked; Anna's mobile 320-147-6590, Roberto's mobile 328-425-5648, www.toursbyroberto .com, toursbyroberto@gmail.com).

Federica Olla is a smart young guide with a knack for creative teaching (€55/hour, mobile 338-133-9525, info@ollaeventi.com).

Bus Tour—Wine & Tours runs half-day guided bus tours from Siena into Chianti, Montalcino, Montepulciano, and San Gimignano country—including winery visits and tastings—and the Tuscan countryside (€38, 10 percent discount with this book, daily 14:00–19:00, four different 5-hour tours, leave from Piazza Gramsci, office at Via Il Casato di Sotto 12, tel. 0577-46091, www .enocuriosi.com, info@wineandtours.it).

Siena

- ❶ Sottopassaggio la Lizza (Underground Bus Depot, Bag Storage & Bus Tickets)
- ❷ Libreria Senese Bookstore
- ❸ Feltrinelli Bookstore
- ❹ Palio Viaggi Travel Agency
- ❺ Wine & Tours
- ❻ Tuscan Wine School

SIENA

Sights in Siena

▲▲▲Il Campo: Siena's Main Square

Il Campo is the heart—geographically and metaphorically—of
Siena. The square fans out from the City Hall (Palazzo Pubblico)
to create an amphitheater, where the
citizens are the stars.

Originally, this area was just a field
(campo) located outside the former city
walls. You can still see some of the old
blocks made of volcanic tuff incorporated into today's red-brick Caffè Fonte
Gaia (along the right side of the square
as you face City Hall).

As the city expanded, Il Campo
eventually became the historic junction
of Siena's various competing districts, or
contrade, and the old marketplace. The
brick surface is divided into nine sections, representing the council
of nine merchants and city bigwigs who ruled medieval Siena. The
square and its buildings are the color of the soil upon which they
stand...a color known to Crayola-users and other artists as "Burnt
Sienna."

The City Hall and its 330-foot tower dominate the square. In
medieval Siena, this secular building was the center of the city,
and the whole focus of Il Campo still flows down to it. The **City
Tower** (Torre del Mangia), Italy's
tallest secular tower, was named
after a hedonistic watchman who
consumed his earnings like a glut-
ton consumes food—his chewed-
up statue is in the courtyard, to the
left as you enter.

The chapel located at the base
of the tower was built in 1348
as thanks to God for ending the
Black Death (after it killed more than a third of the population).
It should also be used to thank God that the tower—just plunked
onto the building with no extra foundation—still stands. These
days, the chapel is used solely to bless the Palio contestants, and
the tower's bell only rings for the race.

The *Fountain of Joy (Fonte Gaia),* by Jacopo della Quercia,
marks the square's high point. Find the snake-handler woman,
the two naked guys about to be tossed in, and the pigeons politely
waiting their turn to tightrope gingerly down slippery spouts to
slurp a drink from wolves' snouts. The relief panel on the left (as

you face the fountain) shows God creating Adam by helping him to his feet. It's said that this reclining Adam influenced Michelangelo when he painted his Sistine Chapel ceiling. This fountain is a copy—you can see most of the original fountain in an interesting exhibit at Siena's Santa Maria della Scala (described later).

To say that Siena and Florence have always been competitive is an understatement. In medieval times, a statue of Venus stood on Il Campo. After the plague hit Siena, the monks blamed the pagan statue. The people cut it to pieces and buried it along the walls of Florence.

Picture Il Campo during the famous Palio horse races (every year on July 2 and Aug 16). Ten snorting horses and their nervous riders (selected from 17 *contrade*, or neighborhoods) line up near the Antica Siena shop (right side of square) to await the starting signal.

Then they race like crazy three times around the perimeter (the gray pavement), which is covered with dirt. Mattresses pad the sharpest turns. Spectators waving the banners of their neighborhoods cram (for free) into the center of the square or, if they have the money, watch from temporary bleachers or the balconies above. Every possible vantage point and perch is packed with people straining to see the action. The winner crosses the line, and 1/17th of Siena goes berserk for the next 365 days.

▲Civic Museum (Museo Civico)—At the base of the tower is Siena's City Hall, the spot where secular government got its start in early Renaissance Europe. There you'll find city government still at work, along with a sampling of local art.

In the following order, you'll see: the Sala Risorgimento, with dramatic scenes of Victor Emmanuel II's unification of Italy (surrounded by statues that don't seem to care); the chapel, with impressive inlaid-wood chairs in the choir; and the Sala del Mappamondo, with Siena's first fresco, Simone Martini's *Maestà* (*Enthroned Virgin*—a groundbreaking depiction of a down-to-earth Madonna), facing the faded *Guidoriccio da Fogliano* (a mercenary providing a more concrete form of protection).

SIENA

Siena's Palio

In the Palio, the feisty spirit of Siena's 17 *contrade* (neighborhoods) lives on. Each *contrada* has a parish church, well, or fountain, and sometimes even a historical museum. Each is represented by a mascot (porcupine, unicorn, wolf, etc.) and unique colors worn proudly by residents.

Contrada pride is evident year-round in Siena's parades and colorful banners, lamps, and wall plaques. (If you hear the thunder of distant drumming, run to it for some medieval action, often featuring flag-throwers.) You are welcome to participate in these lively neighborhood festivals. Buy a scarf in *contrada* colors, grab a glass of Chianti, munch on some *panforte,* and join in the merriment.

Contrada passion is most visible twice a year—on July 2 and August 16—when the city erupts during its world-famous horse race, the Palio di Siena. Ten of the 17 neighborhoods compete (chosen by rotation and lot), hurling themselves with medieval abandon into several days of trial races and traditional revelry. Jockeys—usually from out of town—are considered hired guns, no better than paid mercenaries. Bets are placed on which *contrada* will win...and lose. Despite the shady behind-the-scenes dealing, on the big day the horses are taken into their *contrada's* church to be blessed. ("Go and return victorious," says the priest.) It's considered a sign of luck if a horse leaves droppings in the church.

On the evening of the race, Il Campo is stuffed to the brim with locals and tourists. Dirt is brought in and packed down to create the track's surface, while mattresses pad the walls of surrounding buildings. The most treacherous spots are the sharp

Next is the Sala della Pace—where the city's fat cats met. Looking down on the oligarchy during their meetings were two fascinating frescoes showing the *Effects of Good and Bad Government*, by Ambrogio Lorenzetti. Notice the whistle-while-you-work happiness of the utopian community ruled by the utopian government (in the better-preserved fresco) against the fate of a community ruled by politicians with more typical values (in a terrible state of disrepair). The message: Without justice, there can be no prosperity.

Take a moment to savor one of those to-sigh-for rural panoramas out the window of the Sala della Pace. The view is essentially the same as the one from the top of the big stairs you'll pass as you exit—enjoy it from here.

Cost and Hours: 7.50, €12 combo-ticket

corners, where many a rider bites the dust. One lap around the course is about a third of a mile (350 meters); three laps make a full circuit. In this literally no-holds-barred race—which lasts just over a minute—a horse can win even without its rider (jockeys perch precariously without saddles on the sweaty horses' backs, and often fall off).

The winning neighborhood is the scene of grand celebrations afterward. Winners receive a *palio* (banner), typically painted by a local artist and always featuring the Virgin Mary. But the true prize is proving that your *contrada* is *numero uno,* and mocking your losing rival.

All over town, sketches and posters depict the Palio. This is not some folkloristic event—it's a real medieval moment. If you're packed onto the square with 60,000 people, all hungry for victory, you won't see much, but you'll feel it. Bleacher and balcony seats are expensive, but it's free to join the masses in the square. Be sure to go with an empty bladder as there are no WCs, and be prepared to surrender any sense of personal space.

While the actual Palio packs the city, you could side-trip in from Florence to see the horse-race trials—called *prove* (proh-vay)—on any of the three days before the main event (usually at 9:00 and about 19:30, free seats in bleachers). For more information, visit www.ilpalio.org.

includes City Tower, €11 combo-ticket includes Santa Maria della Scala, daily March–Oct 10:00–19:00—may be open later in summer, Nov–Feb 10:00–17:15, last entry 45 minutes before closing, tel. 0577-292-615.

▲**City Tower (Torre del Mangia)**—Siena gathers around its City Hall more than its church. Medieval Siena was a proud republic, and this tall tower is the exclamation point of its "declaration of

independence." Its 300 steps get pretty skinny at the top, but the reward is one of Italy's best views.

Cost and Hours: €7, €12 combo-ticket includes Civic Museum, daily March–Oct 10:00–19:00, Nov–Feb 10:00–16:00, last entry 45 minutes before closing, closed in rain, limited to 30 tourists at a time so be prepared for long lines—avoid midday crowds, often sold out, free and mandatory bag check.

Near Il Campo

▲**Pinacoteca**—If you're into medieval art, you'll likely find this quiet, uncrowded colorful museum delightful. The museum walks you through Siena's art chronologically, from the 12th through the 16th century, when a revolution in realism was percolating in Tuscany. For the casual sightseer, the Sienese art in the Civic and Duomo museums is adequate. But art fans enjoy this opportunity to trace the evolution of Siena's delicate and elegant works, from stiff, gold-backed icon-like Madonnas to curvy, graceful Madonnas to Italian Renaissance. Concentrate on pieces by Duccio (artist of the *Maestà* in the Duomo Museum), Simone Martini (who did the *Maestà* in the Civic Museum), the brothers Ambrogio and Pietro Lorenzetti (Ambrogio created the *Effects of Good and Bad Government* in the Civic Museum), Pinturicchio (who did the frescoes in the Piccolomini Library in the Duomo), and Domenico Beccafumi (who inlaid pavement in the Duomo).

Cost and Hours: €4, Sun–Mon 9:00–13:00, Tue–Sat 10:00–18:00, last entry 30 minutes before closing, free and mandatory bag check, tel. 0577-281-161 or 0577-286-143. To reach the museum from Il Campo, walk out Via di Città and go left on Via San Pietro.

Siena's Cathedral Area

▲▲▲**Duomo**—If the Campo is the heart of Siena, the Duomo (or cathedral) is its soul. The white-and-dark-green-striped church, sitting on an artificial platform atop Siena's highest point, is visible for miles around. The current  structure dates back to 1215, with the major decoration done during Siena's heyday from 1250 to 1350. This ornate but surprisingly secular shrine to the Virgin Mary is stacked with colorful art inside and out, from the inlaid-marble floors to the stained-glass windows. The interior is a Renaissance riot of striped columns, intricate marble inlays, Michelangelo statues, and Bernini sculptures. In the Piccolomini Library, a series of captivating frescoes by the Umbrian painter Pinturicchio tells the story of Aeneas Piccolomini, Siena's consummate Renaissance Man, who became Pope Pius II.

Cost and Hours: €3 includes cathedral and Piccolomini

Library; €10 "My Name is Duccio" combo-ticket also includes the Duomo Museum (sold 100 yards away at the museum, allows you to skip cathedral line), Crypt, and Baptistery. There's a €5 audioguide for the church and the library (€7/2 people); an €8 combo-audioguide also covers the Duomo Museum (€12/2 people, ID required for deposit). The Duomo and library are both open March–Sept Mon–Sat 10:30–19:30, June–Aug until 20:00, Sun 13:30–17:30; Oct–Feb Mon–Sat 10:30–18:00, Sun 13:30–17:30; last entry 30 minutes before closing. Modest dress is required to enter, but paper ponchos are provided if needed.

SIENA

◑ Self-Guided Tour: In the **nave,** the heads of 172 popes—who reigned from Peter to the 12th century—peer down from above, looking over the fine inlaid art on the floor. With a forest of striped columns, a coffered dome, a large stained-glass window at the far end (it's a copy—the original is viewable up close in the nearby Duomo Museum), and an art gallery's worth of early Renaissance art, this is one busy interior. If you look closely at the popes, you'll see the same four faces repeated over and over.

For almost two centuries (1373–1547), 40 artists paved the marble floor with scenes from the Old Testament, allegories, and intricate patterns. The earliest designs are simple black-and-white with engraved details, but the later ones use inlay technique with many colored marbles. The series starts near the entrance with historical allegories; the larger, more elaborate scenes surrounding the altar are mostly stories from the Old Testament. Many of the floor panels are roped off to prevent further wear and tear.

Grab a seat under the dome. It sits on a 12-sided base, but its "coffered" ceiling is actually a painted illusion. Get oriented to the array of sights by thinking of the church floor as a big 12-hour clock. You're the middle, and the altar is high noon: You'll find the *Slaughter of the Innocents* roped off on the floor at 10 o'clock, Pisano's pulpit between two pillars at 11 o'clock, a copy of Duccio's round stained-glass window at high noon, Bernini's chapel at 3 o'clock, the Piccolomini Altar with the Michelangelo statue (next to doorway leading to a shop, snacks, and WC) at 7 o'clock, the Piccolomini Library at 8 o'clock, and a Donatello statue at 9 o'clock.

Nicola Pisano's octagonal Carrara marble **pulpit** (1268) rests on the backs of lions, symbols of Christianity triumphant. Like the lions, the Church eats its catch (devouring paganism) and nurses its cubs. The seven relief panels tell the life of Christ in rich detail. (Buy light from the coin-op machine.) This is a copy of the original window, which was moved to the Duomo Museum a couple of years ago. The famous rose window was created in 1288 and dedicated to the Virgin Mary.

Look for the *Slaughter of the Innocents* inlaid pavement panel. Herod (left), sitting enthroned amid Renaissance arches, orders the massacre of all babies to prevent the coming of the promised Messiah. It's a chaotic scene of angry soldiers, grieving mothers, and dead babies, reminding locals that a republic ruled by a tyrant will experience misery.

Donatello's rugged *St. John the Baptist* in his famous rags stands in a chapel to the right of the library. To understand why Giovanni Lorenzo Bernini is considered the greatest Baroque sculptor, step into the sumptuous **Bernini Chapel.** This last work in the cathedral (1659) is enough to make even a Lutheran light a candle. Move up to the altar and look back at the two Bernini statues: Mary Magdalene in a state of spiritual ecstasy, and St. Jerome playing the crucifix like a violinist lost in beautiful music.

Over the altar is the *Madonna del Voto,* a Madonna and Child painted by Duccio and adorned with a real crown of gold and jewels. Tilting her head, she looks out sympathetically. This is the Mary to whom the Palio is dedicated, dear to the hearts of the Sienese. The faithful's prayers to Mary are accompanied by offerings, found outside the chapel, hanging on the wall to the left as you exit.

The **Piccolomini Altar** (left wall, marble altarpiece decorated with statues) was designed for the tomb of the Sienese-born Pope Pius III. It's most interesting for Michelangelo's statue of St. Paul (lower right, who is clearly more interesting than the bland, bored popes above him). Paul has the look of Michelangelo's *Moses,* the broken-nosed self-portrait of the sculptor himself, and the relaxed hand of his *David.* It was the chance to sculpt *David* in Florence that convinced Michelangelo to abandon the Siena project.

The brilliantly frescoed **Piccolomini Library** captures the exuberant, optimistic spirit of the 1400s, when humanism and the Renaissance were born. The never-restored frescoes look nearly as vivid now as the day they were finished 550 years ago. (With the bright window light, candles were not necessary in this room—and didn't sully the art with soot.) The painter Pinturicchio (c. 1454–1513) was hired to celebrate the life of one of Siena's hometown boys—a man many call "the first humanist," Aeneas Piccolomini (1405–1464), who became Pope Pius II. Start from the window and work clockwise, following 10 scenes framed with arches, as if Pinturicchio were opening a window onto the spacious 3-D world we inhabit. The library also contains intricately decorated, illuminated music scores, and a statue (a Roman copy of a Greek original) of the Three Graces.

Exit the Duomo, and make a U-turn to the left, walking alongside the church to Piazza Jacopo della Quercia to view the

unfinished cathedral. The nave of the Duomo was supposed to be where the piazza is today. Worshippers would have entered the church from the far end of the piazza through the unfinished wall. (Look way up at the highest part of the wall. That's the viewpoint accessible from inside the Duomo Museum.)

After rival republic Florence began its grand cathedral (1296), proud Siena planned to build one even bigger, the biggest church in all Christendom. Construction began in the 1330s on an extension off the right side of the existing Duomo (today's cathedral would have been used as a transept). Some of the nave's green-and-white-striped columns were built, and are now filled in with a brick wall. The wall connecting the Duomo with the museum of the cathedral was as far as Siena got before a plague hit, killing the city's ability to finish the project. Round white stones in the pavement mark where a row of pillars would have been. Look through the unfinished entrance facade, note blue sky where the stained-glass windows would have been, and ponder the struggles, triumphs, and failures of the human spirit.

▲▲**Duomo Museum (Museo dell'Opera e Panorama)**—
Located at the back of the Duomo on the right, Siena's most enjoyable museum was built to house the cathedral's art. The ground floor is filled with the cathedral's original Gothic sculptures by Giovanni Pisano (who spent 10 years in the late 1200s carving and orchestrating the decoration of the cathedral) and a fine Donatello *Madonna and Child*. A slender, tender Mary gazes down at her chubby-cheeked baby, and her sad eyes say that she knows the eventual fate of her son.

Until a couple of years ago, this original window was located above and behind the Duomo's altar. Now the church has a copy, and art-lovers can enjoy a close-up look at this masterpiece.

The rose window—20 feet across, made in 1288—is dedicated (like the church and the city itself) to the Virgin Mary, and combines elements from rigid Byzantine icons with a budding sense of 3-D realism.

Upstairs to the left awaits a private audience with Duccio's *Maestà* (*Enthroned Virgin*, 1311). Grab a seat and study one of the great pieces of medieval art. The flip side of the *Maestà* (displayed on the opposite wall) features 26 smaller panels—the medieval equivalent of pages—showing colorful scenes from the Passion of Christ.

Climb onto the Panorama del Facciatone for a surprise view of Siena. At the landing just before the top floor, turn right and walk past the rooms, going through the small doorway to the stairwell. Climb down the steps and then up about 60 claustrophobic spiral stairs to the first viewpoint. You can continue up another similar spiral staircase to reach the very top. Look back over toward the Duomo and consider this: If grandiose plans for the church had been completed, you'd be looking straight down the nave.

Cost and Hours: €6; €10 "My Name is Duccio" combo-ticket also includes the Duomo, Crypt, and Baptistery; €3 for worthwhile 40-minute audioguide; €8 combo-audioguide includes Duomo and the library—rentable only at the Duomo, €12/2 people, ID required for deposit; daily March–Sept 9:30–20:00, Oct–Feb 10:00–17:00, tel. 0577-283-048, www.operaduomo.siena.it.

▲**Baptistery**—Siena is so hilly that there wasn't enough flat ground on which to build a big church. What to do? Build a big church anyway and prop up the overhanging edge with the Baptistery. This dark and quietly tucked-away cave of art is worth a look for its cool tranquility bronze panels and angels by Ghiberti, Donatello, and others that adorn the pedestal of the baptismal font (€3; €10 "My Name is Duccio" combo-ticket also includes Duomo, Duomo Museum, and Crypt; daily 9:30–19:00, last entry 30 minutes before closing).

The nearby cathedral "crypt" entrance (halfway up the stairs between the Baptistery and the Duomo Museum) is important archaeologically—several frescoed rooms have been discovered here within the last 10 years. It may be of little interest to the average tourist, but fresco fans will enjoy it.

Cost and Hours: €6, also covered by €10 "My Name is Duccio" combo-ticket, daily 9:30–19:30.

▲**Santa Maria della Scala**—This museum (opposite the Duomo entrance) was used as a hospital until the 1980s. Its labyrinthine 12th-century cellars—carved out of volcanic tuff and finished with brick—go down several floors, and during medieval times were used to store supplies for the hospital upstairs. Today, the hospital and its cellars are filled with museum exhibits, including these main attractions: the fancily frescoed Pellegrinaio Hall (ground floor), most of the original *Fountain of Joy,* St. Catherine's Oratory chapel (first basement), and the Etruscan collection in the Archaeological Museum (second basement). Just inside the complex is the Church of the Santissima Annunziata (which you can see for free by entering from the square, through the left-side wooden door opposite the Duomo entrance).

Cost and Hours: €6, €11 combo-ticket includes Civic Museum, daily 10:30–18:30, last entry 30 minutes before closing, bookstore, café, tel. 0577-534-511, www.santamariadellascala.com.

Pellegrinaio Hall: Sumptuously frescoed, this hall shows medieval Siena's innovative health care and social welfare system in action (c. 1442, wonderfully described in English). Starting in the 11th century, the hospital nursed the sick and cared for abandoned children, as is vividly portrayed in these frescoes. The good works paid off, as bequests and donations poured in, creating the wealth that's evident throughout this building.

Fountain of Joy **Exhibit:** Downstairs you'll find an engaging exhibit on Jacopo della Quercia's early 15th-century *Fountain of Joy (Fonte Gaia)*—and the disassembled pieces of the original fountain itself. In the 19th century, after serious deterioration, the ornate fountain was dismantled and plaster casts were made. (From these casts, they formed the replica that graces Il Campo today.) Here you'll see the eroded original panels paired with their restored casts, along with the original statues that once stood on the edges of the fountain.

On the same floor, pop into **St. Catherine's Oratory,** the small chapel where she prayed and received visions. A holy nail thought to be from Jesus' cross is on the altar.

Archaeological Museum: Descend into the cavernous second basement under groin vaults to be alone with piles of ancient Etruscan stuff excavated from tombs dating centuries before Christ (displayed in a labyrinthine exhibit). Remember, the Etruscans dominated this part of Italy before the Roman Empire swept through—some historians think even Rome originated as an Etruscan town.

Siena's San Domenico Area

Church of San Domenico—This huge brick church is worth a quick look. The spacious, plain interior (except for the colorful flags of the city's 17 *contrade*, or neighborhoods) fits the austere philosophy of the Dominicans and invites meditation on the thoughts and deeds of St. Catherine. Walk up the steps in the rear to see paintings from the life of St. Catherine, patron saint of Siena. Halfway up the church on the right, find a metal bust of St. Catherine, a small case housing her thumb (sometimes loaned out to other churches), and a reliquary on the lowest shelf containing the chain she used to scourge herself. In the chapel (15 feet to the left) surrounded with candles, you'll see Catherine's actual head atop the altar. Through the door just beyond are the sacristy and the bookstore.

Cost and Hours: Free, daily March–Oct 7:00–18:30, Nov–Feb 9:00–18:30, gift shop tel. 0577-286-848, www.basilicacateriniana.com. A WC (€0.50) is at the far end of the parking lot, to the right as you face the church entrance.

Sanctuary of St. Catherine—Step into Catherine's cool and peaceful home. Siena remembers its favorite hometown gal, a simple, unschooled, but mystically devout soul who, in the mid-1300s, helped convince the pope to return from France to Rome. Because of her intervention, Catherine is honored today as Europe's patron saint. Pilgrims have visited her home since 1464, and architects and artists have greatly embellished what was probably once a humble home (her family worked as wool-dyers). Enter through the courtyard, and walk down the stairs at the far end. The church on your right contains the wooden crucifix upon which Catherine was meditating when she received the stigmata. The chapel on your left was originally the kitchen. Go down the stairs to the left of the kitchen to reach the saint's room. Catherine's bare cell is behind wrought-iron doors. Much of the art throughout the sanctuary depicts scenes from her life.

Cost and Hours: Free, daily 9:30–19:00, a few downhill blocks toward the center from San Domenico—follow signs to *Santuario di Santa Caterina*—at Costa di Sant'Antonio 6, tel. 0577-288-175.

Shopping and Nightlife in Siena

Shopping

The main drag, Via Banchi di Sopra, is a cancan of fancy shops. The big local department store is **Upim** (Mon–Sat 8:30–20:00, Sun 10:00–20:00, Piazza Matteotti).

For easy-to-pack souvenirs, get some of the colorful scarves/flags that depict the symbols of Siena's 17 different neighborhoods (such as the wolf, the turtle, and the snail). They're good for gifts or to decorate your home (sold in varying sizes at souvenir stands).

Sweets: All over town, **Prodotti Tipici** shops sell Sienese specialties. Siena's claim to caloric fame is its *panforte*, a rich,

St. Catherine of Siena
(1347–1380)

The youngest of 25 children born to a Sienese cloth-dyer, Catherine began experiencing heavenly visions as a child.

At 16 she became a Dominican nun, locking herself away for three years in a room in her family's house. She lived the life of an ascetic, which culminated in a vision wherein she married Christ. Catherine emerged from solitude to join her Dominican sisters, sharing her experiences, caring for the sick, and gathering both disciples and enemies. At age 23, she lapsed into a spiritual coma, waking with the heavenly command to spread her message to the world. She wrote essays and letters to kings, dukes, bishops, and popes, imploring them to find peace for a war-ravaged Italy. While visiting Pisa during Lent of 1375, she had a vision in which she received the stigmata, the wounds of Christ.

Still in her twenties, Catherine was invited to Avignon, France, where the pope had taken up residence. With her charm, sincerity, and reputation for holiness, she helped convince Pope Gregory XI to return the papacy to the city of Rome. Catherine also went to Rome, where she died young. She was canonized in the next generation (by a Sienese pope), and her relics were distributed to churches around Italy.

SIENA

chewy concoction of nuts, honey, and candied fruits that impresses even fruitcake-haters. There are a few varieties: *Margherita*, dusted in powdered sugar, is more fruity, while *panpepato* has a spicy, peppery crust. Locals prefer a chewy white macaroon-and-almond cookie called *ricciarelli*.

Nightlife

Join the evening *passeggiata* (peak strolling time is 19:00) along Via Banchi di Sopra with gelato in hand.

The **Enoteca Italiana** is a good wine bar in a cellar in the Fortezza. To get there, enter the Fortezza via the bridge, cross the running track, and—after passing a tree—go left down a ramp (sample glasses in three different price ranges: €3, €4, and €6.50; Mon–Sat 12:00–24:00, closed Sun; bottles available from all over Italy, snacks served when the bar's pricey restaurant is between mealtimes; outside terrace, tel. 0577-228-832).

Sleeping in Siena

Finding a room in Siena is tough during Easter (April 24 in 2011) or the Palio (July 2 and Aug 16). Many hotels won't take reservations until the end of May for the Palio, and even then they might require a four-night stay. If you're traveling any other time of year, you should still call ahead, as all the guidebooks list Siena's few budget places. While day-tripping tour groups turn the town into a Gothic amusement park in midsummer, Siena is basically yours in the evenings and off-season.

Most of the listed hotels lie between Il Campo and the Church of San Domenico. Part of Siena's charm is its lively, festive character—this means that all hotels can be plagued with noise, even (and sometimes especially) the hotels in the pedestrian-only zone. If tranquility is important for your sanity, ask for a room that's off the street, or consider staying at one of the recommended places outside the center.

Simple Places near Il Campo

Most of these listings are forgettable but inexpensive, and just a horse wreck away from one of Italy's most wonderful civic spaces.

$$ Palazzo Masi is a modern B&B run by husband-and-wife team Alizzardo and Daniela. Just steps away from Il Campo, it has six pleasant, quiet rooms—some furnished with antiques—and shared common areas on the second and third floors of a renovated

---

Sleep Code

(€1 = about $1.25, country code: 39)

S = Single, **D** = Double/Twin, **T** = Triple, **Q** = Quad, **b** = bathroom, **s** = shower only. Breakfast is not included unless noted. If your hotel doesn't provide breakfast, eat at a bar on Il Campo or near your hotel. Credit cards are generally accepted, but I note in the listings if they aren't. (If not, there are ATMs all over town.) Hotel staff generally speak English unless noted otherwise.

To help you easily sort through these listings, I've divided the rooms into three categories based on the price for a standard double room with bath:

$$$ Higher Priced—Most rooms €130 or more.
$$ Moderately Priced—Most rooms between €90-130.
$ Lower Priced—Most rooms €90 or less.

Prices can change without notice; verify the hotel's current rates online or by email. For other updates, see www .ricksteves.com/update.

Siena Hotels

1. Palazzo Masi & Launderette
2. To Palazzo Bruchi B&B
3. Piccolo Hotel Etruria
4. Albergo Tre Donzelle
5. Locanda Garibaldi
6. Hotel Cannon d'Oro
7. To Hotel Duomo & Pensione Palazzo Ravizza
8. To Hotel Villa Elda & Hotel Villa Liberty
9. Hotel Chiusarelli
10. Alma Domus
11. Albergo Bernini
12. Internet Cafés (2)
13. Launderette

SIENA

medieval 14th-century townhouse (D-€80, Db-€120, these rates promised to readers through 2011 if you book direct, discounts for 4 or more nights, cash only, free Wi-Fi, take the road to the far right of City Hall as you're facing it and head down Casato di Sotto about 50 yards to #29, mobile 349-600-9155, www.palazzo masi.com, info@palazzomasi.it).

$$ Palazzo Bruchi B&B offers six tranquil rooms in a 17th-century palazzo overlooking the Tuscan countryside. There's one fancy, spacious room *(luxe)* that features Old World heavy walnut furnishings and period paintings. The other six rooms are smaller and simpler, with bright, cheery decor and views of the quiet interior courtyard. Camilla takes good care of her guests (Sb-€90, Db-€100, *luxe* Db/Tb-€150, Tb-€120–175, Qb-€200, 4 percent cash discount, includes breakfast, free Internet access and Wi-Fi; take Via Banchi di Sotto until it turns into Via Pantaneto, located on left, just before the Church of San Giorgio at #105; tel. & fax 0577-287-342, www.palazzobruchi.it, masignani@hotmail.com).

$$ Piccolo Hotel Etruria has 20 decent air-conditioned rooms but not much soul. The hotel is overpriced for what it is, though well-located and sleepable (S-€50, Sb-€55, Db-€110, Tb-€138, Qb-€170, optional breakfast-€6, curfew at 1:00 in the morning, next to recommended Albergo Tre Donzelle at Via Donzelle 1–3, tel. 0577-288-088, fax 0577-288-461, www.hoteletruria.com, info @hoteletruria.com, Fattorini family).

$ Albergo Tre Donzelle is a fine budget value with 20 plain, institutional, well-worn rooms. Although the showers have seen better days, these may be the cheapest rooms in the center. Don't hang out here...think of Il Campo, a block away, as your terrace (S-€38, D-€49, Db-€60, T-€70, Tb-€85, no rooms available for Palio; with your back to the tower, head away from Il Campo toward 2 o'clock to Via Donzelle 5; tel. 0577-280-358, www .tredonzelle.com, info@tredonzelle.com).

$ Locanda Garibaldi is a modest, characteristically Sienese place. Gentle Marcello rents seven pleasant rooms up a funky, artsy staircase (Db-€75, Tb-€95, only takes reservations a month in advance, half a block downhill from Il Campo at Via Giovanni Dupre 18, tel. 0577-284-204, Marcello and Sonia speak a little English).

$ Hotel Cannon d'Oro, a few blocks up Via Banchi di Sopra, has 30 airy and comfortable rooms, but is a bit noisy and group-friendly (Sb-€71, Db-€90, Tb-€115, Qb-€136, these discounted prices good with this book through 2011, family deals, includes breakfast, a couple blocks from the bus hub at Via Montanini 28, tel. 0577-44-321, fax 0577-280-868, www.cannondoro.com, info @cannondoro.com, Maurizio).

Sleeping Fancy, Southwest of Il Campo

These two classy and well-run places are a 10-minute walk from Il Campo.

$$$ Hotel Duomo has 20 spacious rooms and a bizarre floor plan (Sb-€105, Db-€130, Db suite-€180, Tb-€180, Qb-€230, includes breakfast, air-con, elevator, Internet access, picnic-friendly roof terrace, discounted parking; follow Via di Città, which becomes Via Stalloreggi, to #38; tel. 0577-289-088, fax 0577-43-043, www.hotelduomo.it, booking@hotelduomo.it, Svetlana and Vasilika). If arriving by train, take a taxi (€8) or bus #3 to the Porta Tufi stop, just a few minutes' walk from the hotel; if driving, go to Porta San Marco, turn right, and follow signs to the hotel—drop your bags, then park in the nearby Il Campo lot.

$$$ Pensione Palazzo Ravizza is elegant and friendly, with an aristocratic feel, a peaceful garden, and a Steinway in the upper lounge. It was a noble's luxurious residence, where John F. Kennedy once stayed (Sb-€150, small loft Db-€130, standard Db-€170, superior Db-€200, Tb-€240, family suites-€300, see website for room differences, rooms in back overlook countryside, includes breakfast, air-con, elevator, cable Internet in rooms, Wi-Fi in public spaces, free parking, Via Piano dei Mantellini 34, tel. 0577-280-462, fax 0577-221-597, www.palazzoravizza.com, bureau @palazzoravizza.it, Ariol).

Near San Domenico Church

These hotels are within a 10-minute walk northwest of Il Campo. Albergo Bernini and Alma Domus, which offer views of the old town and cathedral, are about the best values in town.

$$$ Hotel Villa Elda rents 11 bright and light rooms in a newly renovated villa. Classy, stately, and overpriced, it's in a fine neighborhood just a few minutes' walk past the Church of San Domenico (Db-€89–170, more with view, extra person-€20, includes breakfast, air-con, garden and view terrace, Viale Ventiquattro Maggio 10, tel. 0577-247-927, www.villaeldasiena.it, info@villaeldasiena.it).

$$$ Hotel Chiusarelli, with 48 recently renovated rooms in a beautiful Neoclassical villa, has a handy location but is on a very busy street, making it a last resort. Expect traffic noise at night— ask for a quieter room in the back (can be guaranteed with reservation). The bells of San Domenico are your 7:00 wake-up call (Sb-€98, Db-€138, Tb-€175, ask for Rick Steves discount when you book, air-con, Wi-Fi, rental bikes-€4/half-day, across from San Domenico at Viale Curtatone 15, tel. 0577-280-562, fax 0577-271-177, www.chiusarelli.com, info@chiusarelli.com).

$$ Hotel Villa Liberty, a bit farther out, is a former private mansion that was renovated in 2010. It has 18 big, bright, comfortable rooms and lots of street noise (Sb-€70, Db-€100–130, Tb-€130–160, junior suite-€160–180, air-con, elevator, free Wi-Fi, bar, courtyard, free and easy street parking, facing fortress at Viale V. Veneto 11, tel. 0577-44-966, fax 0577-44-770, www.villaliberty .it, info@villaliberty.it).

$ Alma Domus is a church-run hotel offering 43 clean, quiet little rooms for a steal. Bright lamps, quaint balconies, fine views, grand public rooms, top security, and a pleasant atmosphere make this a great value—but they offer only a limited number of doubles. The 10:00 checkout time is strict, but they will store your luggage in their secure courtyard (Sb-€45, Db-€75, Tb-€95, Qb-€110, breakfast included, ask for view room—*con vista*, central air-con, elevator, Internet access; from San Domenico, walk downhill toward the view with the church on your right, turn left down Via Camporegio, make a U-turn at the little chapel down the brick steps to Via Camporegio 37; tel. 0577-44-177, fax 0577-47-601, www.hotelalmadomus.it, info@ hotelalmadomus.it).

$ Albergo Bernini makes you part of a Sienese family in a modest, clean home with nine traditional rooms (ask for a quiet room away from the restaurant). Giovanni, wife Daniela, and their three daughters welcome you to their spectacular view terrace for breakfast and picnic lunches and dinners (Sb-€78, D-€65, Db-€85, less in winter, optional breakfast-€7.50, cash only, non-smoking, free Wi-Fi, on the main Il Campo–San Domenico drag at Via della Sapienza 15, tel. & fax 0577-289-047, www.albergobernini .com, hbernin@tin.it).

Farther from the Center

City buses will get you to any of the following places.

$$$ Hotel Santa Caterina is a three-star 18th-century place that is professionally run with real attention to quality. Most of the hotel's 22 comfortable rooms were recently renovated, and there's a delightful garden outside (Sb-€115, small Db-€115, Db-€155, Tb-€195, prices promised with this book through 2011—ask for special Rick Steves rate when you reserve, includes buffet breakfast, air-con, fridge in room, elevator, garden side is quieter, but street side—with multipaned windows—isn't bad, parking-€15/ day—request when you reserve, 100 yards outside Porta Romana city gate at Via E.S. Piccolomini 7, tel. 0577-221-105, fax 0577-271-087, www.hscsiena.it, info@hscsiena.it, Lorenza and Andrea). To get to and from downtown Siena, catch shuttle bus #A. To connect with the bus and train stations, take bus #2 (which becomes #17 at Piazza del Sale).

$$$ Frances' Lodge Relais is a small farmhouse B&B less than a mile out of Siena. Franca and Franco rent six modern rooms and one apartment suite in a rustic-yet-elegant old place with an inviting breakfast room, peaceful garden, eight acres of olive trees and vineyards, and great views of Siena and its countryside—even from the swimming pool (small Db-€170, Db-€190, Db suite-€200, Tb-€210–220, Tb suite-€250, Qb suite-€300, these prices promised to Rick Steves readers through 2011, includes great breakfast, air-con-€10, Internet access, free parking, Strada di Valdipugna 2, tel. & fax 0577-42379, mobile 337-671-608, www .franceslodge.it). It's an easy five-minute bus ride from the center (shuttle bus #B) plus a five-minute walk, or €10 by taxi. Consider having an al fresco picnic dinner there, complete with view.

$$ Hotel Porta Romana is at the edge of town off a busy road. Fourteen rooms face the open countryside, and breakfast is served in the garden (Sb-€90, Db-€110, Qb-€130, extra person-€20, 10 percent Rick Steves discount if you book direct, cash preferred, Internet access, free parking, 50 yards from convenient connection to town center via shuttle bus #A—desk has tickets, Via E.S. Piccolomini 35, tel. 0577-42299, fax 0577-232-905, www .hotelportaromana.com, info@hotelportaromana.com, Marco and Evelia).

$$ Hotel San Marco, in a new and characterless building just outside Porta San Marco, has 28 pleasing modern rooms with all the comforts. While it's easiest to drive here, city bus #54 stops 100 yards from the hotel every 15 minutes (Db-€120, discounts for 3 or more nights, air-con, Wi-Fi, free parking, Via Massetana 70, tel. 0577-271-556, fax 0577-271-826, www.sanmarcosiena.it, info @sanmarcosiena.it).

$ Guidoriccio Youth Hostel, which has 100 cheap beds and an institutional ambience, welcomes anyone (€20/bed in doubles, triples, and dorms with sheets; co-ed rooms, includes breakfast, Internet access, self-service laundry-€6, lock-out 10:00–14:00; take bus #10 or #77 from train station or bus #10 or #15 from Piazza Gramsci—about 20 minutes to Via Fiorentina 89 in Stellino neighborhood; tel. 0577-52212, fax 0577-50277, www.ostellosiena .it, info@ostellosiena.it).

Outside of Siena

The following accommodations are set in the lush, peaceful countryside surrounding Siena, and are best for those traveling by car.

$$$ Borgo Argenina is a well-maintained, pricey splurge of a B&B. Run by helpful Elena Nappa, it's 20 minutes north of Siena by car in the Chianti region (Db-€170, beautiful gardens, tel. 0577-747-117, www.borgoargenina.it, info@borgoargenina.it).

$$ Il Canto del Sole is a lovingly restored 18th-century farmhouse turned family-friendly B&B located about six miles outside of the Porta Romana city gate. Run by Laura, Luciano, and their son Marco, it features six bright and airy rooms and two apartments with original antique furnishings, a saltwater swimming pool, a game room, and bike rentals (Db-€90–110, Tb-€130, extra bed-€15, apartment-€180–220, air-con in swimming pool–facing rooms and apartment only, Wi-Fi, Val di Villa Canina 1292, 53014 Loc. Cuna, tel. 0577-375-127, fax 0577-373-378, www.ilcantodel sole.com, info@ilcantodelsole.com). An optional five-course dinner is available by request for €20 (wine is extra).

$ Agriturismo Poggio Salvi has three pleasant, spacious apartments—rentable only by the week in high season—set in a grassy field near the tiny burg of Poggio Salvi, 15 minutes southwest of Siena. Dwellings are separate, with modern conveniences (rentals from Sat–Sat, €625/2 people and €970/4 people during high season, Internet access, Loc. Poggio Salvi 249, 53010 San Rocco a Pilli, tel. & fax 0577-349-443, mobile 333-290-7890, www .poggiosalvi.net, info@poggiosalvi.net).

Eating in Siena

Sienese restaurants are reasonable by Florentine and Venetian standards. You can enjoy ordering high on the menu here without going broke.

Dining in the Old Town

Antica Osteria Da Divo is *the* place for a dressy and atmospheric €45 meal. The kitchen is creative, the ambience is candlelit, and the food is fresh and top-notch. While the cuisine is flamboyant and almost over-the-top, they serve up my favorite splurge dinner in town. Chef Pino is fanatic about fresh ingredients, enjoys giving traditional dishes his creative spin, and is understandably proud of his desserts (Wed–Mon 12:00–14:30 & 19:00–22:30, closed Tue, reservations smart; facing Baptistery door, take the far right street and walk one long curving block to Via Franciosa 29; tel. 0577-284-381). Those dining here with this book can finish with a complimentary biscotti and *vin santo* or coffee (upon request).

Hostaria Il Carroccio seats guests in an artsy sea-foam-green dining room and serves elegantly presented traditional "slow food" recipes with innovative flair at affordable prices. Musician Sting's wife Trudie Styler (they have a home in Tuscany) pops in now and again with buddies such as Bruce Springsteen to sample the homemade desserts (€7 pastas, €15 *secondi,* €30 tasting *menu*—minimum two people, cash only, reservations wise, Thu–Tue 12:30–15:00 & 19:30–22:00, closed Wed, Via Casato di Sotto 32, tel. 0577-41-165, sweet Renata and Mauro).

Osteria Boccon del Prete puts an artistic spin on Tuscan

Siena Restaurants

1. Antica Osteria Da Divo
2. Hostaria Il Carroccio
3. Osteria Boccon del Prete
4. Trattoria La Torre, Key Largo Bar, Ciao Cafeteria & Spizzico Pizza
5. To Taverna San Giuseppe
6. To Osteria Nonna Gina
7. Trattoria Papei
8. Ristorante Guidoriccio
9. Osteria la Chiacchera
10. Osteria Trombicche
11. La Taverna Di Cecco
12. Locanda Garibaldi
13. Pizzeria La Speranza & Bar Paninoteca San Paolo
14. Bar il Palio
15. Il Bandierino
16. Osteria Liberamente
17. Costarella Gelateria
18. Antica Pizzicheria al Palazzo della Chigiana
19. Consorzio Agrario Siena Grocery
20. Enoteca Italiana

favorites using the freshest seasonal ingredients. Their sultry dining room is intimate and tiny, making reservations a must (Mon–Sat 12:30–15:00 & 19:30–22:00, closed Sun, Via S. Pietro 17, tel. 0577-280-388).

Eating Traditional and Rustic in the Old Town

Trattoria La Torre is a thriving *casalinga* (home-cooking) eatery, popular for its homemade pasta, plates of which entice eaters as they enter. The sound of its busy open kitchen adds to the conviviality. Ten tables are packed under one medieval brick arch. Ask for a written menu, or study the one in the window before entering; otherwise, the owner likes to just recite his long string of dishes (Fri–Wed 12:00–15:00 & 19:00–22:00, closed Thu, just steps below Il Campo at Via Salicotto 7, tel. 0577-287-548, Alberto Boccini).

Taverna San Giuseppe, a local favorite, offers modern Tuscan cuisine in a chic grotto atmosphere. Check the posters tacked around the entry for daily specials. Reserve or arrive early to get a table (€8 pastas, €18 *secondi,* Mon–Sat 12:00–14:30 & 19:00–22:00, closed Sun, reservations wise, air-con, 7-minute climb up street to the right of City Hall at Via Giovanni Dupre 132, tel. 0577-42-286, Matteo).

Osteria Nonna Gina wins praise from locals for its good-quality, rustic cuisine and reasonable prices. The front room is more charming than the cellar (€8 pastas, €9 *secondi,* Tue–Sun 12:30–14:30 & 19:30–22:30, closed Mon, 10-minute walk from Il Campo—two blocks beyond Hotel Duomo—at Piano dei Mantellini 2, tel. 0577-287-247).

Trattoria Papei is a Sienese favorite, featuring a bright, bustling family atmosphere and friendly servers dishing out generous portions of rib-stickin' Tuscan specialties and grilled meats (daily 12:00–15:00 & 19:00–22:30, closed Mon off-season, Piazza del Mercato 6, tel. 0577-280-894; Signora Giuliana rules the kitchen, while Amadeo speaks English).

Ristorante Guidoriccio, just a few steps below Il Campo, feels warm and welcoming. You'll get smiling service from Ercole and Elisabetta (€8 pastas, €13 *secondi,* Mon–Sat 12:30–14:30 & 19:00–22:30, closed Sun, air-con, Via Giovanni Dupre 2, tel. 0577-44-350).

Osteria la Chiacchera is a youthful hole-in-the-brick-wall that plays hip music and serves "peasant food" at peasant prices on simple tables and paper placemats. It's an eat-it-and-beat-it, pasta-slinging place, with rickety outside tables clinging to the steep, stepped lane (€5.50 pastas, €7 *secondi,* Wed–Mon 12:00–15:30 & 19:00–24:00, closed Tue, great cakes, skip the *trippa*—tripe, down the street to the left of Albergo Bernini at Costa di San Antonio 4, tel. 0577-280-631, Anna).

Osteria Trombicche is cheap and small, with tight indoor seating and two tiny outdoor tables from which to watch the street scene. They serve fast, hearty food to a young crowd (€5 *ribollita*—bean-and-vegetable soup, €6–12 vegetarian sampler plates, hand-cut prosciutto, Mon–Sat 11:00–22:00, closed Sun, Via delle Terme 66, tel. 0577-288-089).

La Taverna Di Cecco is a clean, comfortable little eatery where earnest Luca serves tasty dishes made from fresh ingredients for a fair price. Try the yummy salads and traditional Sienese specialties (€8 pastas, €12 *secondi*, daily 12:00–16:00 & 19:00–24:00, Via Cecco Angiolieri 19, tel. 0577-288-518).

Locanda Garibaldi, just around the corner from Il Campo, gives you a chance to imagine Siena before the tourist hordes discovered it. Join Marcello, kindly wife Sonia, and their son Simone for an unpretentious Sienese meal in a rustic setting, while the TV murmurs quietly in the corner. The pasta is handmade, the house wine is cheap, and the almond pie *(torta di mandorle)* is sweet and crunchy (€6 pastas, €9 *secondi*, €20 fixed-price meal with house wine, Sun–Fri 12:00–14:00 & 19:00–21:00, closed Sat, Via Giovanni Dupre 18, tel. 0577-284-204).

Eating on Il Campo

If you choose to eat (or drink) on perhaps the finest town square in Italy, you'll pay a premium, meet waiters who don't need to hustle, and get mediocre food. And yet I recommend it. The clamshell-shaped square is lined with venerable cafés, bars, restaurants, and pizzerias. **Caffè Fonte Gaia,** long the classic place to see and be seen, is now a bit tired. **Pizzeria La Speranza** serves good but pricey pizzas with full-frontal views. **Bar il Palio** is best for drinks (straight prices, no cover, decent waiters, great perch). For value, everyone agrees: it's **Il Bandierino,** with the square's best food but worst view. Their *pici* (pee-chee), a fat Sienese spaghetti, is good (€9 salads, €11 pizzas, €11 pastas; no cover but a 20 percent service fee, daily 11:00–23:00, tel. 0577-282-217). For a trendy vibe popular with young people, pick the dynamic little **Osteria Liberamente** (fine wine by the glass, cocktails with good tapas, breakfasts, noisy music inside but great outdoor tables, rotating art exhibit, tastings on Wed, open daily 12:00–late, tel. 0577-274-733, Pino).

If your hotel doesn't serve breakfast or if you'd like something more memorable, consider breakfast on Il Campo—there are plenty of options. A cappuccino and a *cornetto* (croissant) run about €5–6.

Drinks or Snacks from Balconies Overlooking Il Campo

Three places have skinny balconies with benches overlooking the main square for their customers. Sipping a coffee or nibbling a pastry here while marveling at the Il Campo scene is one of my favorite things to do in Europe. And it's very cheap. Survey these three places from Il Campo (from the base of the tower, imagine a 12-hour clock—they are at 10 o'clock, high noon, and 3 o'clock, respectively).

The little **Costarella Gelateria,** on the corner of Via di Città and Costa dei Barbieri, has good ice cream, drinks, and light snacks such as cute little €1.50 sandwiches (Fri–Wed 8:00–late, closes at 22:30 and all day Thu in off-season, Via di Città 33).

Bar Paninoteca San Paolo has a youthful pub ambience and a row of stools overlooking the square. It serves big salads and 50 kinds of sandwiches, hot and cold (€3.50 each, €0.50 extra if you sit outside, order and pay at the counter, food served daily 12:00–2:00, on Vicolo di S. Paolo at the stairs leading down to the top of Il Campo—look for "great hot sandwiches" written on a brown canopy).

Key Largo Bar has two benches in the corner offering a great secret perch. Buy your drink or snack at the bar (no extra charge to sit), climb upstairs, and slide the ancient bar to open the door. Suddenly you're imagining Palio ponies zipping wildly around the corner (daily 7:00–23:00 or until 24:00 in summer, on the corner of Via Rinaldini).

Eating Cheaply in the Center

Antica Pizzicheria al Palazzo della Chigiana may be the official name, but I bet locals just call it Antonio's. For most of his life, frenzied Antonio has carved salami and cheese for the neighborhood. Most of the day, a hungry line spills onto the street as locals wait for their sandwiches—meat and cheese sold by weight—with a good bottle of Chianti (Italian law dictates that he must sell you a bottle of wine and lend you the glasses). Antonio and his boys offer a big cheese-and-meat plate (about €18 gets you 30 minutes of eating) and pull out a tiny tabletop in the corner so you can munch or sip while standing and watch the ham-hock-y scene. He's also got a small table outside (daily 8:00–20:00, Via di Città 95, tel. 0577-289-164). Even if you don't get a sandwich, pop in to inhale the commotion or peruse Antonio's gifty traditional edibles.

Ciao Cafeteria, at the bottom of Il Campo, offers good-value self-service lunches, but no ambience or views (daily 12:00–15:00). The crowded **Spizzico,** a pizza counter in the front half of Ciao, serves huge, inexpensive quarter-pizzas; on sunny days, people take the pizza—trays and all—out on Il Campo for a picnic (daily

11:00–21:00, to left of City Tower as you face it).

Budget eaters look for *pizza al taglio* shops, scattered throughout Siena, selling pizza by the slice. Of all the grocery shops, the biggest is **Consorzio Agrario Siena.** Ask them to make you up a *panino* (Mon–Sat 8:00–19:30, sometimes open Sun, a block off Piazza Matteotti, toward Il Campo at Via Pianigiani 5).

Siena Connections

Siena has sparse train connections but is a great hub for buses to the hill towns, though frequency drops on Sundays and holidays. For most, Florence is the gateway to Siena. Even if you are a railpass-user, connect these two cities by bus—it's faster than the train, and Siena's bus station is more convenient and central than its train station.

By Train

Siena's train station is at the edge of town.

From Siena by Train to: Florence (direct trains hourly, 1.5–2 hours, €6.20; bus is better), **Pisa** (2/hour, 1.75 hours, change at Empoli, €7), **Assisi** (8/day, 4–5 hours, most involve 2 changes, bus is faster), **Rome** (1–2/hour, 3.25–3.75 hours, transfer in Florence or Chiusi, €13–21 depending on type of train), **Orvieto** (12/day, 2–2.5 hours, change in Chiusi). For more information, visit www.trenitalia.com.

By Bus

The main bus companies are Sena (www.sena.it) and Tra-In (skip Tra-In's notoriously unreliable website—it's better to get schedule info in person). On schedules, the fastest buses are marked *rapida*. I'd stick with these. Some buses depart Siena from Piazza Gramsci; others leave from the train station (confirm when you buy your ticket). Note that if a schedule lists your departure point as either Via Tozzi or Piazza la Lizza, you actually catch the bus at Piazza Gramsci (Via Tozzi is the street that runs alongside Piazza Gramsci, and Piazza la Lizza is the name of the bus-hub square). Confusing? *Assolutamente!*

Tickets and Information: You can get tickets for Tra-In buses and Sena buses at the train station's bus-ticket kiosk (cash only, Mon–Sat 6:15–20:15, Sun 7:30–12:30 & 14:30–18:30). You can also buy tickets at **Sottopassaggio la Lizza,** located under Piazza Gramsci—look for stairwells to the underground passageway in front of NH Excelsior Hotel (credit cards accepted; Tra-In bus office: Mon–Sat 7:00–19:30, Sun 7:30–19:30, tel. 0577-204-246, www.trainspa.it; Sena bus office: Mon–Sat 7:15–19:45, closed Sun, tel. 0577-208-282, www.sena.it; on Sundays, when the Sena bus-ticket office is closed, buy tickets next door at Tra-In office). If necessary, you can buy tickets from the driver, but it costs €5 extra.

Services: Sottopassaggio la Lizza also has luggage storage (€5.50/day, carry-on-sized luggage no more than 33 pounds, open daily 7:00–19:00, no overnight storage), posted bus schedules, TV monitors listing all imminent departures for several bus companies, and WCs (€0.50).

By Bus to: Florence (2/hour, 1.25-hour *corse rapide* buses are faster than the train, avoid the 2-hour *diretta* buses unless you have time to enjoy the beautiful scenery en route, €7, by Tra-In bus, tickets available at *tabacchi* shops if bus-ticket office is closed, Florence-bound buses depart from in front of NH Excelsior Hotel on Piazza Gramsci), **San Gimignano** (8/day, 1.25 hours, €5.50, by Tra-In bus, tickets sometimes available at *tabacchi* shops), **Assisi** (daily at 16:40, 2 hours, €12, by Sena bus, bus departs from the train station; terminates 3 miles below Assisi at Santa Maria degli Angeli, where a city bus finishes the ride), **Rome** (8/day, 3 hours, €21, by Sena bus, arrives at Rome's Tiburtina station on Metro line B with easy connections to the central Termini train station), **Milan** (3/day, 4 hours, €31, by Sena bus, departs from Siena's train station, arrives at Milan's Cadorna Station with Metro access and direct trains to Malpensa Airport), **Pisa's Galileo Galilei Airport** (2/day, 1.75 hours, €14, by Tra-In bus, via Poggibonsi); to reach the town center of **Pisa,** the train is better (see earlier).

ASSISI

Assisi is famous for its hometown boy, St. Francis, who made very good. While Francis the saint is interesting, Francesco Bernardone the man is even more so, and mementos of his days in Assisi are everywhere—where he was baptized, a shirt he wore, a hill he prayed on, and a church where a vision changed his life.

About the year 1200, this simple friar from Assisi countered the decadence of Church government and society in general with a powerful message of non-materialism and a "slow down and smell God's roses" lifestyle. Like Jesus, Francis taught by example, living without worldly goods and aiming to love all creation. A huge monastic order grew out of his teachings, which were gradually embraced (some would say co-opted) by the Church. Christianity's most popular saint and purest example of simplicity is now glorified in beautiful churches, along with his female counterpart, St. Clare. In 1939, Italy made Francis one of its patron saints.

Francis' message of love, simplicity, and sensitivity to the environment has a broad and timeless appeal. But every pilgrimage site inevitably gets commercialized, and Francis' legacy is now Assisi's basic industry. In summer, this Umbrian town bursts with flash-in-the-pan Francis fans and Franciscan knickknacks. Those able to see past the glow-in-the-dark rosaries and bobblehead friars can actually have a "travel on purpose" experience.

Planning Your Time

Assisi is worth a day and a night. Its old town has a half-day of sightseeing and another half-day of wonder. The essential sight is the Basilica of St. Francis. For a good visit, take my self-guided "Welcome to Assisi" walk, ending at the Basilica of St. Francis.

Schedule time to wander the back streets and linger on the main square, Piazza del Comune.

Most visitors are day-trippers. While the town's a zoo by day, it's a delight at night. Assisi after dark is closer to a place Francis could call home.

Orientation to Assisi

Crowned by a ruined castle, Assisi spills downhill to its famous Basilica of St. Francis. The town is beautifully preserved and rich in history. A 5.5-magnitude earthquake in 1997 did more damage to the tourist industry than to the town's buildings. Fortunately, tourists—whether art-lovers, pilgrims, or both—have returned, drawn by Assisi's special allure.

The city sprawls across a ridge that rises from a flat plain. The Basilica of St. Francis sits at the low end of town; Piazza Matteotti (with bus station and parking lot) is at the high end; and the main square, Piazza del Comune, lies in between. Via San Francesco runs from Piazza del Comune to the basilica. Capping the hill above the town is a ruined castle called the Rocca Maggiore, and rising above that is Mount Subasio. The town is small, and slopes uphill from west to east. Walking uphill from the basilica to Piazza Matteotti takes 30 minutes, while the downhill journey takes about 15 minutes. Some Francis sights lie outside the city walls, both in the valley beneath the ridge and in the hills above.

Tourist Information

The TI is in the center of town on Piazza del Comune (Mon–Sat 8:00–14:00 & 15:00–18:00, Sun 10:00–13:00 & 14:00–17:00 except Sept–May Sun 9:00–13:00, tel. 075-813-8680).

The **Assisi Card** is free to hotel guests staying in town; otherwise it costs €2 from the TI, or from *tabacchi* and other stores around town. The card doesn't give discounted admission to any sites, but it does get you reduced parking fees at the Piazza Matteotti garage, and a 10 percent discount in numerous restaurants, bars, and shops around town (www.assisicard.com).

If you're interested in Assisi's Roman roots, ask at the TI if the excavations of the recently discovered **Domus Romane** (Roman houses) are open yet to the public. If so, they may be worth a look for their original frescoes and mosaic floors (under Piazza del Comune).

Arrival in Assisi

By Train and Bus: City buses connect Assisi's train station with the old town of Assisi on the hilltop (2/hour, 15 minutes, €1), stopping at Piazzale Giovanni Paolo II (near Basilica of St. Francis),

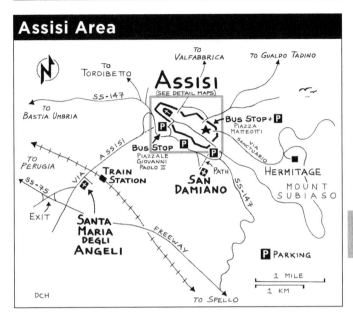

Assisi Area

TO VALFABBRICA

TO GUALDO TADINO

TO TORDIBETTO

ASSISI
(SEE DETAIL MAPS)

SS-147

TO BASTIA UMBRIA

BUS STOP P
PIAZZA MATTEOTTI

P

VIA SANCTUARIO

ASSISI

TO PERUGIA

BUS STOP
PIAZZALE GIOVANNI PAOLO II

P

SS-75

VIA

TRAIN STATION

PATH
SAN DAMIANO

SS-147

HERMITAGE

MOUNT SUBIASO

EXIT

SANTA MARIA DEGLI ANGELI

FREEWAY

P **PARKING**

1 MILE

1 KM

DCH

TO SPELLO

ASSISI

then Largo Properzio (near Basilica of St. Clare), and finally Piazza Matteotti (top of old town). Buses usually leave from the train station at :15 and :45 past the hour (buy tickets at the train station's newsstand). You can check bags at the newsstand (€3/12 hours, daily 6:00–19:00), but not in the old town.

Going from the old town to the train station, buses usually run from Piazza Matteotti at :10 and :40 past the hour (stopping outside Porta Nuova at Largo Properzio a couple minutes later, and in Piazzale Giovanni Paolo II a few minutes after that).

At Piazzale Giovanni Paolo II (the big parking lot #A for cars and buses below the Basilica of St. Francis), there are two bus stops *(fermata bus):* one sign reads *per f.s. S.M. Angeli, Linea C* (to the train station; this is also where the bus headed for Piazza Matteotti stops—check the front of the bus for its destination), and the other is for Linea B, a short line that runs through the center of the old town to Piazza del Comune. Hop on a bus marked *Piazza Matteotti* if you're exhausted after your basilica visit and need a sweat-free five-minute return to the top of the old town (near many of my recommended hotels).

Taxis from the train station to the old town cost about €15. Extra charges for luggage, night service, and additional people (four is customary) are legitimate. When departing the old town, you'll find taxi stands at Piazzale Giovanni Paolo II, the Basilica of St. Francis, the Basilica of St. Clare, and Piazza del Comune (or have your hotel call for you, tel. 075-813-100). Expect to pay a minimum of €10 for any ride.

By Car: Drivers just coming in for the day should follow the signs to several handy parking lots. Piazza Matteotti's wonderful underground parking garage is at the top of the town (which comes with bits of ancient Rome in the walls; €1/hour, €16/24 hours, or €10/24 hours with Assisi Card, daily 7:00–21:00, until 23:00 in summer). Another big lot, Parking Giovanni Paolo II, is 200 yards below the Basilica of St. Francis (€1/hour for the first two hours, €1.50/hour thereafter). The Parking Mojano lot, while below the wall, comes with an escalator that transports you nearly to the Basilica of St. Clare (€1.50/hour, €12/day).

Helpful Hints

Combo-Ticket: One €8 ticket covers three minor sights: Rocca Maggiore (castle), Pinacoteca (paintings), and the newly restored Roman Forum (*biglietto cumulativo*, valid for 1 day, may include audioguide). It's available at these three sights, but not from the TI. The Assisi Card, which is sold at the TI, doesn't grant discounts on any sights (see "Tourist Information," earlier).

Best Shopping: Tacky knickknacks line the streets leading to the Basilica of St. Francis. For better shops (with local handicrafts), head to Via San Rufino and Corso Mazzini (both just off Piazza del Comune, shops described later in the "Welcome to Assisi" self-guided walk). A Saturday-morning market fills Piazza Matteotti (which has a good parking garage).

Festivals: Assisi annually hosts several interesting festivals commemorating St. Francis and life in the Middle Ages. **Festa di Calendimaggio** is a springtime medieval festival featuring costume parades, concerts, and competitions among Assisi's rival neighborhoods (www.calendimaggiodiassisi.it). Rustic medieval "taverns" pop up around the center offering *porchetta* (roasted pig) and *vino* (starts the first Thu–Sun in May). The **Settimana Francescana** commemorates the beginning of the end of Francis' life, when he made his way for the last time to the Porziuncola Chapel (Sept 28). This week-long celebration culminates in the **Festa di San Francesco,** which marks his death with religious processions, special services, and an arts, crafts, and folklore fair (Oct 3–4). The TI has an *Info Assisi* booklet with details on upcoming festivals and celebrations.

Internet Access: Facing the Cathedral of San Rufino, the recommended **Caffè Duomo** offers free Internet access to anyone ordering even just a drink (otherwise €2.50/hour, daily 7:30–23:00, snacks, Piazza San Rufino 5, tel. 075-815-5209).

Laundry: Belleblu' Lavanderia has a few self-service machines (€5/wash, €4/dry, Mon–Fri 9:00–18:00, Sat 9:00–13:00, closed

St. Francis of Assisi
(1181/82-1226)

In 1202, young Francesco Bernardone donned armor and rode out to battle the Perugians (residents of Umbria's capital city). The battle went badly, and 20-year-old Francis was captured

and imprisoned for a year. He returned a changed man. He avoided friends and his father's lucrative business, and spent more and more time outside the city walls fasting, praying, and searching for something.

In 1206, a vision changed his life, culminating in a dramatic confrontation. He stripped naked before the town leaders, threw his clothes at his father—turning his back on the comfortable material life—and declared his loyalty to God alone.

Idealistic young men flocked to Francis, and they wandered Italy like troubadours, spreading the joy of the Gospel to rich and poor. Francis became a cult figure, attracting huge crowds. They'd never seen anything like it—sermons preached outdoors, in the local language (not Church Latin), making God accessible to all. Francis' new order of monks was also extremely non-materialist, extolling poverty and simplicity. Despite their radicalism, the order eventually gained the pope's own approval and spread through the world. Francis, who died in Assisi at the age of 45, left a legacy of humanism, equality, and love of nature that would eventually flower in the Renaissance.

In Francis' Sandal-Steps

1. Baptized in Assisi's **Cathedral of San Rufino** (then called St. George's).
2. Raised in the family home just off Piazza del Comune (now the **Chiesa Nuova**).
3. Heard call to "rebuild church" in **San Damiano.** (The crucifix of the church is now in the **Basilica of St. Clare.**)
4. Settled and established his order of monks at the **Porziuncola Chapel** (today's St. Mary of the Angels Basilica).
5. Met Clare. (Her tomb and possessions are at the **Basilica of St. Clare.**)
6. Received the pope's blessing for his order (1223 document in the **Basilica of St. Francis' relic chapel**).
7. Had many visions and was associated with miracles during his life (depicted in **Giotto's frescoes** in the Basilica of St. Francis' upper level).
8. Died at the **Porziuncola,** his body later interred beneath the **Basilica of St. Francis.**

Sun, Via Borgo Aretino 6a, tel. 075-816-084).

Travel Agencies: You can purchase train and most bus tickets (except for Siena) at **Agenzia Viaggi Stoppini,** between Piazza del Comune and the Basilica of St. Clare (Mon–Fri 9:00–12:30 & 15:30–18:30, Sat 9:00–12:00, closed Sun, Corso Mazzini 31, tel. 075-812-597). Fabrizio, who runs the agency, is patient with tourists' needs and charges exactly what you'd pay at the train station for tickets.

Bus tickets for Siena and many other destinations are sold at **Agenzia Viaggi Mavitur** (Mon–Fri 8:30–13:00 & 15:00–18:30, Sat 8:30–13:00, closed Sun, Via Frate Elia 1b, below the Basilica of St. Francis, tel. 075-812-377). This agency sells tickets only for buses and planes, not trains. Some tickets can be bought on the bus, though it'll cost you an extra couple of euros (see "Assisi Connections," at the end of this chapter).

Local Guide: Giuseppe Karabotis is a good, licensed guide (€110/2 hours, mobile 328-867-0567, iokarabot@tele2.it); if he's busy, he can recommend other guides.

Getting Around Assisi

Cute electrical minibuses, labeled *Linea A* and *Linea B,* connect the top of the town with the bottom. While it's only a 15-minute stroll down the hill, the climb back up can have you looking for a lift. Before boarding, confirm the destination (below the Basilica of St. Francis at the Porta San Francisco, Piazza del Comune, or Piazza Matteotti). You can buy a bus ticket (good on any city bus) at a newsstand or kiosk for €1, or get a ticket from the driver for €1.50.

Self-Guided Walk

▲▲Welcome to Assisi

There's much more to Assisi than St. Francis and what the blitz tour groups see. This walk covers the town from Piazza Matteotti at the top, down to the Basilica of St. Francis at the bottom. To get to Piazza Matteotti, ride the bus from the train station (or from Piazzale Giovanni Paolo II) to the last stop; drive there (underground parking with Roman ruins); or hike five minutes uphill from Piazza del Comune.

• *Start 50 yards beyond Piazza Matteotti (away from city center—see map).*

❶ The Roman Amphitheater

A lane named Via Anfiteatro Romano leads to a cozy circular neighborhood built around a Roman amphitheater—a reminder that Assisi was once an important Roman town. Circle the amphitheater counterclockwise. Imagine how colorful the town laundry

Welcome to Assisi Walk

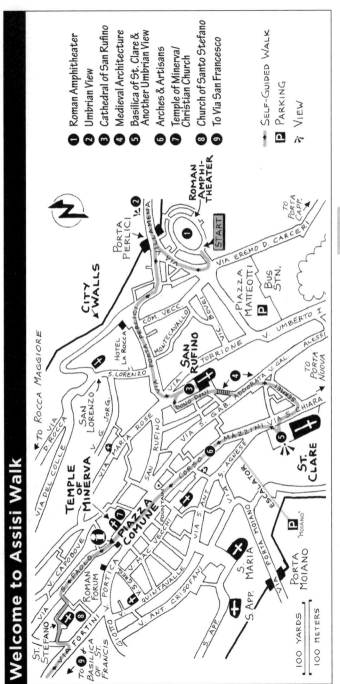

1 Roman Amphitheater
2 Umbrian View
3 Cathedral of San Rufino
4 Medieval Architecture
5 Basilica of St. Clare & Another Umbrian View
6 Arches & Artisans
7 Temple of Minerval Christian Church
8 Church of Santo Stefano
9 To Via San Francesco

◆ Self-Guided Walk
🅿 Parking
ᐳ View

ASSISI

basin (on the right) must have been in previous generations, when the women of Assisi gathered here to do their wash. Adjacent to the laundry is a small rectangular pool filled with water; above it are the coats of arms of Assisi's leading families. A few steps farther, hike up the stairs to the top of the hill for an aerial view of the oval amphitheater. The Roman stones have long been absorbed into the medieval architecture. It was Roman tradition to locate the amphitheater outside of town...which this used to be. While the amphitheater dates from the first century A.D., the buildings filling it today were built in the 13th and 14th centuries.

• *Continue on, enjoying the grand view of the fortress in the distance. The lane leads down to a city gate and an...*

❷ Umbrian View

Step outside of Assisi at the Porta Perlici for a commanding view. Umbria, called the "green heart of Italy," is the country's geographical center and only landlocked region. Enjoy the various shades of green: silver green on the valley floor (olives), emerald green (grapevines), and deep green on the hillsides (evergreen oak trees). Also notice Rocca Maggiore ("big fortress"), which provided townsfolk a refuge in times of attack, and, behind you atop the nearer hill, Rocca Minore ("little fortress"), which provides the town's young lovers a little privacy. The quarry (under the Rocca Maggiore) was a handy source for Assisi's characteristic pink limestone.

• *Go back through the gate and follow Via Porta Perlici downhill—it's immediately on your right—into town (toward Hotel La Rocca). Enjoy the higgledy-piggledy architecture (this neighborhood has some of the most photogenic back lanes in town). You'll pass a wall containing an aqueduct (on the left) that goes back to Roman times. It still brings water from a mountain spring into the city (push the brass tap for a taste). After about 200 yards, turn left through a medieval town gate (with Hotel La Rocca on your right). Just after the hotel, you'll pass a second gate dating from Roman times. Follow Via*  *Porta Perlici downhill until you hit a fine square facing a big church. (Caffè Duomo, facing Piazza San Rufino, is a nice place for a drink or snack; it also has free Internet access for customers.)*

❸ Cathedral of San Rufino

Trick question: Who's Assisi's patron saint? While Francis is one of Italy's patron saints, Rufino (the town's first bishop, martyred and buried here in the third century) is Assisi's. The cathedral (seat

of the local bishop) is 11th-century Romanesque with a Neoclassical interior. Although it has what is considered to be one of the best and purest Romanesque facades in all of Umbria, the big triangular top of it (just a decorative wall) was added in Gothic times. Study the lions at the base of the facade: One is eating a Christian martyr, reminding worshippers of the courage of early Christians.

Enter the church (Mon–Fri 7:00–12:30 & 14:30–19:00, Sat–Sun 7:00–19:00, tel. 075-812-283). While the front of the church is an unremarkable mix of 17th- and 18th-century Baroque and Neoclassical, the rear (near where you enter) has several points of interest. Notice first the two fine statues: St. Francis and St. Clare (by Giovanni Dupré, 1888). To your right is an old baptismal font (in the corner with the black iron grate). In about 1182, a baby boy was baptized in this font. His parents were upwardly mobile Francophiles who called him Francesco ("Frenchy"). In 1194, a nobleman baptized his daughter Clare here. Eighteen years later, their paths crossed in this same church, when Clare attended a class and became mesmerized by the teacher—Francis. Traditionally, the children of Assisi are still baptized here.

The striking glass panels in the floor reveal foundations preserved from the ninth-century church that once stood here. You're walking on history. After the 1997 earthquake, structural inspectors checked the church from ceiling to floor. When they looked under the paving stones, they discovered graves (until Napoleon decreed otherwise, it was common practice to bury people in churches). Underneath that level, they found Roman foundations and some animal bones (suggesting the possibility of animal sacrifice). There might have been a Roman temple here; churches were often built upon temple ruins. As you're standing at the back of the church facing the altar, look left to the Roman cistern (inside the great stone archway). If you take the three steps down, an automatic light should go on. Marvel at the fine stonework and Roman engineering. In the Middle Ages, this was the town's emergency water source when under attack.

Underneath the church, incorporated into the Roman ruins, are the foundations of an earlier Church of San Rufino, now the crypt and Diocesan museum. When open, you can go below to see the saint's sarcophagus and the small museum featuring the cathedral's art from centuries past (€3, mid-March–mid-Oct Thu–Tue 10:00–13:00 & 15:00–18:00, in winter closes at 17:30, closed Wed except in Aug, tel. 075-812-712, www.assisimuseodiocesano.com).

• *Leaving the church, take a sharp left (on Via Dono Doni), following the sign for Santa Chiara. After 20 yards, take a right and go down the stairway to see some...*

❹ Medieval Architecture

At the bottom of the stairs, notice the pink limestone pavement, part of the surviving medieval town. The arches built over doorways indicate that the buildings date from the 12th through the 14th centuries, when Assisi was booming. Italian cities such as Assisi—thriving on the north–south trade between northern Europe and Rome—were in the process of inventing free-market capitalism, dabbling in democratic self-rule, and creating the modern urban lifestyle. The vaults you see that turn lanes into tunnels are reminders of medieval urban expansion (mostly 15th century). While the population grew, people wanted to live within its protective walls. Medieval Assisi had several times the population density of today's Assisi.

Notice the blooming balconies; Assisi holds a flower competition each June.

• *Continue steeply downhill. When you arrive at a street, turn left, going slightly uphill for a block, then take the low road at the Y, and head down Via Sermei. Continue ahead, following the S. Chiara sign downhill to the big church.*

❺ Basilica of St. Clare (Basilica di Santa Chiara)

Dedicated to the founder of the Order of the Poor Clares, this Umbrian Gothic church is simple, in keeping with the nuns' dedication to a life of contemplation (daily 6:30–12:00 & 14:00–19:00, until 18:00 in winter). In Clare's lifetime, the order was located in the humble Church of San Damiano, in the valley below, but after Clare's death, they needed a bigger and more glorious building. The church was built in 1265, and the huge buttresses were added in the next century. The interior's fine frescoes were whitewashed in Baroque times.

The Chapel of the Crucifix of San Damiano, on the right, has the wooden crucifix that changed Francis' life. In 1206, an emaciated, soul-searching, stark-raving Francis knelt before this crucifix (then located in the Church of San Damiano) and asked for guidance. The crucifix spoke: "Go and rebuild my Church, which you can see has fallen into ruin." Francis followed the call.

Stairs lead from the nave down to the tomb of St. Clare. Her tomb is at the far end (the image is wax; her bones lie underneath). As you circulate with the crowd of pilgrims, notice the paintings on the walls depicting spiritual lessons from Clare's life and death (see sidebar). At the opposite end of the crypt (back between the stairs, in a large glassed-in area) are important relics: the saint's

St. Clare
(1194–1253)

The 18-year-old rich girl of Assisi fell in love with 30-year-old Francis' message, and made secret arrangements to meet him. The night of Palm Sunday, 1212, she slipped out of her father's mansion in town and escaped to the valley below. A procession of friars with torches met her and took her to (what is today) the St. Mary of the Angels Basilica. There, Francis cut her hair, clothed her in a simple brown tunic, and welcomed her into a life of voluntary poverty. Clare's father begged, ordered, and physically threatened her to return, but she would not budge.

Clare was joined by other women who banded together as the Poor Clares. She spent the next 40 years of her life within the confines of the convent of San Damiano: barefoot, vegetarian, and largely silent. Her regimen of prayer, meditation, and simple manual labor—especially knitting—impressed commoners and popes, leading to her canonization almost immediately after her death. St. Clare is often depicted carrying a monstrance (a little temple holding the Eucharist wafer).

ASSISI

robes, hair (in a silver box), and an enormous tunic she made—along with relics of St. Francis (including a blood-stained stocking he wore after receiving the stigmata). The attached cloistered community of the Poor Clares has flourished for 700 years.

• *Leave the church and belly up to the viewpoint at the edge of the square for...*

Another Umbrian View

On the left is the convent of St. Clare (global headquarters of all the Poor Clares). Below you lies the olive grove of the Poor Clares, which has been there since the 13th century. In the distance is a grand Umbrian view. Assisi overlooks the richest and biggest valley in otherwise hilly and mountainous Umbria. The municipality of Assisi has a population of 25,000, but only 3,500 people live in the old town. The lower town grew up with the coming of the railway in the 19th century. In the haze, the blue-domed church is St. Mary of the Angels (Santa Maria degli Angeli, described later), the cradle of the Franciscan order. A popular pilgrimage site today, it marks the place where St. Francis lived and worked.

Spanish-speaking Franciscans settled in California. Three of their missions grew into major cities: Los Angeles (named after this church), San Francisco (named after St. Francis), and Santa Clara (named after St. Clare).

• *From the church square, step out into Via Santa Chiara. You can see gates in both directions.*

❻ Arches and Artisans

The gate over the road behind the church dates from 1265. (Beyond it, you can just see the crenellations of the 1316 Porta Nuova, which marks the final expansion of Assisi.) Toward the city center (on Via Santa Chiara, the high road), an arch marks the site of the Roman wall. These three gates represent the town's three walls, illustrating how much the city has grown since ancient times.

Walk uphill along Via Santa Chiara (which becomes Corso Mazzini) to the city's main square. The street is lined with interesting shops selling traditional embroidery, religious souvenirs, and gifty local edibles. About 20 yards before the arch, at #1b, a plaque over the door explains that the old printing press (a national monument now, just inside the door) was used to make fake documents for Jews escaping the Nazis in 1943 and 1944.

The shops on Corso Mazzini, on the stretch between the gate and the main square, show off many local crafts. As you browse, watch for the following shops: Galleria d'Arte Pena (on the left, #20) sells the medieval fantasy townscapes of Paolo Grimaldi, a local painter who runs this shop with his brother. A helpful travel agency is across the street (Agenzia Viaggi Stoppini; see "Helpful Hints," earlier). Next, the shop L'Ulivo Sculture (on the left at #14d) sells olive-wood carvings, as does Poiesis, across the street at #23. It's said that St. Francis made the first nativity scene to help humanize and, therefore, teach the Christmas message. That's why you'll see so many crèches in Assisi. (Even today, nearby villages are enthusiastic about their "living" manger scenes, and Italians everywhere enjoy setting up elaborate crèches in churches for Christmas.) Adjacent to #14 is a bakery, Bar Sensi, selling the traditional raisin-and-apple strudel called *rocciata* (€3.50 each). Farther along on the left (at #9) is Il Duomo, selling religious art, manger scenes, and crucifixion figurines. Across the street, on the right, is a respected embroidery shop. And on the square (at #34, opposite the flags), La Bottega dei Sapori is worth a visit for edible and drinkable souvenirs.

You've walked up what was, in ancient times, the main drag into town. Ahead of you, the six fluted Corinthian columns of the Temple of Minerva marked the forum (today's Piazza del Comune). Sit at the fountain on the piazza for a few minutes of people-watching—don't you love Italy? Within a few hundred yards of this square, on either side, were the medieval walls. Imagine the commotion of 5,000 people confined within these walls. No wonder St. Francis needed an escape for some peace and quiet.

• *Now, head over to the temple on the square.*

❼ Temple of Minerva/Christian Church

Assisi has always been a spiritual center. The Romans went to great
lengths to make this first-century B.C. Temple of Minerva a cen-
terpiece of their city. Notice the columns that cut into the stairway.
It was a tight fit here on the hilltop. In ancient times, the stairs
went down—about twice as far as they do now—to the main drag,
which has gradually been filled in over time. The Church of Santa
Maria sopra ("over") Minerva was added in the ninth century. The
bell tower is from the 13th century. Pop inside the temple/church
(Mon–Sat 7:15–19:30, Sun 8:00–19:30, closes at sunset and midday
in winter).

Today's interior is 17th-century Baroque. Flanking the altar
are the original Roman temple floor stones. You can even see the
drains for the bloody sacrifices that took place here. Behind the
statues of Peter and Paul, the original Roman embankment peeks
through.

Across the square at #11, step into the 16th-century frescoed
vaults from the old market. Notice the Italian flair for design.
Even this smelly market was once finely decorated. The art style
was "grotesque"—literally, a painting in a grotto. This was painted
sometime after 1492. How do art historians know? Because it features turkeys—first seen in Europe after Columbus returned with
his bag of exotic souvenirs. The turkeys painted here may have
been that bird's European debut.

• *From the main square, hike past the temple up the high road, Via San
Paolo. After 200 yards, a sign directs you down a lane to the...*

❽ Church of Santo Stefano

Surrounded by cypress, fig, and walnut trees, Santo Stefano—which
used to be outside the town walls in the days of St. Francis—is a
delightful bit of offbeat Assisi. Legend has it that Santo Stefano's
bells miraculously rang on October 3, 1226, the day St. Francis
died. Step inside. This is the typical rural Italian Romanesque
church—no architect, just built by simple stonemasons who put
together the most basic design (daily 8:30–21:30, Sept–May until
18:30).

• *The lane zigzags down to Via San Francesco. Turn right and walk
under the arch toward the Basilica of St. Francis.*

❾ Via San Francesco

This was the main drag that led from the town to the basilica holding the body of St. Francis. Francis was a big deal even in his own
day. He died in 1226 and was made a saint in 1228—the same year
that the basilica's foundations were laid—and his body was moved
here by 1230. Assisi was a big-time pilgrimage center, and this
street was its booming main drag. The arch marks the end of what

was Assisi in St. Francis' day. Notice the fine medieval balcony just below the arch. A few yards farther down (on the left), cool yourself at the fountain. The hospice next door was built in 1237 to house pilgrims. Notice the three surviving faces of its fresco: Jesus, Francis, and Clare.

• *Continuing on, you'll eventually reach Assisi's main sight, the Basilica of St. Francis.*

Self-Guided Tour

▲▲▲Basilica of St. Francis

The Basilica di San Francesco is one of the artistic and religious highlights of Europe. In 1226, St. Francis was buried (with the

outcasts he had stood by) outside of his town on the "Hill of the Damned"—now called the "Hill of Paradise." The basilica is frescoed from top to bottom by the leading artists of the day: Cimabue, Giotto, Simone Martini, and Pietro Lorenzetti. A 13th-century historian wrote, "No more exquisite monument to the Lord has been built."

From a distance, you see the huge arcades "supporting" the basilica. These were 15th-century quarters for the monks. The arcades that line the square and lead to the church housed medieval pilgrims.

Cost and Hours: Free entry; lower basilica daily 6:00–18:45, until 17:45 in winter; relic chapel in lower basilica supposedly open 9:00–18:00 but often closed; upper basilica daily 8:30–18:45, until 18:00 in winter. Modest dress is required to enter the church—no sleeveless tops or shorts for men, women, or children.

The church courtyard at the entrance of the lower basilica has an info office (Mon–Sat 9:15–12:00 & 14:15–17:30, closed Sun, tel. 075-819-001). Audioguides (boring and old-school) are available at the kiosk located outside the entrance of the lower basilica (€4–5 donation requested, daily 9:00–17:00, 40 minutes). You can also take an English tour, offered daily except Sunday (€10 donation requested, call or email to reserve, tel. 075-819-0084, www.sanfrancescoassisi.org, assisisanfrancesco@libero.it). The church bookshop, behind the upper and lower basilica, sells the excellent guidebook *The Basilica of Saint Francis—A Spiritual Pilgrimage* (€3, by Goulet, McInally, and Wood; I used it as a source for my self-guided tour). To worship in the basilica, consider joining the Franciscan brothers in the lower basilica in the morning at 7:00

Assisi

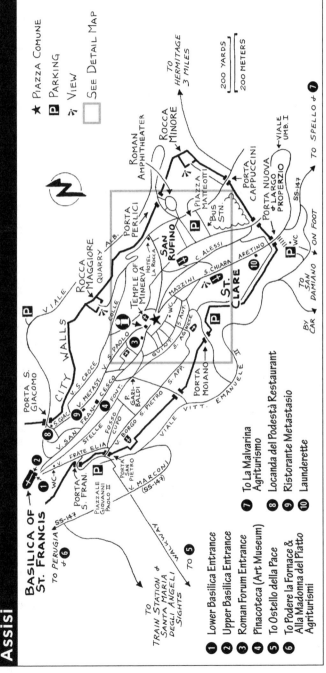

★ PIAZZA COMUNE
P PARKING
🔭 VIEW
☐ SEE DETAIL MAP

200 YARDS
200 METERS

1 Lower Basilica Entrance
2 Upper Basilica Entrance
3 Roman Forum Entrance
4 Pinacoteca (Art Museum)
5 To Ostello della Pace
6 To Podere la Fornace & Alla Madonna del Piatto Agriturismi
7 To La Malvarina Agriturismo
8 Locanda del Podestà Restaurant
9 Ristorante Metastasio
10 Launderette

BASILICA OF ST. FRANCIS

TO PERUGIA + 6
TO SPELLO + 7
TO HERMITAGE 3 MILES

TRAIN STATION & SANTA MARIA DEGLI ANGELI SIGHTS

ROCCA MAGGIORE
ROCCA MINORE
ROMAN AMPHITHEATER

CITY WALLS

PORTA S. GIACOMO
PORTA PERLICI
PORTA CAPPUCCINI
PORTA NUOVA + LARGO PROPERZIO
PORTA MOIANO
PORTA S. FRAN.
PORTA SAN PIETRO

SAN RUFINO
Temple of MINERVA
ST. CLARE
S. CHIARA

PIAZZA MATTEOTTI
BUS STN.

PIAZZALE GIOVANNI PAOLO II

VIALE VITT. EMANUELE II
VIALE UMB. I

TO SAN DAMIANO

BY CAR
ON FOOT

ASSISI

or 11:00, or experience a sung Mass Sundays at 10:30. English and additional sung Mass services don't follow a set schedule. Call the basilica to find out when English-speaking pilgrimage groups or choirs have reserved Masses and attend with them (tel. 075-819-001). You can also call to ask about upcoming concerts (tel. 075-819-0032).

Overview

The Basilica of St. Francis, a theological work of genius, can be difficult for the 21st-century tourist/pilgrim to appreciate.

Since the basilica is the reason that most people visit Assisi, and the message of St. Francis has even the least-devout blessing the town Vespas, I've designed this self-guided tour with an emphasis on the place's theology (rather than art history).

A disclaimer before we start: Just as Francis used many Bible legends to help teach the Christian message, legends from the life of Francis were used in later ages to teach the same message. Are they true? In general, probably not. Are they in keeping with Francis' message? Yes. Do I share legends here as if they are historic? Sure.

The church has three parts: the upper basilica, the lower basilica, and the saint's tomb (below the lower basilica). In the 1997 earthquake, the lower basilica—with walls nearly nine feet thick—was unscathed. The upper basilica, with bigger windows and walls only three feet thick, was damaged. Following a restoration, the entire church reopened to visitors in late 1999.

To get oriented, stand at the lower entrance in the courtyard. Opposite the entry to the lower basilica is the information center. (There are two different pay WCs within a half block—up the road in a squat building, and halfway down the big piazza on the left.)

Enter through the grand doorway of the lower basilica. Just inside, decorating the top of the first arch, look up and see St. Francis, who greets you with a Latin inscription. Sounding a bit like John Wayne, he says the equivalent of "Slow down and be joyful, pilgrim. You've reached the Hill of Paradise. And, if you're observant and thoughtful, this church will knock your spiritual socks off."

• *Start with the tomb. Enter the nave and turn left; midway down the nave, follow signs to your right and go downstairs to the tomb.*

The Tomb

The saint's remains are above the altar in the stone box with the iron ties. In medieval times, pilgrims came to Assisi because St. Francis was buried here. Holy relics were the "ruby slippers" of medieval Europe. Relics gave you power—they answered your prayers and won your wars—and ultimately helped you get back to your eternal Kansas. Assisi made no bones about promoting the saint's relics, but hid his tomb for obvious reasons of security. His

The Franciscan Message

Francis' message caused a stir. Not only did he follow Christ's teachings, he adopted his lifestyle, living as a poor, wandering preacher. He traded a life of power and riches for one of obedience, poverty, and chastity. He was never ordained as a priest, but his influence on Christianity was monumental.

The Franciscan existence (Brother Sun, Sister Moon, and so on) is a space where God, man, and the natural world frolic harmoniously. Francis treated every creature—animal, peasant, pope—with equal respect. He and his "brothers" (*fratelli,* or friars) slept in fields, begged for food, and exuded the joy of non-materialism. Franciscan friars were known as the "Jugglers of God," modeling themselves on French troubadours (*jongleurs,* or jugglers) who roved the countryside singing, telling stories, and cracking jokes.

In an Italy torn by conflict between towns and families, Francis promoted peace and the restoration of order. (He set an example by reconstructing the crumbled San Damiano chapel.) While the Church was waging bloody Crusades, Francis pushed ecumenism and understanding. Even today the leaders of the world's great religions meet here for summits.

This richly decorated basilica seems to contradict the teachings of the poor monk it honors, but it was built as an act of religious and civic pride to remember the hometown saint. It was also designed—and still functions—as a pilgrimage center and a splendid classroom. Though monks in robes may not give off an "easy-to-approach" vibe, the Franciscans of today are still God's jugglers (and most of them speak English).

Here is Francis' message, in his own words:

The Canticle of the Sun
Good Lord, all your creations bring praise to you!
Praise for Brother Sun, who brings the day. His radiance reminds us of you!
Praise for Sister Moon and the stars, precious and beautiful.
Praise for Brother Wind, and for clouds and storms and rain that sustain us.
Praise for Sister Water. She is useful and humble, precious and pure.
Praise for Brother Fire who cheers us at night.
Praise for our sister, Mother Earth, who feeds us and rules us.
Praise for all those who forgive because you have forgiven them.
Praise for our sister, Bodily Death, from whose embrace none can escape.
Praise and bless the Lord, and give thanks, and, with humility, serve him.

body was buried secretly while the basilica was under construction, and over the next 600 years, the exact location was forgotten. When the tomb was to be opened to the public in 1818, it took a month and a half to find his actual remains.

Francis' four closest friends and first followers are memorialized in the corners of the room. Opposite the altar, up four steps in between the entrance and exit, notice the small copper box behind the metal grill. This contains the remains of Francis' rich Roman patron, Jacopa dei Settesoli. She traveled to see him on his deathbed, but was turned away because she was female. Francis waived the rule and welcomed "Brother Jacopa" to his side.

The candles you see are the only real candles in the church (others are electric). Pilgrims pay a coin, pick up a candle, and place it at the tomb. Franciscans will light it later.

• *Climb back to the lower nave.*

Nave of Lower Basilica

Appropriately Franciscan—subdued and Romanesque—this nave was frescoed with parallel scenes from the lives of Christ (right) and Francis (left), connected by a ceiling of stars. Unfortunately, after the church was built and decorated, side chapels needed to be erected to provide mausoleums for the rich families that patronized the work of the order. Huge arches were cut out of some scenes, but others survive. In the fresco directly above the entry to the tomb, Christ is being taken down from the cross (just the bottom half of his body can be seen, to the left), and it looks like the story is over. Defeat. But in the opposite fresco (above the tomb's exit), we see Francis preaching to the birds, reminding the faithful that the message of the Gospel survives.

These stories directed the attention of the medieval pilgrim to the altar, where he could meet God through the sacraments. The church was thought of as a community of believers sailing toward God. The prayers coming out of the nave (*navis,* or ship) fill the triangular sections of the ceiling—called *vele,* or sails—with spiritual wind. With a priest for a navigator and the altar for a helm, faith propels the ship.

Stand behind the altar (toes to the bottom step, facing the entrance) and look up. The three scenes in front of you represent the creed of the Franciscans: Directly above the tomb of St. Francis, you'll see to the right, ***Obedience*** (Francis appears twice, wearing a rope harness and kneeling in front of Lady Obedience); to the left, ***Chastity*** (in a tower of purity held up by two angels); and straight ahead, ***Poverty.*** Here Jesus blesses the marriage as Francis slips a ring on Lady Poverty. In the foreground, two "self-sufficient" yet pint-size merchants (the new rich of a thriving northern Italy) are throwing sticks and stones at the bride. But Poverty, in her patched

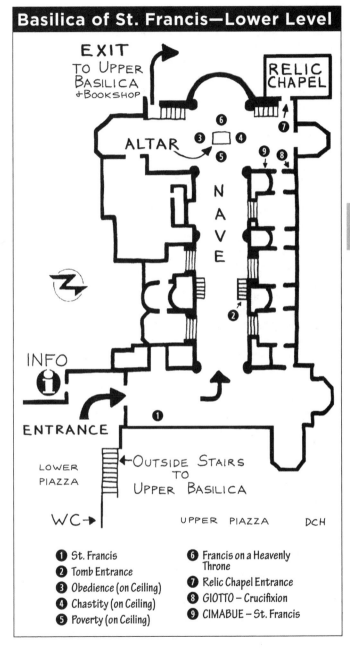

Basilica of St. Francis—Lower Level

EXIT
TO UPPER
BASILICA
+BOOKSHOP

RELIC
CHAPEL

ALTAR

NAVE

INFO

ENTRANCE

LOWER
PIAZZA

OUTSIDE STAIRS
TO
UPPER BASILICA

WC →

UPPER PIAZZA

DCH

❶ St. Francis
❷ Tomb Entrance
❸ Obedience (on Ceiling)
❹ Chastity (on Ceiling)
❺ Poverty (on Ceiling)

❻ Francis on a Heavenly Throne
❼ Relic Chapel Entrance
❽ GIOTTO – Crucifixion
❾ CIMABUE – St. Francis

ASSISI

wedding dress, is fertile and strong, and even those brambles blossom into a rosebush crown. The three knots of the rope that tie the Franciscan robe symbolize obedience, chastity, and poverty.

Putting your heels to the altar and bending back like a drum major, look up for a peek at the reward for a life of obedience, chastity, and poverty: **Francis on a heavenly throne** in a rich, golden robe. He traded a life of earthly simplicity for glory in heaven.

• *Now, turn to the right and march to the corner, where steps lead down into the...*

Relic Chapel

This chapel is filled with fascinating relics (which a €0.50 flier explains in detailed English). Step in and circle the room clockwise. You'll see the silver chalice and plate that Francis used for the bread and wine of the Eucharist (in small, dark windowed case set into wall, marked *Calice e Patena*). Francis believed that his personal possessions should be simple, but the items used for worship should be made of the finest materials. In the corner display case is a small section of the itchy haircloth *(cilizio)*—not sheep's wool, but cloth made from scratchy horse or goat hair—worn by Francis as penitence. In the next corner are the tunic and slippers that Francis donned during his last days. Next, find a prayer (in a fancy silver stand) that St. Francis wrote for Brother Leo, signed with his tau cross. The last letter in the Hebrew alphabet, tav ("tau" in Greek) is symbolic of faithfulness to the end. Francis signed his name with this simple capital-T-shaped character. Next is a papal document (1223) legitimizing the Franciscan order and assuring his followers that they were not risking a (deadly) heresy charge. Finally, see the tunic that was lovingly patched and stitched by followers of the five-foot, four-inch-tall St. Francis.

Before leaving the chapel, notice the modern paintings done in the last year or so by local artists. Over the entrance, Francis is shown being born in a stable like Jesus (by Capitini). Scenes from the life of Clare and Padre Pio (a Capuchin priest, huge in Italy, who was sainted in 2002) were painted by Stefanelli and Antonio.

• *Return up the stairs to the...*

Transept of Lower Basilica

This church brought together the greatest Sienese (Lorenzetti and Simone Martini) and Florentine (Cimabue and Giotto) artists of the day. Look around at the painted scenes. In 1300, this was radical art—believable homespun scenes, landscapes, trees, real people. Study **Giotto's painting of the Crucifixion,** with the eight sparrow-like angels. For the first time, holy people are expressing emotion: One angel turns her head sadly at the sight of Jesus, and another scratches her hands down her cheeks, drawing blood.

Mary (lower left), previously in control, has fainted in despair. The Franciscans, with their goal of bringing God to the people, found a natural partner in Europe's first modern (and therefore naturalist) painter, Giotto.

To grasp Giotto's Renaissance leap, compare his work with the painting to the right, by Cimabue. It's Gothic, without the 3-D architecture, natural backdrop, and slice-of-life reality of Giotto's work. **Cimabue's St. Francis** (far right) shows the saint with the stigmata—Christ's marks of the Crucifixion. Contemporaries described Francis as being short, with a graceful build, dark hair, and sparse beard. (This is considered the most accurate portrait of Francis—done according to the description of one who knew him.) The sunroof haircut (tonsure) was standard for monks of the day. According to legend, the brown robe and rope belt were inventions of necessity. When Francis stripped naked and ran away from Assisi, he grabbed the first clothes he could, a rough wool peasant's tunic and a piece of rope, which became the uniform of the Franciscan order. To the left, at eye level under the sparrow-like angels, are paintings of saints and their exquisite halos (by Simone Martini or his school).

Francis' friend, "Sister Bodily Death," was really not all that terrible. In fact, Francis would like to introduce you to her now (above and to the right of the door leading into the relic chapel). Go ahead, block the light from the door with this book and meet her. Before his death, Francis added a line to *The Canticle of the Sun:* "Praise for our sister, Bodily Death, from whose embrace none can escape."

• *Now cross the transept to the other side of the altar (enjoying some of the oldest surviving bits of the inlaid local-limestone flooring—c. 13th century) and find the staircase going up. Immediately above the stairs is Pietro Lorenzetti's* Francis Receiving the Stigmata. *(Francis is considered the first person ever to earn the marks of the cross through his great faith and love of the Church.) Make your way to the...*

Courtyard

The courtyard overlooks the 16th-century cloister, the heart of this monastic complex. The courtyard functioned as a cistern to collect rainwater, supplying enough for 200 monks (today, there are about 40). The Franciscan order emphasizes teaching. This place functioned as a kind of theological center of higher learning designed to rotate monks in for a six-month stint, then send them back home more prepared and inspired to preach effectively. That explains the complex narrative of the frescoes wallpapering the walls and halls here. The treasury *(Museo del Tesoro)* to the left of the bookstore is free (donation requested) and features ornately

Basilica of St. Francis—Upper Level

ASSISI

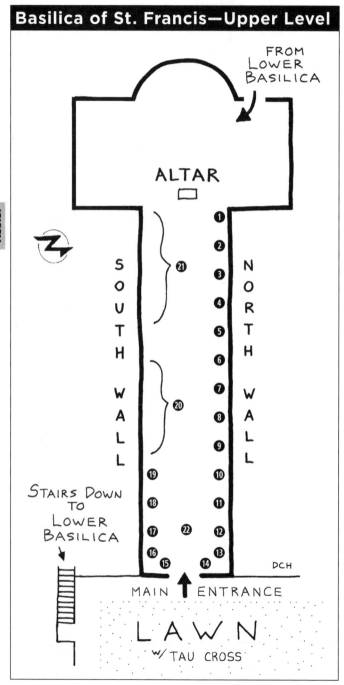

FROM LOWER BASILICA

ALTAR

SOUTH WALL

NORTH WALL

STAIRS DOWN TO LOWER BASILICA

MAIN ENTRANCE

DCH

LAWN w/ TAU CROSS

Basilica Key

❶ A Common Man Spreads his Cape before Francis

❷ Francis Offers his Cape to a Needy Stranger

❸ Francis is Visited by the Lord in a Dream

❹ Francis Prays to the Crucifix

❺ Francis Relinquishes his Possessions

❻ The Pope has a Dream

❼ The Pope Confirms the Franciscan Order

❽ A Vision of the Flaming Chariot

❾ A Vision of Thrones

❿ Exorcism of Demons in Arezzo

⓫ St. Francis Before the Sultan

⓬ Ecstasy of St. Francis

⓭ The Crèche at Greccio

⓮ Miracle of the Spring

⓯ Sermon to the Birds

⓰ The Knight of Celano Invites Francis to his Deathbed

⓱ Preaching for Pope Honorius III

⓲ The Apparition at Arles

⓳ Francis Receives the Stigmata

⓴ Francis' Death, Funeral, and Canonization

㉑ Three "Post Mortem Miracles" Associated with St. Francis

㉒ Tan Patches on Ceiling (1997 Earthquake Damage)

decorated chalices, reliquaries, vestments, and altarpieces.

• *From the courtyard, climb the stairs (next to the bookshop) to the...*

Upper Basilica

Built later than its counterpart below, the brighter upper basilica is considered the first Gothic church in Italy (started in 1228).

Local guides say it has the oldest stained glass in Italy (behind the apse), but the basilica's draw for art-lovers is that it was practically wallpapered by Giotto and his assistants in about 1297–1300. Or perhaps it was subcontracted to other artists—scholars debate it. The gallery of frescoes shows 28 scenes from the life of St. Francis. The events are a mix of documented history and folk legend.

• *Get oriented by facing the basilica's main altar. Working clockwise, start on the right-hand (north) wall. Note that the subtitles in the black strip below the frescoes describe each scene in clear Latin—and affirm my interpretation.*

❶ **A common man spreads his cape before Francis** in front of the Temple of Minerva on Piazza del Comune. Before his conversion, young Francis was the model of Assisian manhood—handsome, intelligent, and well-dressed, befitting the son of a wealthy cloth dealer. Above all, he was liked by everyone, a natural charmer who led his fellow teens in nights of wine, women, and song. Medieval pilgrims understood a deeper meaning in this scene: The "eye" of God (symbolized by the rose window in the Temple of Minerva) looks over 20-year-old Francis, a dandy "imprisoned" in his own selfishness (the Temple—with barred windows—was once a prison).

❷ **Francis offers his cape to a needy stranger** (next panel). Francis was always generous of spirit. He became more so after being captured in battle and held for a year as a prisoner of war, then suffering from illness. Charity was a Franciscan forte.

❸ **Francis is visited by the Lord in a dream.** Still unsure of his calling, Francis rode off to the Crusades. One night, he dreams of a palace filled with armor marked with crosses. Christ tells him to leave the army—to become what you might consider the first "conscientious objector"—and go home to wait for a non-military assignment in a new kind of knighthood. He returned to Assisi and, though reviled as a coward, would end up fighting for spiritual wealth, not earthly power and riches.

❹ **Francis prays to the crucifix** in the Church of San Damiano. After months of living in a cave, fasting, and meditating, Francis kneels in the run-down church and prays. The crucifix speaks, telling him: "Go and rebuild my Church, which you can see has fallen into ruin." Francis hurried home and sold his father's cloth to pay for God's work. His furious father dragged him before the bishop.

❺ **Francis relinquishes his possessions.** In front of the bishop and the whole town, Francis strips naked and gives his dad his clothes, credit cards, and time-share on Capri. Francis raises his hand and says, "Until now, I called you father. From now on, my only father is my Father in Heaven." He then ran off into the hills, naked and singing. In this version, Francis is covered by the bishop, symbolizing his transition from a man of the world to a man of the Church. Notice the disbelief and concern on the bishop's advisors' faces; subtle expressions like these wouldn't have made it into other medieval frescoes of the day.

❻ **The pope has a dream.** Francis headed to Rome, seeking the pope's blessing on his fledgling movement. Initially rebuffing Francis, the pope then dreams of a simple, barefooted man propping up his teetering Church, and then...

❼ **The pope confirms the Franciscan order,** handing Francis and his gang the document now displayed in the relic chapel.

Francis' life was surrounded by visions and miracles, shown in three panels in a row: (❽) **A vision of the flaming chariot,** (❾) **A vision of thrones,** and (❿) **Exorcism of demons in Arezzo.**

• *Next see...*

❶ St. Francis before the sultan. Francis' wandering ministry took him to Egypt during the Crusades (1219). He walked unarmed into the Muslim army camp. They captured him, but the sultan was impressed with Francis' manner and let him go, reportedly whispering, "I'd convert to your faith, but they'd kill us both." Here the sultan gestures from his throne.

❷ Ecstasy of St. Francis. This oft-painted scene shows the mystic communing with Christ.

❸ The Crèche at Greccio. A creative teacher, Francis invents the tradition of manger scenes in 1223.

• *Around the corner, see the...*

❹ Miracle of the spring. Shown here getting water out of a rock to quench a stranger's thirst, Francis felt closest to God when in the hills around Assisi, seeing the Creator in the creation.

❺ Sermon to the birds. In his best-known miracle, Francis is surrounded by birds as they listen to him teach. Francis embraces all levels of creation. One interpretation of this scene is that the birds, which are of different species, represent the diverse flock of humanity and nature, all created and beloved by God and worthy of each other's love.

• *Continue to the south wall for the rest of the panels.*

Despite the hierarchical society of his day, Francis was welcomed by all classes, shown in these three panels: (**❻**) **The knight of Celano invites Francis to his deathbed;** (**❼**) **Preaching for Pope Honorius III,** who listens carefully; and (**❽**) **The apparition at Arles,** which illustrates how Francis could be in two places at once (something only Jesus and saints can pull off). The proponents of Francis, who believed he was destined for sainthood, show him performing the necessary miracles.

❾ Francis receives the stigmata. It's September 17, 1224,

and Francis is fasting and praying on nearby Mount Alverna when a six-winged angel (called a seraph) appears with holy laser-like powers to burn in the marks. For the strength of his faith, Francis is given the marks of his master, the "battle scars of love"...the stigmata. These five wounds Christ suffered during crucifixion (nails in palms and feet, lance in side) marked Francis' body for the rest of his life.

The next panels (**❿**) deal with **Francis' death, funeral, and canonization.** The last panels (**⓫**) show **miracles** associated with the saint after his death, proving that he's in heaven and bolstering his eligibility for sainthood.

Before you leave the front entrance, look up at the ceiling and the walls near the rose window to see (**㉒**) **large tan patches.** In 1997, when a 5.5-magnitude quake hit Assisi, it shattered the upper basilica's frescoes into 300,000 fragments that had to be meticulously picked up and pieced back together. Shortly after the quake, two monks and two art scholars were standing here when an aftershock shook the ceiling frescoes down, killing them.

Outside, on the lawn, are the Latin *pax* (peace) and the Franciscan tau cross. For a drink or snack, the Bar San Francisco (facing the upper basilica) is handy. For *pax,* take the high lane back to town, up to the castle, or into the countryside.

Sights in Assisi

▲Roman Forum (Foro Romano)—For a look at Assisi's Roman roots, tour the Roman Forum, which is actually under Piazza del Comune. The floor plan is clearly explained in English, as are the surviving odd bits and obscure pieces. During your visit, you'll walk on an ancient Roman road.

Cost and Hours: €4, included in €8 combo-ticket that also covers next two sights, daily 10:00–13:00 & 14:30–19:00, closes at 17:00 in winter; from Piazza del Comune, go one-half block down Via San Francesco—it's on your right; tel. 075-815-5077.

Pinacoteca—This small museum attractively displays its 13th- to 17th-century art (mainly frescoes), with general English information in nearly every room. There's a damaged Giotto Madonna and a rare secular fresco (to the right of the Giotto art), but it's mainly a peaceful walk through a pastel world—best for art-lovers.

Cost and Hours: €3, included in €8 combo-ticket, daily 10:00–18:00, June–Aug until 19:00, Nov–Feb closes at 17:00, Via San Francesco, no building number—look for banner above entryway, on main drag between Piazza del Comune and Basilica of St. Francis, tel. 075-815-5077.

▲Rocca Maggiore—The "big castle" offers a good look at a 14th-century fortification and a fine view of Assisi and the Umbrian countryside. If you're pinching your euros, the view is just as good from outside the castle. There's talk of restoring some rooms in their original medieval style, possibly in time for your visit.

Cost and Hours: €5, included in €8 combo-ticket, daily from 10:00 until an hour before sunset—about 19:15 in summer, tel. 075-815-5077.

Commune with Nature—For a picnic with the same birdsong and views that inspired St. Francis, leave the tourists behind and hike to the Rocca Minore (small private castle, not tourable) above Piazza Matteotti.

In Santa Maria degli Angeli

This modern part of Assisi sits in the flat valley below the hill town (see "Assisi Area" map, earlier). It has two sights: the basilica that marks the spot where Francis lived, worked, and died; and the church where the crucifix spoke to him.

▲▲St. Mary of the Angels Basilica (Basilica Patriarcale di Santa Maria degli Angeli in Porziuncola)—This huge basilica,

towering above the buildings below Assisi, was built in the 16th century around the tiny but historic Porziuncola Chapel (now directly under the dome). The last part of the church's Italian name ("in Porziuncola") means literally "over the Porziuncola Chapel." After Francis' conversion, some local monks gave him this *porziuncola*, or "small portion"—a little land with a fixer-upper chapel. Francis lived here after he founded the Franciscan Order in 1208, and this was where he consecrated St. Clare as a Bride of Christ. What would humble Francis think of the huge church—Christianity's 10th largest— that was built over his tiny chapel?

Behind the chapel on the right, find the Cappella del Transito, which marks the site of Francis' death on October 3, 1226. Francis died as he'd lived—simply, in a small hut located here. On his last night on earth, he invited some friars to join him in a Last Supper–style breaking of bread. Then he undressed, lay down on the bare ground, and began to recite Psalm 141, "Lord, I cry unto thee." He spoke the last line, "Let the wicked fall into their own traps, while I escape"...and he passed on.

Follow *Roseto* signs to the rose garden. Francis, fighting a temptation that he never named, once threw himself onto the roses. As the story goes, the thorns immediately dropped off. Thornless roses have grown here ever since.

When you reach the statue of Francis petting a sheep, look to the right, through the window at the rose garden. The Rose Chapel (Cappella delle Rose) is built over the place where Francis lived.

In the autumn, a room in the next hallway displays a giant animated nativity scene (a reminder to pilgrims that Francis first established the tradition of manger scenes as a teaching aid). The bookshop has some works in English, while the Porziuncola Museum features a few monastic cells of interest to pilgrims, a model of Assisi during Francis' lifetime, and religious art and objects from the basilica (€2.50, museum open May–mid-Sept Tue–Sun 9:30–12:30 & 15:30–19:00, mid-Sept–April Tue–Sun 9:30–12:30 & 15:00–18:00, closed Mon, tel. 075-805-1419, www.porziuncola.org).

Cost and Hours: The basilica is free to enter and open Mon–Sat 6:15–12:50 & 14:30–19:30; it opens 30 minutes later on Sun (tel. 075-805-11). A little TI kiosk is across the street from the souvenir stands (generally daily 10:00–12:30 & 16:00–18:30, tel. 075-804-4554). As you face the church, the best WC is on your right.

Getting There: To get to St. Mary of the Angels Basilica from Assisi's train station, it's a five-minute walk (exit station left, take first left at McDonald's—you'll see the dome in the distance). When you leave the basilica, you can catch a bus that goes to the station and on to Assisi's old town (leaving church, stop is on your right). The orange city buses run twice hourly (buses to the old town depart the basilica at :10 and :40 after the hour; tickets cost €1 if you buy at *tabacchi* or the newsstand near the TI, €1.50 if you buy from driver; 20-minute ride up to old town). It's efficient to visit this basilica either on your way to the old town of Assisi or when you leave.

Museo Pericle Fazzini—This new museum, housed in the arcaded building opposite St. Mary of the Angels Basilica, features works by the contemporary Italian sculptor Pericle Fazzini. The collection includes bronzes of St. Francis and the original sketch of "The Resurrection"—Fazzini's famous bronze of Jesus rising from a nuclear-bomb crater, commissioned by the pope for the audience hall of the Vatican.

Cost and Hours: €5, Tue–Sun 10:00–13:00 & 16:00–19:00, closed Mon, tel. 075-804-4586, www.museo.periclefazzini.it.

Church of San Damiano—Located in the valley beneath the Basilica of St. Clare, this church and convent was where Francis received his call and where Clare spent her days as Mother Superior of the Poor Clares. Today, there's not much to see, but it's a relatively peaceful escape from touristy Assisi. Drivers can zip right there, while walkers descend pleasantly from Assisi for 15 minutes through an olive grove.

In 1206, Francis was inside the church when he heard the

wooden crucifix order him to rebuild the church. (The crucifix in San Damiano is a copy; the original is now displayed in the Basilica of St. Clare.) Francis initially interpreted these miraculous words as a call to rebuild crumbling San Damiano. He sold his father's cloth for money to fix the church. (The church we see today, however, was rebuilt later by others.) Eventually, Francis realized the call was to revitalize the Christian Church at large.

As he approached the end of his life, Francis came to San Damiano to visit his old friend Clare. She set him up in a simple reed hut in the olive grove where, in September 1225, he was inspired to write his poem *The Canticle of the Sun*.

Cost and Hours: Daily, 10:00–12:00 & 14:00–18:00, closes at 16:30 in winter, tel. 075-812-273, www.assisiofm.org; start walking from Porta Nuova parking lot at south end of town and follow the signs.

Outside of Assisi

Hermitage (Eremo delle Carceri)—If you want to follow further in St. Francis' footsteps, take a trip up the rugged slopes of nearby Mount Subasio to the humble hermitage Francis and his followers retreated to for solitude. The highlight is a look at the tiny, dank cave where Francis would retire for private prayer.

Cost and Hours: Free, daily 6:30–19:00, until 17:30 off-season, tel. 075-812-301, www.eremocarceri.it. Guided visits may be available.

Getting There: There is no public transportation right to the top; either drive, take a taxi, or hike. Starting from Assisi's Porta Cappuccini gate, it's a stiff three-mile, 1.5-hour hike with an elevation gain of 800 feet. The Linea A bus from Piazza del Comune will cut your hike by 30 minutes; get off at the Camping Fortemaggiore stop. Wear sturdy shoes and bring water. A souvenir kiosk at the entrance sells drinks and sandwiches.

Sleeping in Assisi

Assisi accommodates large numbers of pilgrims on religious holidays. Finding a room at any other time should be easy. Few hotels are air-conditioned. Locals suggest that you keep your windows closed in the middle of the day so that your room will be as cool as possible in the evening.

Hotels and Rooms

$$$ Hotel Umbra, a quiet villa in the middle of town, has 24 spacious rooms with great views and fine accommodations (Sb-€75, standard Db-€110, superior Db-€123, Tb-€155, 10 percent cash discount for 2 or more nights with this book, air-con, elevator,

---

Sleep Code

(€1 = about $1.25, country code: 39)
S = Single, **D** = Double/Twin, **T** = Triple, **Q** = Quad, **b** = bathroom,
s = shower only. Unless otherwise noted, credit cards are
accepted, English is spoken, and breakfast is included.
  To help you sort easily through these listings, I've divided
the rooms into three categories based on the price for a
standard double room with bath:

$$$ Higher Priced—Most rooms €100 or more.
 $$ Moderately Priced—Most rooms between €55–100.
  $ Lower Priced—Most rooms €55 or less.

  Prices can change without notice; verify the hotel's
current rates online or by email. For other updates, see www
.ricksteves.com/update.

---

peaceful garden and view sun terrace, most rooms have views,
good restaurant, dinner only, closed Dec–Feb, just off Piazza del
Comune under the arch at Via degli Archi 6, tel. 075-812-240,
fax 075-813-653, www.hotelumbra.it, info@hotelumbra.it, family
Laudenzi).

  $$ Hotel Ideale, on a ridge overlooking the valley, offers 14
airy, modern rooms (all with views, 10 with balconies), a tranquil
garden setting, and free parking (Sb-€50, Db-€90, prices good
with this book through 2011, 10 percent discount for stays of 3 or
more nights, may be cheaper off-season, air-con, confirm your
arrival time especially if it's after 17:00, Piazza Matteotti 1, tel. 075-
813-570, fax 075-813-020, www.hotelideale.it, info@hotelideale
.it, friendly sisters Lara and Ilaria). The hotel is close to the bus
stop (and parking lot) at Piazza Matteotti at the top end of town.

  $$ Hotel Belvedere, a great value, is a modern building with
16 big, spacious rooms—nine come with sweeping views (Sb-€45,
Db-€65, breakfast-€5, elevator, large communal view terrace,
2 blocks past Basilica of St. Clare at Via Borgo Aretino 13, tel.
075-812-460, fax 075-816-812, www.assisihotelbelvedere.it, info
@assisihotelbelvedere.it, run by Enrico and Mary from New Jersey).

  $$ La Pallotta offers seven clean, bright rooms and a com-
munal view room on the top floor (Sb-€45, Db-€75, free Internet
access, Wi-Fi, free use of washer and clothesline, free hot drinks
and cake at teatime, free use of an Assisi audioguide; a block off
Piazza del Comune at Via San Rufino 6—go up a short flight of
stairs outside building, above the arch, to reach entrance; tel. & fax
075-812-307, www.pallottaassisi.it, pallotta@pallottaassisi.it, help-
ful Stefano, Serena, and family). They also have a good restaurant

Assisi Hotels & Restaurants

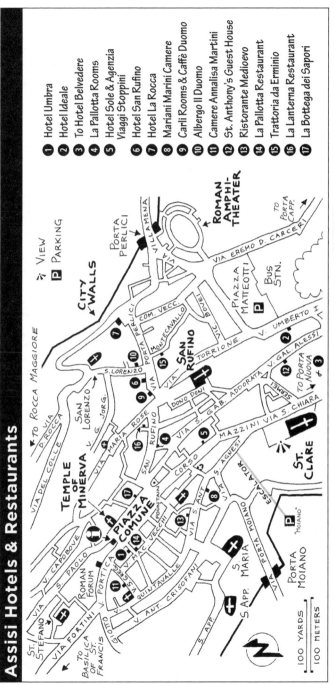

1. Hotel Umbra
2. Hotel Ideale
3. To Hotel Belvedere
4. La Pallotta Rooms
5. Hotel Sole & Agenzia Viaggi Stoppini
6. Hotel San Rufino
7. Hotel La Rocca
8. Mariani Marini Camere
9. Carli Rooms & Caffè Duomo
10. Albergo Il Duomo
11. Camere Annalisa Martini
12. St. Anthony's Guest House
13. Ristorante Medioevo
14. La Pallotta Restaurant
15. Trattoria da Erminio
16. La Lanterna Restaurant
17. La Bottega dei Sapori

ASSISI

(see "Eating in Assisi," later).

$$ Hotel Sole, renting 38 rooms in a 15th-century building, is tired and forgettable. Service comes with a shrug, but the location is central. Half of its rooms are in a newer annex across the street (Sb-€45, Db-€65, Tb-€85, breakfast-€5, ask for a discount, easy parking, 100 yards before Basilica of St. Clare at Corso Mazzini 35, tel. 075-812-373, fax 075-813-706, www.assisihotelsole.com, info@assisihotelsole.com).

$$ Hotel San Rufino offers a great locale, solid stone quality, and 11 comfortable rooms (Sb-€46, Db-€56, Tb-€75, breakfast-€4; from Cathedral of San Rufino, follow sign to Via Porta Perlici 7; tel. & fax 075-812-803, www.hotelsanrufino.it, info@hotelsan rufino.it). Their nine-room annex, Albergo Il Duomo (listed later), saves you about €6 a night for a double with no loss in comfort.

$$ Hotel La Rocca, on the peaceful top end of town, has 32 solid and modern rooms in a medieval shell (Sb-€43, Db-€56, Tb-€75, breakfast-€4, parking-€6, sunny rooftop terrace, 3-minute walk from Piazza Matteotti at Via Porta Perlici 27, tel. & fax 075-812-284, www.hotelarocca.it, info@hotelarocca.it).

$ Mariani Marini Camere, in a utilitarian building rebuilt after the earthquake, rents 10 basic, perfectly sleepable rooms. While there's a tiny sun deck and a little reception area, it's an extremely basic place (Db-€45 for two or more nights, €50 for one-night stay, extra bed-€10, cash only, Via A. Cristofani 5, tel. and fax 075-812-508, mobile 348-733-2610, www.cameremarianimarini .com, info@cameremarianimarini.com, Antonio and Fabrizio).

$ Carli Rooms has six shiny, spacious, new rooms in a solid, minimalist place above a shop (Sb-€37, Db-€48, Qb-€60, show this book to get these prices, family lofts, Wi-Fi, free parking nearby, facing the Duomo at Via Porta Perlici 1, tel. 075-812-490, mobile 339-531-1366, carliarte@live.it, Carli).

$ Albergo Il Duomo is tidy and *tranquillo,* with nine rooms on a stair-stepped lane one block up from San Rufino. Check in at Hotel San Rufino (Sb-€40, Db-€50, breakfast-€4, Vicolo San Lorenzo 2, tel. & fax 075-812-742, www.hotelsanrufino.it, info @hotelsanrufino.it).

$ Camere Annalisa Martini is a cheery home in the town's medieval core that swims in vines, roses, and cats. Annalisa enthusiastically accommodates her guests with a picnic garden, a washing machine (€7/small load, includes line drying), a communal refrigerator, and six homey rooms (S-€27, Sb-€30, D-€38, Db-€42, Tb-€58, Qb-€68, cash only but credit card required for deposit, 3 rooms share 2 bathrooms, no breakfast; 1 block from Piazza del Comune—go downhill toward basilica, turn left on Via San Gregorio to #6; tel. & fax 075-813-536, cameremartini @libero.it, Mamma Rosignoli—"roh-sin-YOH-lee"—doesn't speak English, but Annalisa does).

$ *Hostel:* Francis probably would have bunked with the peasants in Assisi's **Ostello della Pace** (€17 beds in 4- to 8-bed rooms, €19/person in private 2- to 4-person rooms with bath, dinner-€10.50, laundry service-€3.50, lockout 9:30–16:00, midnight curfew; get off bus at Piazzale Giovanni Paolo II, then walk 15 minutes downhill to Via di Valecchie 177; tel. & fax 075-816-767, www.assisihostel.com, assisi.hostel@tiscali net.it).

Sweet Dreams in a Convent

Assisi is filled with convents, most of which rent rooms to pilgrims and travelers. While you don't need to be a pilgrim or even a Christian to be welcome, it's just common sense to stay in a convent *only* if you're approaching Assisi with a contemplative mindset. Convents feel institutional, house many groups, and are not particularly cheap—but they come with all the facilities you might need to enjoy a spirit-filled visit to Assisi.

$$ St. Anthony's Guest House is where the Franciscan Sisters of the Atonement (including several Americans and Canadians) offer a very warm and tranquil welcome. Their oasis of peace is just above the Basilica of St. Clare. With only 35 beds in 20 rooms at a reasonable price, they book up literally months in advance (Sb-€40–45, Db-€60–65, Tb-€80–85, 2-night minimum, cash only for short stays, no problem if couples want to share a bed, 23:00 curfew, closed mid-Nov–Feb, library, views, picnic garden, parking-€3 donation/day, just below Piazza Matteotti at Via Galeazzo Alessi 10, tel. 075-812-542, fax 075-813-723, atoneassisi@tiscali.it).

Agriturismi near Assisi

If you're looking for some rest and relaxation on your journey, retire to the country at a farmhouse.

$$ Podere la Fornace is a renovated farmhouse in the tiny village of Tordibetto, just a few miles outside Assisi. The five apartments have 1–3 bedrooms, full kitchens, and a living room that can sleep an extra person. Local wine, olive oil, and pasta are available on-site (Db-€65–110, apartment-€80–195, price depends on size and season, 2-night minimum, games for children, swimming pool, bikes, cooking lessons, Via Ombrosa 3, tel. 075-801-9537, mobile 338-990-2903, fax 075-801-9630, www.lafornace .com, info@lafornace.com).

$$ Alla Madonna del Piatto is a six-room *agriturismo* located about five miles outside of Assisi, with impressive views of the countryside. The Dutch-Italian owners have taken a centuries-old farm into the modern age, making organic olive oil on the premises and offering cooking classes that include visits to the market.

Ruurd and Letizia offer useful tips on sightseeing, the culture, dining, and wineries in the area (Db-€80–115, 2-night minimum, non-smoking, closed Dec–mid-March, at Via Petrata 37 in the parish of Pieve San Nicolò, tel. 075-819-9050, mobile 328-702-5297, www.incampagna.com, letizia.mattiacci@gmail.com).

$$ La Malvarina *agriturismo* invites visitors to its farm, where the owners keep horses, raise their own poultry, harvest truffles, tend sheep for cheesemaking, and produce their own extra-virgin organic olive oil, honey, and marmalade. The 13 rooms and three apartments are homey and comfortable. Guests can take cooking lessons with Mamma Maria, enjoy walking tours of the countryside, join guided visits to nearby Umbrian hill towns, or just relax by the swimming pool and enjoy the views of the countryside (Db-€95, Tb-€110, Qb-€140, apartments-€100—or €660/week, cooking lessons-€25/person up to 4 people, €100/lesson more than 4 people, optional 5-course dinner with wine-€30, Via Pieve di Sant'Apollinare 32, tel. & fax 075-806-4280, www.malvarina.it, info@malvarina.it; Claudio, Filippo, and Piera).

Eating in Assisi

I've listed decent, central, good-value restaurants. Assisi's food is heavy and rustic. Locals brag about their sausage and love to grate truffles on pasta. To bump up any meal, consider a glass or bottle of the favorite homegrown red wine, Sagrantino de Montefalco. Umbria's answer to Brunello (although many here would say it's Brunello that has to measure up to Sagrantino), it stirs dancing girls and flames.

Fine Dining

Ristorante Medioevo is my vote for your best splurge. With heavy but spacious cellar vaults, this restaurant is an elegant, accessible playground of gastronomy. William Ventura will guide you to the best of Umbrian cuisine. He features traditional cuisine with a modern twist, dictated by what's in season. While his first passion is cooking, his second is music—mellow jazz and bossa nova give a twinkle to the medieval atmosphere. Dishes are well-presented, knives are sharpened at your table, beef and game dishes are the specialties, and the wonderful Sagrantino wine is served by the glass (€10 pastas, €14 *secondi*, Tue–Sun 12:30–15:00 & 19:30–22:45, closed Mon; from the fountain on Piazza del Comune, hike downhill two blocks to Via Arco dei Priori 4; tel. 075-813-068).

La Pallotta, a local favorite run by a friendly and hardworking family, offers delicious, well-presented regional specialties, such as *piccione* (squab, a.k.a. pigeon) and *coniglio* (rabbit). Margarita is in charge of the kitchen. Reservations are smart (€8 pastas, €10 *secondi*, interesting €25 fixed-price sampler of local specialties, Wed–Mon 12:15–14:30 & 19:00–21:30, closed Tue, vegetarian options, a few steps off Piazza del Comune across from temple/church at Vicolo della Volta Pinta 2, tel. 075-812-649).

Casual Eateries

Trattoria da Erminio is charming, with peaceful tables on a tiny square, or indoor seating under a big medieval brick vault. Run by Federico and his family for three generations, it specializes in local meat cooked on an open-fire grill. They have good Umbrian wines—before you order, ask Federico for a taste of the Petranera wine (€12 grilled meats, €13–22 tourist fixed-price meal featuring local recipes based on seasonal produce—changes weekly, Fri–Wed 12:00–14:30 & 19:00–21:00, closed Thu; from Piazza San Rufino, go a block up Via Porta Perlici and turn right to Via Montacavallo 19; tel. 075-812-506).

At **Locanda del Podestà,** chef Selvio cooks up tasty grilled Umbrian sausages, *gnocchi alla locanda,* and all manner of truffles, while Romina graciously serves happy diners who know a good value. Try the tasty *scottaditto* ("scorch your fingers") lamb chops (€7 pastas, €12 *secondi,* Thu–Tue 12:00–14:30 & 19:00–21:30, closed Wed and Jan, 5-minute walk uphill along Via Cardinale Merry del Val from basilica, San Giacomo 6c, tel. 075-816-553).

Ristorante Metastasio, just up the street from Podestà, has Assisi's best view terrace for dining (€9 pastas, €12 *secondi,* closed Wed, Via Metastasio 9, tel. 075-816-525).

Caffè Duomo, which faces the Cathedral of San Rufino, has a cozy interior with a jazzy ambience and great outdoor seating. It's run by enthusiastic young stallions, has a good selection of beers, and offers free Internet access to anyone ordering even just a drink. They also sell sandwiches and ice cream (daily 7:30–23:00, Piazza San Rufino 5, tel. 075-815-5209, Francesco and Ada speak English). Across the street, you can get pizza by the slice.

La Lanterna, up a small alleyway at the top of Via San Rufino, is a sleek, newly renovated eatery where you can dine by candlelight. Their €18 fixed-price meal (served all day), consisting of a starter, *secondo,* and side dish, is a good deal. It's run by a Neapolitan family who also make tasty pizzas in their wood-fired oven. Show this book for a free after-dinner *limoncello* from Luigi (daily 12:00–15:30 & 18:00–23:00, Via San Rufino 39, tel. 075-816-399, chef Massimiliano speaks English).

Picnic on the Main Square

There are many little grocery stores *(alimentari)* nearby.

Try **La Bottega dei Sapori** for a picnic of Umbrian treats: good prosciutto sandwiches and specialty items, including truffle paste and olive oil. Friendly Fabrizio, who is a slow-food enthusiast, may give you a taste. He also stocks the best Umbrian wines at good-to-go prices—nice if you have an appointment with your terrace for sunset (daily 9:00–20:00, closed Jan–Feb, Piazza del Comune 34, tel. 075-812-294).

Assisi Connections

From Assisi by Train to: Rome (13/day, 2–3.5 hours, 5 direct, most others change in Foligno), **Florence** (6/day direct, 2–3 hours), **Orvieto** (roughly hourly, 2–2.5 hours, with transfer in Terantola), **Siena** (8/day, 4–4.5 hours, most involve 2 transfers; bus is faster), **Cortona** (every 2 hours, 70 minutes to Camucia-Cortona station). The train-station ticket office is often closed until 13:30; on those mornings only, a ticket machine is available. You can get train information and tickets from Agenzia Viaggi Stoppini in the middle of town. Train station tel. 075-804-0272 (generally unresponsive; you're better off asking at Agenzia Viaggi Stoppini or checking online at www.trenitalia.com).

By Bus: Several different bus companies offer service to **Rome** (2/day, 3 hours, €16, pay driver, departs from Piazzale Giovanni Paolo II below the basilica, arrives at Rome's Tiburtina station—the train makes much more sense), **Siena** (2/day at about 10:45 and 17:00, Nov–April no morning departure, 2 hours, €12). You can't buy Siena tickets from the driver; you must buy them at Assisi's Agenzia Viaggi Mavitur at Via Frate Elia 1b. The 17:00 bus to Siena leaves from Porta San Pietro; the 10:45 bus departs from St. Mary of the Angels Basilica (stopping immediately at the side of the church).

Don't take the bus to **Florence;** the train is better. To see either **Gubbio** or **Todi** as a side-trip from Assisi, you'll need a car—bus schedules don't accommodate day-trippers. Day trips to **Spello, Perugia,** and **Lake Trasimeno** also aren't doable by bus, but you can do them by train.

By Plane: Perugia/San Egidio Airport, about 10 miles from Assisi, has daily connections to London Stansted airport (on Ryanair) and to Milan. No public transport runs between Assisi and the airport; a taxi costs about €25 (tel. 075-592-141, www.sangallo.it/perugiaairport).

PRACTICALITIES

This section covers just the basics on traveling in Italy (for much more information, see *Rick Steves' Italy 2011*). You can find free advice on specific topics at www.ricksteves.com/tips.

Money

Italy uses the euro currency: 1 euro (€) = about $1.25. To convert prices in euros to dollars, add about 25 percent: €20 = about $25, €50 = about $65. (Check www.oanda.com for the latest exchange rates.)

The standard way for travelers to get euros is to withdraw money from a cash machine (called a *bancomat* in Italy) using a debit or credit card, ideally with a Visa or MasterCard logo. Before departing, call your bank or credit-card company: Confirm that your card will work overseas, ask about international transaction fees, and alert them that you'll be making withdrawals in Europe.

To keep your valuables safe, wear a money belt. But if you do lose your credit or debit card, report the loss immediately to the respective global customer-assistance centers. Call these 24-hour US numbers collect: Visa (410/581-9994), MasterCard (636/722-7111), and American Express (623/492-8427).

Phoning

Smart travelers use the telephone to reserve or reconfirm rooms, reserve restaurants, get directions, research transportation connections, confirm tour times, phone home, and lots more.

To call Italy from the US or Canada: Dial 011-39 and then the local number. (The 011 is our international access code, and 39 is Italy's country code.)

To call Italy from a European country: Dial 00-39 followed by the local number. (The 00 is Europe's international access code.)

To call within Italy: Just dial the local number.

To call from Italy to another country: Dial 00 followed by the country code (for example, 1 for the US or Canada), then the area code and number. If you're calling European countries whose phone numbers begin with 0, you'll usually have to omit that 0 when you dial.

Tips on Phoning: To make calls in Italy, you can buy two different types of phone cards—international or insertable—sold locally at newsstands. Cheap international phone cards, which work with a scratch-to-reveal PIN code at any phone, allow you to call home to the US for pennies a minute, and also work for domestic calls within Italy. Insertable phone cards, which must be inserted into public pay phones, are reasonable for calls within Italy (and work for international calls as well, but not as cheaply as the international phone cards). Calling from your hotel-room phone is usually expensive, unless you use an international phone card. A mobile phone—whether an American one that works in Italy, or a European one you buy when you arrive—is handy, but can be pricey. For more on phoning, see www.ricksteves.com/phoning.

Emergency Telephone Numbers in Italy: For English-speaking **police** help, dial 113. To summon an **ambulance**, call 118. For passport problems, call the **US Embassy** (in Rome, 24-hour line—tel. 06-46741) or **US Consulates** (Milan—tel. 02-290-351, Florence—tel. 055-266-951, Naples—tel. 081-583-8111); or the **Canadian Embassy** (in Rome, tel. 06-854-441) or **Canadian Consulates** (Naples—tel. 081-401-338, Padua—tel. 049-876-4833). For other concerns, get advice from your hotel.

Making Hotel Reservations

To ensure the best value, I recommend reserving rooms in advance, particularly during peak season. Email the hotelier with the following key pieces of information: number and type of rooms; number of nights; date of arrival; date of departure; and any special requests. (For a sample form, see www.ricksteves.com/reservation.) Use the European style for writing dates: day/month/year. For example, for a two-night stay in July, you could request: "1 double room for 2 nights, arrive 16/07/11, depart 18/07/11." Hoteliers typically ask for your credit-card number as a deposit.

Given the economic downturn, hoteliers are willing and eager to make a deal. I'd suggest emailing several hotels to ask for their best price. Comparison-shop and make your choice.

In general, hotel prices can soften if you do any of the following: offer to pay cash, stay at least three nights, mention this book, or travel off-season. You can also try asking for a cheaper room (for example, with a bathroom down the hall), or offer to skip breakfast.

Eating

Italy offers a wide array of eateries. A *ristorante* is a formal restaurant, while a *trattoria* or *osteria* is usually more traditional and simpler (but can still be pricey). Italian "bars" are not taverns, but small cafés selling sandwiches, coffee, and other drinks. An *enoteca* is a wine bar with snacks and light meals. Take-away food from pizza shops and delis (such as a *rosticcería* or *tavola calda*) makes an easy picnic.

Italians eat dinner a bit later than we do; better restaurants start serving around 19:00. A full meal consists of an appetizer (antipasto), a first course (*primo piatto*, pasta or soup), and a second course (*secondo piatto*, expensive meat and fish dishes). Vegetables *(verdure)* may come with the *secondo* or cost extra, as a side dish *(contorni)*. The euros can add up in a hurry, but you don't have to order each course. My approach is to mix antipasti and *primi piatti* family-style with my dinner partners (skipping *secondi*). Or, for unexciting but basic values, look for a *menù turistico* (or *menù del giorno*), a three- or four-course, fixed-price meal deal.

Good service is relaxed (slow to an American). You won't get the bill until you ask for it: *"Il conto?"* Most restaurants include a service charge in their prices (check the menu for *servizio incluso*—generally around 15 percent). To reward good service, you can round up to the nearest euro. If a service charge is not included, you can tip 5 to 10 percent.

At bars and cafés, getting a drink while standing at the bar *(banco)* is cheaper than drinking it at a table *(tavolo)* or sitting outside *(terrazza)*. This tiered pricing system is clearly posted on the wall. Sometimes you'll pay at a cash register, then take the receipt to another counter to claim your drink.

Transportation

By Train: In Italy, most travelers find it's cheapest simply to buy train tickets as they go. To see if a railpass could save you money, check www.ricksteves.com/rail. To research train schedules, visit Germany's excellent all-Europe website, http://bahn.hafas.de/bin/query.exe/en, or Italy's www.trenitalia.it/en/index.html.

You can buy tickets at train stations (at the ticket window or at automated machines with English instructions) or from travel agencies. Before boarding the train, you must validate your train documents by stamping them in the yellow box near the platform. Strikes *(sciopero)* are common and generally announced in advance (but a few sporadic trains still run—ask around).

By Car: It's cheaper to arrange most car rentals from the US. For tips on your insurance options, see www.ricksteves.com/cdw. Theft insurance is mandatory in Italy ($10–15/day). Bring your driver's license. For route planning, try www.viamichelin.com.

Italy's freeway *(autostrada)* system is slick and speedy, but you'll pay about a dollar for every 10 minutes of use. Be warned that car traffic is restricted in many city centers—don't drive or park in any area that has a sign reading *Zona Traffico Limitato* (*ZTL,* often shown above a red circle)...or you might be mailed a ticket later. A car is a worthless headache in cities—park it safely (get tips from your hotel). As break-ins are common, be sure all of your valuables are out of sight and locked in the trunk, or even better, with you or in your hotel room.

Helpful Hints

Theft Alert: Italy has particularly hardworking pickpockets. Assume beggars are pickpockets and any scuffle is simply a distraction by a team of thieves. If you stop for any commotion or show, put your hands in your pockets before someone else does. Better yet, wear a money belt.

Time: Italy uses the 24-hour clock. It's the same through 12:00 noon, then keep going: 13:00, 14:00, and so on. Italy, like most of continental Europe, is six/nine hours ahead of the East/West Coasts of the US.

Business Hours: Many businesses are open throughout the day Monday through Saturday, but some businesses close for lunch (roughly 13:00-15:30), particularly in smaller towns.

Sights: Opening and closing hours of sights can change unexpectedly; confirm the latest times with the local tourist information office or its website. Some major churches enforce a modest dress code (no bare shoulders or shorts) for everyone, even children.

Holidays and Festivals: Italy celebrates many holidays, which can close sights and attract crowds (book hotel rooms ahead). For information on holidays and festivals, check Italy's website: www.italiantourism.com. For a simple list showing major—though not all—events, see www.ricksteves.com/festivals.

Numbers and Stumblers: What Americans call the second floor of a building is the first floor in Europe. Europeans write dates as day/month/year, so Christmas is 25/12/11. Commas are decimal points and vice versa—a dollar and a half is 1,50, and there are 5.280 feet in a mile. Italy uses the metric system: A kilogram is 2.2 pounds; a liter is about a quart; and a kilometer is six-tenths of a mile.

Resources from Rick Steves

This Snapshot guide is excerpted from *Rick Steves' Italy 2011,* which is one of more than 30 titles in my series of guidebooks on European travel. I also produce a public television series, *Rick Steves' Europe,* and a public radio show, *Travel with Rick Steves.* My website, www.ricksteves.com, offers free travel information, free vodcasts and podcasts of my shows, free audio tours of major sights in Europe (for you to download onto an iPod or other MP3 player), a Graffiti Wall for travelers' comments, guidebook updates, my travel blog, an online travel store, and information on European railpasses and our tours of Europe.

Additional Resources

Tourist Information: www.italiantourism.com
Passports and Red Tape: www.travel.state.gov
Travel Insurance Tips: www.ricksteves.com/insurance
Packing List: www.ricksteves.com/packlist
Cheap Flights: www.skyscanner.net
Airplane Carry-on Restrictions: www.tsa.gov/travelers
Updates for This Book: www.ricksteves.com/update

How Was Your Trip?

If you'd like to share your tips, concerns, and discoveries after using this book, please fill out the survey at www.ricksteves.com/feedback. Thanks in advance—it helps a lot.

Italian Survival Phrases

Good day.	**Buon giorno.**	bwohn JOR-noh
Do you speak English?	**Parla inglese?**	PAR-lah een-GLAY-zay
Yes. / No.	**Sì. / No.**	see / noh
I (don't) understand.	**(Non) capisco.**	(nohn) kah-PEES-koh
Please.	**Per favore.**	pehr fah-VOH-ray
Thank you.	**Grazie.**	GRAHT-seeay
You're welcome.	**Prego.**	PRAY-go
I'm sorry.	**Mi dispiace.**	mee dee-speeAH-chay
Excuse me.	**Mi scusi.**	mee SKOO-zee
(No) problem.	**(Non) c'è un problema.**	(nohn) cheh oon proh-BLAY-mah
Good.	**Va bene.**	vah BEHN-ay
Goodbye.	**Arrivederci.**	ah-ree-vay-DEHR-chee
one / two	**uno / due**	OO-noh / DOO-ay
three / four	**tre / quattro**	tray / KWAH-troh
five / six	**cinque / sei**	CHEENG-kway / SEHee
seven / eight	**sette / otto**	SEHT-tay / OT-toh
nine / ten	**nove / dieci**	NOV-ay / deeAY-chee
How much is it?	**Quanto costa?**	KWAHN-toh KOS-tah
Write it?	**Me lo scrive?**	may loh SKREE-vay
Is it free?	**È gratis?**	eh GRAH-tees
Is it included?	**È incluso?**	eh een-KLOO-zoh
Where can I buy / find...?	**Dove posso comprare / trovare...?**	DOH-vay POS-soh kohm-PRAH-ray / troh-VAH-ray
I'd like / We'd like...	**Vorrei / Vorremmo...**	vor-REHee / vor-RAY-moh
...a room.	**...una camera.**	OO-nah KAH-meh-rah
...a ticket to ___.	**...un biglietto per ___.**	oon beel-YEHT-toh pehr
Is it possible?	**È possibile?**	eh poh-SEE-bee-lay
Where is...?	**Dov'è...?**	DOH-veh
...the train station	**...la stazione**	lah staht-seeOH-nay
...the bus station	**...la stazione degli autobus**	lah staht-seeOH-nay DAYL-yee OW-toh-boos
...tourist information	**...informazioni per turisti**	een-for-maht-seeOH-nee pehr too-REE-stee
...the toilet	**...la toilette**	lah twah-LEHT-tay
men	**uomini, signori**	WOH-mee-nee, seen-YOH-ree
women	**donne, signore**	DON-nay, seen-YOH-ray
left / right	**sinistra / destra**	see-NEE-strah / DEHS-trah
straight	**sempre diritto**	SEHM-pray dee-REE-toh
When do you open / close?	**A che ora aprite / chiudete?**	ah kay OH-rah ah-PREE-tay / keeoo-DAY-tay
At what time?	**A che ora?**	ah kay OH-rah
Just a moment.	**Un momento.**	oon moh-MAYN-toh
now / soon / later	**adesso / presto / tardi**	ah-DEHS-soh / PREHS-toh / TAR-dee
today / tomorrow	**oggi / domani**	OH-jee / doh-MAH-nee

In the Restaurant

I'd like...	Vorrei...	vor-REHee
We'd like...	Vorremmo...	vor-RAY-moh
...to reserve...	...prenotare...	pray-noh-TAH-ray
...a table for one / two.	...un tavolo per uno / due.	oon TAH-voh-loh pehr OO-noh / D●
Non-smoking.	Non fumare.	nohn foo-MAH-ray
Is this seat free?	È libero questo posto?	eh LEE-bay-roh KWEHS-toh POH-
The menu (in English), please.	Il menù (in inglese), per favore.	eel may-NOO (een een-GLAY-zay) pehr fah-VOH-ray
service (not) included	servizio (non) incluso	sehr-VEET-seeoh (nohn) een-KLO
cover charge	pane e coperto	PAH-nay ay koh-PEHR-toh
to go	da portar via	dah POR-tar VEE-ah
with / without	con / senza	kohn / SEHN-sah
and / or	e / o	ay / oh
menu (of the day)	menù (del giorno)	may-NOO (dayl JOR-noh)
specialty of the house	specialità della casa	spay-chah-lee-TAH DEHL-lah KAH●
first course (pasta, soup)	primo piatto	PREE-moh peeAH-toh
main course (meat, fish)	secondo piatto	say-KOHN-doh peeAH-toh
side dishes	contorni	kohn-TOR-nee
bread	pane	PAH-nay
cheese	formaggio	for-MAH-joh
sandwich	panino	pah-NEE-noh
soup	minestra, zuppa	mee-NEHS-trah, TSOO-pah
salad	insalata	een-sah-LAH-tah
meat	carne	KAR-nay
chicken	pollo	POH-loh
fish	pesce	PEH-shay
seafood	frutti di mare	FROO-tee dee MAH-ray
fruit / vegetables	frutta / legumi	FROO-tah / lay-GOO-mee
dessert	dolci	DOHL-chee
tap water	acqua del rubinetto	AH-kwah dayl roo-bee-NAY-toh
mineral water	acqua minerale	AH-kwah mee-nay-RAH-lay
milk	latte	LAH-tay
(orange) juice	succo (d'arancia)	SOO-koh (dah-RAHN-chah)
coffee / tea	caffè / tè	kah-FEH / teh
wine	vino	VEE-noh
red / white	rosso / bianco	ROH-soh / beeAHN-koh
glass / bottle	bicchiere / bottiglia	bee-keeAY-ray / boh-TEEL-yah
beer	birra	BEE-rah
Cheers!	Cin cin!	cheen cheen
More. / Another.	Ancora un po.' / Un altro.	ahn-KOH-rah oon poh / oon AHL-troh
The same.	Lo stesso.	loh STEHS-soh
The bill, please.	Il conto, per favore.	eel KOHN-toh pehr fah-VOH-ray
tip	mancia	MAHN-chah
Delicious!	Delizioso!	day-leet-seeOH-zoh

For more user-friendly Italian phrases, check out *Rick Steves' Italian Phrase Book & Dictionary* or *Rick Steves' French, Italian, and German Phrase Book*.

Free mobile app (and podcast)

With the **Rick Steves Audio Europe** app, your iPhone or smartphone becomes a powerful travel tool.

This exciting app organizes Rick's entire audio library by country—giving you a playlist of all his audio walking tours, radio interviews, and travel tips for wherever you're going in Europe.

Let the experts Rick interviews enrich your understanding. Let Rick's self-guided tours amplify your guidebook. With Rick in your ear, Europe gets even better.

Thanks Facebook fans for submitting photos while on location! From top: John Kuijper in Florence, Brenda Mamer with her mother in Rome, Angel Capobianco in London, and Alyssa Passey with her friend in Paris.

Find out more at ricksteves.com/audioeurope

▶ Plan Your Trip

Browse thousands of articles and a wealth of money-saving tips for planning your dream trip. You'll find up-to-date information on Europe's best destinations, packing smart, getting around, finding rooms, staying healthy, avoiding scams and more.

▶ Eurail Passes

Find out, step-by-step, if a railpass makes sense for your trip—and how to avoid buying more than you need. Get a bunch of free extras!

▶ Graffiti Wall & Travelers' Helpline

Learn, ask, share—our online community of savvy travelers is a great resource for first-time travelers to Europe, as well as seasoned pros.